Frederick Law Olmsted

ESSENTIAL TEXTS

DATE DUE

			PRINTED IN U.S.A.

Frederick Law Olmsted

ESSENTIAL TEXTS

Edited by Robert Twombly

W. W. Norton & Company
New York • London

This book is dedicated to landscape architects, students, and instructors everywhere who are too often relegated to secondary status—"yes, some trees would be nice out back, if they don't cost too much." And for those architects who think this is as it should be: Consider what Frederick Law Olmsted had to say and, depending, take heart or take stock.

For information about special discounts for bulk purchases, please contact W. W. Norton Special Sales at specialsales@wwnorton.com or 800-233-4830

Manufacturing by Edwards Brothers, Lillington
Book design by Jonathan D. Lippincott
Page makeup by Ken Gross
Production manager: Leeann Graham

Library of Congress Cataloging-in-Publication Data

Olmsted, Frederick Law, 1822–1903.
 Frederick Law Olmsted : essential texts / edited by Robert Twombly.
  p. cm.
 Includes bibliographical references and index.
 ISBN 978-0-393-73310-5 (pbk.)
 1. Landscape architecture. I. Twombly, Robert C. II. Title.
 SB472.4.O46 2010
 712.092—dc22

                                        2009049382

ISBN: 978-0-393-73310-5 (pbk.)

W. W. Norton & Company, Inc.500 Fifth Avenue, New York, N.Y. 10110
www.wwnorton.com

W. W. Norton & Company Ltd.Castle House, 75/76 Wells StreetLondon W1T 3QT

0 9 8 7 6 5 4 3 2 1

Contents

Preface and Acknowledgments

It is no exaggeration to say that Frederick Law Olmsted is the best-known and most revered landscape architect in United States history. But he was much more than that. Well regarded for five books based on his travels through England and the American South and Southwest that were published from 1852 to 1861, for his many newspaper and journal essays, and his association with Putnam's Magazine, Olmsted was a high-profile public intellectual and man of letters well before he turned forty.

As if this were not enough, in April 1858 he and Calvert Vaux won the competition to design New York City's Central Park, and slowly but not quite surely, Olmsted became a landscape gardener (the term he preferred to "landscape architect"). Two other careers intervened—more on this in the introduction—before he and Vaux entered into a second collaboration, late in 1865, to design Prospect Park in the still-independent city of Brooklyn. There was now no going back. Despite many other interests, he was from then on, first, foremost, and forever, a landscape gardener.

The firm of "Olmsted, Vaux, & Company" was dissolved in October 1872, although the two men remained on good terms, their professional paths occasionally crossing, until Vaux died in 1895. Their on-and-off partnership from 1858 to 1872 generated innumerable coauthored proposals and reports, including many of great historical importance, but the editor decided to omit them from this volume.

Given the vast number of texts Olmsted wrote on his own, the editor's second decision was to limit inclusion here to speeches and essays intended for public consumption: some youthful observations, Olmsted's thoughts on cities, landscape design, small residential sites, and the history and theory of parks. With the exception of "Plan for a Small Homestead" (Document 4) and his lecture on the Chicago World's Fair (Document 11), in other words, there are no reports or proposals on individual designs, which in any case would mainly interest specialists—horticulturists, for example, would enjoy the plant lists—who may consult them in *The Papers of Frederick Law Olmsted*. (Documents 4 and 11 do, however, enable readers to glimpse the modus operandi with which he approached specific projects.) The principal objective here is to reconstruct his design and social philosophies as they addressed what he believed to be the pressing professional, urban, and national issues of his day.

The editor has corrected misspellings, British and archaic spellings and punctuation, and typesetting errors without indication. Words in brackets are either definitional or the editor's best guess as to what Olmsted in his manuscripts, proofreaders editing them, or both, inadvertently omitted or misread.

I would like to thank those who helped me with this project but are in no way responsible for shortcomings that herein exist: Judy Connorton, librarian at the City College of New York School of Architecture, Urban Design, and Landscape Architecture, as well as her assistant Nilda Sanchez and students aides there; Mary Woolever, archivist, The Ryerson &

Burnham Libraries, The Art Institute of Chicago; and Nancy Green—patient, encouraging, immensely helpful—for the third time my editor at W. W. Norton (I devoutly hope there will be a fourth), as well as her skillful proofreader and other associates.

"Tranquility and Rest to the Mind"

In 1872, at age fifty, Frederick Law Olmsted began designing grounds for the McLean Asylum in Belmont, Massachusetts, "a retreat for the insane" where landscaping intended
to encourage "moderate exercise and tranquil occupation of
the mind" might, he hoped, ameliorate the destructive consequences of too much mental "exertion, heat, excitement or
bewilderment." He could have written much the same—and
did in different words—about his urban parks. In 1898, at age
seventy-six, Olmsted was committed to that very asylum—
known as McLean Hospital after 1892— with symptoms similar to those he had listed twenty-six years earlier, collectively
known as senile dementia. Always an active man, some might
have said hyperactive, often refusing to rest when overtaxed,
he hated being confined, but to be confined in one of his own
creations was even worse, especially because, as he angrily
wrote during one of his rapidly diminishing lucid moments,
"they didn't carry out my plan, confound them!"[1] He died at
McLean five years later, on August 23, 1903, and was buried in
Old North Cemetery in Hartford, Connecticut, his birthplace
eighty-one years before.

The first of his forebears in America, James Olmsted, arrived
in the Massachusetts Bay Colony from England in 1632, but

four years later he migrated with the soon-to-be mightily influential Congregational minister Thomas Hooker to what became Hartford. Six generations of farmers, seamen, soldiers, and businessmen later, John Olmsted, as politically and philanthropically active as his ancestors, was one of the city's most prominent merchants. His wife, Charlotte Law Hull, bore him two sons, Frederick Law on April 26, 1822, and John Hull in 1825, before her untimely death at age twenty-five in February 1826, when Frederick was not quite four. Fourteen months later John married again, to Mary Ann Bull, who gave him seven more children: five daughters and two sons. Of his nine offspring, John's favorite was first-born Frederick.

In 1822, Hartford, the state capital, was a thriving, surprisingly cosmopolitan city of nearly seven thousand people. Located near the geographical center of Connecticut, it was a convenient starting point for regional sightseeing in all directions, including south to Long Island Sound, and small enough for easy access on foot to the surrounding countryside. Beginning when he was six and throughout his teenage years, Frederick and family often traveled around New England and New York State, and he once went with just his father to Washington, D.C., via New York City and Baltimore. His parents indulged his continuous exploration of the countryside, not objecting when several times he got lost and had to spend the night with total strangers. Without doubt, his love of nature began and grew with these family excursions and solitary walks. But William Gilpin (1724–1804) and Uvedale Price (1747–1829), whose books on natural and manmade English landscapes he discovered in the Hartford Young Men's Institute, also played their part.

The Olmsted house was full of books, as were those of neighbors and relatives. Frederick had access to them all, and he read widely. This was not always the case at the common and boarding schools and ministers' homes to which he was sent from age ten to eighteen for formal or tutorial instruction ranging in quality from excellent to abysmal. As he approached maturity in 1840, it is fair to say that despite eight years of schooling he was not well trained in anything, but he was intellectually curious, restless, and eager to begin a career. Through business connections, his father got him a job that August as an apprentice clerk and bookkeeper in a New York City dry goods firm, where he remained until March 1842.

He learned a valuable lesson from his eighteen months in New York: that the world of commerce was not for him. But his stay there was not without consequence. His employers regularly sent him to wharves and ships on business matters, and he could see New York harbor from his residence in Brooklyn Heights. As a boy he had listened with fascination to his relatives' seafaring tales, and he had often visited and vacationed on Long Island Sound, to which he and brother John had occasionally sailed their own boat down the Connecticut River. So it is not surprising, perhaps, that on April 24, 1843, two days before his twenty-first birthday, he set sail from New York aboard a trading ship on a year's voyage to China and back. It is not clear if at that moment he thought seafaring might be his life's work, but long before he returned the next April he knew it would not. Suffice it to say that everything about the affair was, for him as well as his shipmates, miserable.

During the next three years, thanks to his prosperous, generous, and somewhat overindulgent father, Olmsted undertook a program of self-education by auditing lectures for a semester at Yale College, which his brother was attending, and reading widely at home, particularly about geometry, natural philosophy, and agriculture. He decided he wanted to work on a model farm and did so for the summer of 1846 in Onondaga County, New York. Shortly before arriving there, while visiting the Albany office of Luther Tucker, editor of *The Cultivator*, an innovative agricultural magazine, he met landscape designer Andrew Jackson Downing (1815–52), who had just agreed to edit a new monthly, *The Horticulturist*, a meeting the importance of which Olmsted could not have envisioned at the time.

Olmsted's exposure to modern agricultural technology during the summer of 1846 was a turning point in his life, prompting him early the next year to take possession of a 70-acre farm his father acquired for him on Sachem's Head, a rocky promontory jutting into Long Island Sound at Guilford, Connecticut. Buildings and grounds were in terrible condition, but with the help of his reading and travel observations, his work on the model farm, and practical advice from hired hands, he upgraded both while putting in a large vegetable garden. He seems to have taken up farming not to make a profit, although that would have been a plus, but to learn the fundaments of land management and horticulture by "do it yourself" effort. This is borne out in his very first publication, a July 1847 "query" of *The Horticulturist*, wherein he wonders if closely planted quince trees might make a good screen against salt breezes, and asks which shade and ornamental trees and shrubs, and which apple variety (he planned to start an orchard) are best suited to withstand "the influence of the sea." Olmsted certainly learned valuable lessons on Sachem's Head, one of which was that hostile climate and poor soil were best avoided. Another was that he now wanted to make "scientific" agriculture his career. Thus it was that in January 1848 his father purchased a 125-acre, better-situated farm on Staten Island, New York, for $13,000, "a great deal of money," he wrote in his diary. His son named it "South Side."

Olmsted lived there—except for occasional stays in Hartford and almost two years of travel—until he moved to Manhattan in 1857, although the buildings and grounds of South

Side remained in the family until 1866. During that time he reorganized the road system and rebuilt and expanded the residence while transforming what had been wheat fields into a nursery and a fruit and vegetable farm. He moved the service buildings out of sight of the house, reconfiguring its immediate surroundings to include an ornamental flower garden. In January 1852 he reported to *The Horticulturist* that since his arrival he had planted 1,000 pear trees of several varieties, especially recommending the little known Soldat Laboureur—"a very good first (class) pear"—a dozen specimens of which he had imported from France. Basically, Olmsted accomplished three things at South Side: he became a commercial farmer, not making a great deal of money but not losing a great deal either; he helped to organize and was an officer of the Richmond County Agricultural Society, whose mission included the dissemination of modern farming techniques, information on new and better crop varieties, and the improvement of rural architecture; and for the first time he planned—and with his own hands helped to build—a fairly large, albeit uncomplicated, landscaping project. But improving and working the land was not Olmsted's only interest. During his years on Staten Island, he also engaged in a variety of literary activities, the basis of his public reputation before his name and Central Park's became synonymous.

From 1852 to 1861, Olmsted published five books and dozens of newspaper and magazine articles, and for two years he was an "editor," actually a front man of sorts, for the fledgling *Putnam's Magazine*, a journal of opinion and new fiction, founded to compete with *Harper's New Monthly Magazine*, which reprinted material often pirated from other publications. His first book, the outcome of a seven-month tour of the British Isles in 1850, was *Walks and Talks of an American Farmer in England* (1852), two chapters of which appeared in *The Hor-*

ticulturist: "The People's Park at Birkenhead" (Document 1) in May 1851, and an appraisal of English apple orchards in January 1852. Although it did not sell widely, *Walks and Talks* was favorably reviewed in the press, establishing him as a promising newcomer to the world of American letters.

Olmsted's many interests included the economic and social consequences of slavery, the intensifying abolitionist movement, and their impact on the growing sectional crisis in the United States. Because of *Walks and Talks*, the *New-York Daily Times* financed Olmsted's December 1852 to April 1853 trip to southern coastal regions and published his fifty letters, signed "Yeoman," from February 1853 to February 1854; Olmsted revised them for re-publication as *A Journey in the Seaboard Slave States, with Remarks on Their Economy* (1856). Next came *A Journey Through Texas; or, a Saddle-Trip on the Southwestern Frontier* (1857), based on seventeen letters the *Times* printed from March to June 1854 written by Olmsted during a second trip from November 1853 to August 1854. Following that was *Journey in the Back Country* (1860), originally published in the *New York Tribune* in installments from June to September 1857, based on additional material gathered during his southwestern excursion. The *Journey* trilogy was condensed and combined into the two-volume *Cotton Kingdom: A Traveler's Observations on Cotton and Slavery* (1861). These books were widely reviewed and were considered by many—even some on the "pro" side of the slavery issue—to be necessary reading. Having established himself as a prominent public intellectual during the mid to late 1850s, Olmsted could from then on write pretty much anything he pleased on any subject for any number of newspapers and magazines (see Documents 2 and 6 to 8).

One of them was Downing's *The Horticulturist, A Journal of Rural Art and Rural Taste*, which soon after its first issue in July 1846 became the most widely circulated magazine of its type in the United States. Olmsted was its avid reader from the start, published four pieces in it from 1847 to 1852, and periodically corresponded with Downing, who gave him letters of introduction for his 1850 English walking tour. In August 1851, subscriber and editor met for the second time when Olmsted visited Downing's landscape design office in Newburgh, New York. There he also met Calvert Vaux (1824–95), a young London architect Downing had persuaded to migrate to the United States during his own European tour in 1850. (His and Olmsted's paths did not cross.) Downing's determination to integrate house and grounds more holistically—that is, to design estates in their entirety—had prompted him to take on a partner, since his own architectural drafting skills were shaky. Vaux returned to Newburgh with him in September 1850 and sometime during the next twenty-two months, before Downing's tragic death by drowning in July 1852 at age thirty-six, became a principal in "Downing & Vaux, Architects." Vaux remained in town to complete the firm's unfinished business and to accept his own commissions until 1856, when, with wife and young children, he moved to Manhattan.

New York City, in the meantime, after years of public clamor, some of it Downing's, had set aside land for a public park. In June 1856, its commissioners adopted civil engineer Egbert L. Viele's (1825–1902) plan for its development, appointing him engineer-in-chief of the works, and then in September 1857 appointed Olmsted superintendent—under Viele's direction—largely because he was well known for his intelligence and integrity, seemed to be "above" politics, and had prominent, well-placed advocates. It was the superintendent's job to direct the park's police and its labor force in clearing, draining, and grading the land, activities he had undertaken at Sachem's Head but more extensively on Staten Island. At that same meeting the commissioners also decided to set Viele's plan aside and hold an anonymous competition for a better one.

Vaux intended to enter the competition and invited Olmsted to join him despite his inexperience with landscape designing. At first reluctant, not wishing to offend his superior, Olmsted came aboard because of Viele's patronizing comment about his abilities. He and Vaux went to work in January 1858, their "Greensward" entry won in April, and they were hired to execute the plan for Central Park. Because Olmsted was to direct labor and police—that is, be in charge of virtually everything not directly concerned with design—he was appointed "Architect-in-Chief" (in France he would have been called "Chief of the Works," which makes more sense: see Document 9), with an annual salary of $2,500. ("Engineer-in-Chief" Viele thus became Olmsted's subordinate, touching off years of acrimony.)[2] Because Vaux's role preparing architectural and landscaping plans plus working drawings was also considered subordinate, he was named "Assistant Architect" at five dollars per day (approximately $1,500 annually). He was, needless to say, upset and insulted, all the more so when Olmsted did not speak up on his behalf. The situation was somewhat remedied in 1859 when Vaux became "Consulting Architect" at $2,000 a year, but it was not until 1877 that Olmsted publicly stated that no one "has more claim than Mr. Vaux to the design of the Park or to what is termed 'the aesthetic arrangement of the grounds,' " adding that he also "made the original [architectural] studies . . .; and his superintendence of their details was personal, direct, and controlling."[3]

Vaux was a trained architect while Olmsted was not; he had learned and practiced landscape design on at least sixteen "Downing & Vaux" projects, while Olmsted had only the relatively rudimentary South Side to his credit; he had persuaded a reluctant Olmsted to join him on the Greensward plan; and he had played a larger role than Olmsted—as Olmsted himself admitted—conceptualizing Central Park, attending to its landscaping details, and, of course, designing its structures. This is not to say that the design and implementation of Central Park was not a collaboration. No one will ever know the extent of back-and-forth during the four-month gestation period of Greensward and the years the two men spent bringing their proposal to fruition. But just as it might be supposed that if there had been no Downing, there would not have been a Vaux, in terms of landscape design, it might also be supposed that if there had been no Vaux, there would not have been an Olmsted. To this day, many people attribute the design of Central Park solely to Frederick Law Olmsted, having never heard of Calvert Vaux—the same is true of Prospect Park in Brooklyn (see below)—and that beginning with Central Park, Olmsted was forever more and only a landscape designer. But the reality is that after three years as "Architect-in-Chief," at age thirty-nine in 1861, Olmsted had not yet found his calling. It would take a repeat performance by Vaux to find it for him.

Before that happened, Olmsted had two additional careers—held two other quite disparate but immensely challenging positions, it might be more accurate to say. His books on the American South had revealed his deep concern about the sectional conflict that would culminate in the creation of the Confederate States of America in February 1861 and the outbreak of civil war in April. Wanting to be directly involved in the war effort, and presumably in the process of reconciliation to follow, Olmsted took a leave of absence from the park in June to become Executive Secretary of the United States Sanitary Commission, a kind of precursor to the Red Cross, created by federal law that month to contravene the ineffective government Medical Bureau. Its roots lay in an effort to coordinate the work of women volunteers aiding wounded soldiers, but under Olmsted's direction the Commission expanded services beyond basic treatment of casualties to include provision of field hospitals and hospital ships, the ambulances, medicines, doctors, and nurses to supply and staff them, the inspection and improvement of camp living conditions, and a great deal more. Coordinating all that was enormously wearing on Olmsted, physically and psychically.

The Commission's operating headquarters were in Washington, but directing it required constant travel to battle sites, medical facilities, and directorial meetings out of town. Occasionally when in New York, Olmsted visited Vaux and Central Park, always feeling their pull on him to return. Also disconcerting were the immense physical demands the enormous workload made on his somewhat frail and illness-prone physique. But worst was the almost inevitable bureaucratic and administrative infighting for which Olmsted had little tolerance. Conflicting directives from the Board of Commissioners and its Executive Committee, political grandstanding and rivalries, inane regulations, confusing lines of authority and chains of command, all these and more took their toll on Olmsted, who, maybe naively or even arrogantly, thought things should be run his way with no questions asked. There is no doubt he was an effective administrator with well-honed political skills, but he was also impatient with slow movement, questionable policies, and being overruled. Reluctantly perhaps, and against the wishes of those superiors who knew he had performed admirably, Olmsted resigned his post in August 1863 to become Superintendent of the Mariposa Estate, a gold-mining company holding seventy square miles of land in Bear Valley, eighty-five miles southeast of Stockton, California, near what is now Yosemite National Park. Seven months later his family joined him.

Frederick and his brother were very close, and Olmsted

was immensely pleased when John married Mary Cleveland Bryant in 1850. He thought her a wonderful person, and she returned the sentiment, becoming as important to Olmsted as her husband was. John was frailer and more frequently ill than Frederick, who was devastated when John, only thirty-two years old, died in 1857. His death brought Mary and Frederick closer together, not only in mourning but also in affection, so while it may have been unconventional, it was almost preordained that their love would deepen and they would marry, in June 1859. Olmsted's sister-in-law thus became his wife, and his three nieces and nephews became his stepchildren. Mary gave him three more children of their own, a son John in 1860, who died of cholera in infancy; a daughter Marian born in 1861; and a son Henry in 1870, renamed Frederick Law Olmsted Jr. when he was four. When Mary arrived at Mariposa Estate in March 1864, she brought Olmsted's stepchildren and three-year-old Marian with her.

Having his family there helped Olmsted survive what proved to be a rather rough ordeal. Living conditions at Bear Valley, first of all, were crude, to say the least, primitive, virtually barbaric, he thought. So, too, were social relations, which he attributed to untamed frontier conditions, not to any failure of democratic institutions. Early on, the estate's financial situation turned dangerously shaky when it was revealed that surveys predicting extensive gold deposits were seriously flawed, and soon enough mine output began to decline steadily. By September 1865, employees, including Olmsted, were not being paid, stores were closing, crime was increasing, epidemics were widespread, Olmsted himself had been quite sick, and residents were abandoning their ramshackle houses to the local Digger indians. Olmsted, too, decided to leave, and in October he and his family began the six-week trek by steamer from San Francisco to Panama, across the isthmus by train, then steamer again to New York, where they found rooms in an East Fourteenth Street boarding house.

There were at least two positive outcomes of what was otherwise a disastrous twenty-six months at Mariposa. The first was his joining the movement for scenic preservation. Olmsted preferred graceful, gentle, restful landscapes that subtly changed with passage through them—"friendly" landscapes, it might be said, that eased the spirit and soothed the soul, akin to those he had known since childhood in the Northeast. He was not drawn to grandeur or immensity, which he feared might overwhelm, even intimidate. It was not awe he wished to experience, but tranquility. Nevertheless, he was stunned by the majestic beauty of the Yosemite Valley and the giant sequoias in nearby Mariposa Big Tree Grove, both of which were ceded by the federal government to the state of California in 1864. So it was with pleasure that he agreed to chair the commission to oversee their management, which to him meant preservation of natural beauty and resources for public pleasure and scientific inquiry.

The second positive outcome was his tentative return to landscape design. In March 1865 construction began on Mountain View Cemetery in Oakland, California, but his plans the same year for a downtown San Francisco park and for the new College of California in Berkeley, which would have been his first residential community, never left the drawing board. He may also have designed estates for Darius Ogden Mills, founder of the Bank of California, and for George P. Howard, both on the outskirts of San Francisco. And then in July 1865 he learned that he and Vaux had been reappointed landscape architects of Central Park. Although Olmsted had been keeping his hand in, suggesting to some that he would likely resume an interrupted career, he remained uncertain about what the future held. Calvert Vaux, however, had his own ideas.

While in California, Olmsted and Vaux had kept in close touch, but toward the end of Olmsted's tenure there their correspondence gathered momentum. In 1860 the city of Brooklyn had acquired land for a public park, the next year hiring Egbert Viele to plan it. But in 1864 a new park commission president asked Vaux to assess both the suitability of the site and Viele's suggestions for it. When Vaux found both lacking, the president asked how much money he would require to make a completely new design. Fearing that the contentious history with Viele over Central Park might repeat itself, lengthening the design process, Vaux suggested a generous $10,000 and immediately asked Olmsted to join him. Olmsted demurred, saying the money was not enough, especially if difficulties with Viele and his supporters did indeed recur, as he felt they surely would. In June 1865 the park commissioners hired Vaux to make a new plan incorporating his suggestions from the year before. Olmsted again refused to join him, but after receiving exceptionally candid, quite un-Vaux-like letters in July, he changed his mind. Olmsted's position on Central Park, Vaux wrote, was " 'all theirs is ours,' all ours is mine—and all mine is my own, or something like it. To the commission it was, I will work for the Park, but I must have the reputation— and I must have it all—and I must have it immediately and I must have it always." Olmsted had too much desire for control, he wrote, which got in the way of his being an artist. He even accepted the title "Architect-in-Chief" but then walked away, claiming he was "badly used and injured innocently." But, Vaux wrote, all that is history. "You are, and I am . . . necessary to this work" in Prospect Park. Success "depends on you. . . . I am willing to contribute all I can. Are you content to do the same?"

"It is a testimony to the strength of [their] friendship

that Vaux could express these things so forthrightly," Francis R. Kowsky wrote in his biography, which was certainly true because in August 1865 Olmsted accepted the position of landscape architect, along with Vaux, for both Central and Prospect parks. Almost thirty years later Olmsted admitted that but for Vaux he would not have been involved with either undertaking. But for him, "I should not have been a landscape architect. I should have been a farmer."[4] So it was that in December 1865 stationery was delivered to a new office at 110 Broadway: "Olmsted, Vaux & Co. Landscape Architects," it read across the top.

The partnership lasted until October 1872, after which reports about ongoing projects appeared periodically until January 1874, signed "Olmsted & Vaux" instead of "Olmsted, Vaux & Co." The geographical range of their practice from 1865 to 1872—though tilting toward the Northeast and Middle West—was as impressive as its variety. Cities for which they designed, proposed, or advised, or that asked about public parks include Newark, Philadelphia, Buffalo, Chicago, Cincinnati, Providence, New Britain and Hartford, Connecticut, Boston and Fall River, Massachusetts, and Charleston, South Carolina. In New York and Brooklyn alone they took on eight new projects in addition to their work on Central and Prospect parks.

Six governmental agencies approached them for city or regional plans, ranging in scale from laying out townships and street systems in places as widely separated as Westchester County, New York, and Tacoma, Washington, to the landscaping of a single showcase thoroughfare, Chicago's Drexel Boulevard. Possibly the best known of the eleven urban subdivisions and suburban communities with which they were involved is Riverside, Illinois, designed and constructed after 1869 in collaboration with the noted engineer/architect William Le Baron Jenney (1832–1907). Harvard, Yale, Vassar, and Cornell are among eight institutions of higher learning that for one reason or another contacted them, but only Gallaudet College (now University) commissioned them to do a comprehensive plan, which was executed from 1869 to 1872. Four mental institutions were also among their clients, including the New York State Asylum at Buffalo, where the building was designed by Henry Hobson Richardson (1838–86), with whom Olmsted would later collaborate several times. Grounds for the state capitol in Hartford and for a United States army depot in Jeffersonville, Indiana, complete the partners' work list. They designed no private estates.[5]

In addition to this demanding schedule, Olmsted, always attuned to political events of the day, was involved with the planning, and agreed to join the editorial board, of *The Nation* magazine, which began publication in 1865. He wrote for it occasionally (Documents 3 and 6), but his primary responsibility was helping to determine editorial policy. This meant supporting the Freedmen's Bureau's assistance to recently emancipated former slaves, advocating equal rights for all citizens including freedmen and women, fighting for "good government," as political reform was then called, and much more, and on issues touching his professional interests, opposing architect Richard Morris Hunt's (1827–95) proposal for elaborate Central Park gateways and California's decision to cede portions of the Yosemite Valley to squatters. It is possible that Olmsted's ever-increasing prominence may not have pleased Vaux, who did not exactly shun, but preferred to keep his distance from, political issues that did not affect him professionally. The one was a very public figure; the other preferred his privacy.

If this was a bone of contention between them, it was hardly the sole reason for terminating the partnership, certainly not the principal one, and perhaps not a reason at all. They had their differences, to be sure. Vaux continued to resent his partner's garnering most of the credit for Central Park, which he believed, with good reason and notwithstanding Olmsted's disclaimers, should accord to him. He sometimes thought that Olmsted was less interested in the art of making parks—his own priority—than in supervising them, and while content to let his partner be the front man when dealing with politicians and park administrators, he thought Olmsted paid insufficient attention to the daily operation of their own firm's business, about which Vaux was a stickler. Taking outside work, like editing *The Nation*, might well have been another irritant. But the core issue was none of the above; it was the inevitable outcome of their careers beginning to diverge.

By October 1872, primarily but not exclusively on the basis of Central and Prospect parks, Olmsted was nationally known for his landscape design, while Vaux, equally well known in this regard, was (independently of Olmsted) taking on more architectural work, including New York City's American Museum of Natural History, its Metropolitan Museum of Art, and landscape painter Frederic Edwin Church's "Olana" residence and grounds in Hudson, New York. Convinced of his competence in both building and landscape design, but unlike Downing certain he could integrate the two on his own when necessary, Vaux decided to go it alone, hoping also to increase his income. Olmsted had no lack of self-confidence either, nor any doubt that he could now design landscapes as well or better than anyone else. And so for "reasons of mutual convenience," they decided to part company, on good terms certainly, on such good terms that they would later collaborate on a handful of projects, including a public park dedicated to Andrew Jackson Downing—whom both considered their mentor—in Newburgh, New York, begun in 1889 but not completed until two years after Vaux's 1895 death. Neither would accept a fee for his services.

After their separation, Vaux pursued dual careers in architecture and landscape design. Regrettably, his most spectacular conception, the interior of his 1872 competition entry for the Main Pavilion at the 1876 Centennial Exhibition in Philadelphia, did not win; its rendering shows how magnificent it would have been (while another reveals its conventionally fussy "Victorian" exterior).[6] He did distinguish himself, however, with several lodging houses, industrial schools, and small parks sponsored by reform associations to improve living conditions in New York City's poorer neighborhoods. His more upscale buildings included an 1881–84 residence for Samuel J. Tilden (1814–86), governor of New York in 1875–76 and Democratic presidential nominee in 1876. The best known of his landscape projects are grounds for the Canadian Parliament Building (1873-79) in Ottawa, for Bryn Mawr College (1884) in Pennsylvania, for the Grant's Tomb site (1885) in Manhattan, for New York University's Bronx campus (1894), and for the New York Botanical Garden (1895), also in the Bronx. Vaux was a highly regarded, much sought-after designer, to be sure, but as cultivated taste shifted during the 1880s toward classical revivals, his commitment to picturesque styles did not shift with it and his architectural practice declined. He spent much time in his last years organizing his business papers. When he died by drowning in 1895, some who knew him speculated that he had committed suicide. Although unlikely, the speculation itself, given the source, raises questions about his psychic state.

Olmsted's life also changed during the 1880s, but for the better. With his work on the extensive Boston park system under way, and perhaps seeking a more placid living and working environment than New York City offered, especially now that he was approaching his sixties, Olmsted purchased an old farmhouse in Brookline, Massachusetts, in 1883, rejecting an offer by his friend Henry Hobson Richardson, who lived a half mile away, to design something for him. Wanting "Fairsted," as he named it, "to be part of nature herself, rather than . . . foreign to the general character of the place,"[7] he covered it from foundation to roof line with a thick layer of vines and creepers, and rather than build a terrace, his usual way of connecting house to grounds, he added a conservatory with large windows opening to the lawn. The lawn itself he divided by plantings into areas out of sight from each other and the house—"outdoor living rooms" or "open-air apartments," he called them (see Documents 3 to 5 and 10), dotted with tables and chairs depending on the weather. Olmsted added an office wing to Fairsted in the 1890s and lived happily there until 1898. In 1963 it was designated a National Historic Landmark.[8]

With Vaux's departure in 1872, Olmsted changed his firm's name to "Frederick Law Olmsted, Landscape Architect," but in 1884 his stepson John Charles (1852–1920) joined him and the name became "F. L. & J. C. Olmsted" until 1889 when a talented young employee, Henry Sargent Codman (d. 1893), was apparently elevated to junior partner, necessitating the change to "F. L. Olmsted & Co." With Codman's unexpected death while recuperating from an appendectomy in 1893 and the immediate promotion of another talented young employee, Charles Eliot (d. 1897), to full partner, the firm became "Olmsted, Olmsted & Eliot," until 1897—even though Frederick Law Olmsted stopped designing in 1895—the year Eliot died and Olmsted officially retired, when it reverted briefly to "F. L. & J. C. Olmsted," "F. L." now referring to Frederick Law Olmsted Jr. (1870–1957), who came aboard that year. From 1898 to 1961 it was "Olmsted Brothers, Landscape Architects." The 114-year history beginning in 1865 ended when the last successor firm, known as "Olmsted Associates, Inc." despite lacking an Olmsted as principal, closed its doors in 1979.

An 1898 or 1899 photograph shows thirteen male employees

(seven unidentified) standing, sitting, and sprawling in front of the "Olmsted Brothers" office. There is no way to know with certainty if this was the entire workforce, but it likely was. A second photograph from circa 1922 depicts thirty-four employees (including one woman, a secretary) assigned to a single job, the 2,800-acre Palo Verdes Estates, a suburban residential community in Los Angeles County, California, that the firm planned and supervised from 1909 to 1933. There is no way to know what percentage of the firm's workforce this contingent represents. Nor is it possible to determine how many employees Frederick Law Olmsted had at various times while he was in charge. But one thing is certain: in the quarter century separating these two photographs, "Olmsted Brothers" grew exponentially.[9]

That would have been impossible without Olmsted's impressive legacy, measured for the moment only by the extent and variety of his work. During the twenty-three years from 1872 until he unofficially stepped down in 1895, Olmsted and assistants drew thousands of plans for hundreds of executed and unexecuted projects coast to coast. His reputation rested primarily (and still does) on urban parks and park systems, but he also designed dozens of private estates and, when grouped together, a similar number of cemeteries and arboreta, urban subdivisions and suburban communities, grounds for public and commercial buildings, residential institutions like mental hospitals, churches, railroad stations, recreational facilities, expositions, and fairs—in short, for almost every imaginable purpose. He was also instrumental in the creation of scenic reserves, the Niagara Falls Reservation in New York, along with the aforementioned Yosemite Valley in California, being the best known. It is fair to say that well before retirement Olmsted was easily the most highly regarded and respected landscape designer in the United States, and was considered the "father" of American landscape architecture, and on both counts he still is.

His reputation rests not only on the quantity but also on the quality of the work he produced, which, even when neglected, altered, or executed improperly in the first place, remains a constant source of public and private pleasure. But the work itself was informed by his social and design philosophies, which are not always obvious in his writings but are nevertheless embedded there.

Frederick Law Olmsted's upbringing was a privileged one, not that of landed gentry, oceanic traders, or new-to-the-scene large-scale manufacturers who collectively formed the wealthiest sector of American society, but of well-established businessmen and professionals who in today's terms would be considered upper-middle class, a portion of which, like some of their "superiors," were philanthropically oriented, comfortable among the literati, and, perhaps most importantly, civic-minded: concerned with the well-being of the large or small agglomerations in which they lived and for which because of their status they felt responsible. This is not to say they were social reformers. They were, rather, intelligent, well-informed people of conscience who believed in the inevitability of "progress," American style, which meant to them the ever-widening distribution of democracy's benefits thanks to equal opportunity for all, including prosperity and perhaps upward mobility, attainable by anyone who worked hard and lived frugally. They did not believe in collectively generated progress, people banding together in labor unions or radical political parties, for example, or in government provision of services that would now be called "welfare," all of which were considered anti-democratic constraints on individual liberty. Their assumption was that human capacity for self-improvement was potentially unlimited as long as people were left alone to care for themselves by themselves and, if duty called, occasionally help each other out. Olmsted absorbed this manner of thinking, but by the 1850s he began attaching caveats: that certain cooperative movements (see Document 2) and improvement of the physical environment by government action (see below) were also beneficial to democracy.

By the 1840s as Olmsted came of age, the most momentous threat to his social milieu's vision of democracy, the rampaging bull in the china shop, was slavery. But lurking on the horizon was another: industrialization, which brought with it, after the Civil War especially, not only horrible working conditions in factories but also horrible living conditions in cities as urban populations seeking employment expanded rapidly owing to massive migration from rural America and abroad (see Documents 13 and 15). Olmsted was well aware of both, addressing the former with his journalism, his books of the 1850s, and as editor of *The Nation*. The latter he addressed with his parks.

Olmsted did not believe that the pell-mell growth of cities would soon slow and eventually stop, as did many of his contemporaries. Present-day Boston, he argued by way of example in an 1870 lecture (Document 13), would in short order become the tiny hub of an enormous metropolis. And with continued growth, residents' health and morals—his words—would continue to deteriorate. Life expectancy is shorter and illness more prevalent in cities than outside them, he averred, primarily because inadequate sun, foliage, clean air, and opportunity for healthy exercise were exacerbated by pollution and filth. Buildings jammed together on narrow, overcrowded streets, people pushing and jostling each other back and forth, everyone a stranger with "nothing in common"—a condition later generations would label alienation—had already resulted in mutual distrust, the "regard of others in a hard if not always threatening way," a state of mind that had already led to increased delinquency, crime, and diminishing of the civility he and his class so highly cherished. And, if unaddressed, matters would only get worse. Although Olmsted repeatedly stated that throughout history cities had come into being primarily to facilitate commerce, he never openly suggested that commerce was therefore the fundamental, albeit indirect, cause of deteriorating health and morals. But he did say that some city districts should be commerce free. Less densely packed new residential subdivisions was one possibility; open, airy public parks was another.

Olmsted did not directly address the class and ethnic hostility that became increasingly volatile as the nineteenth century progressed. But he was certainly aware of the situation. Consider that Central Park in New York and Prospect Park in Brooklyn "are the only places in those associated cities," he said in that 1870 lecture (Document 13), where

> you will find a body of Christians coming together, and with an evident glee in the prospect of coming together, all classes largely represented, with a common purpose, not at all intellectual, competitive with none, disposing to jealousy and spiritual or intellectual pride toward none, each individual adding by his mere presence to the pleasure of all others, all helping to the greater happiness of each. You may thus often see vast numbers of persons brought closely together, poor and rich, young and old, Jew and Gentile. I have seen a hundred thousand thus congregated, and I assure you that . . . I have looked studiously but vainly among them for a single face completely unsympathetic with the prevailing expression of good nature and light-heartedness.

Olmsted's use of "Christians" as a synonym for "poor and rich, young and old, Jew and Gentile" may seem inappropriate today, but at the time "Christian" was often employed in a secular sense to describe a well-mannered person of good will and intention, as well as humane activity by a group (see Document 6). If, as he believed, public parks actually bestowed a "distinctly harmonizing and refining influence upon the most unfortunate and most lawless classes of the city—an influence favorable to courtesy, self-control, and temperance," then he might be forgiven for thinking that a "Christian" breaching of class, ethnic, and religious barriers was a not unworthy objective.

It is tempting to say, and it has been said, that Olmsted was anti-city and saw parks primarily as agencies of social control: anti-city because he inserted the countryside—or interpretations of it—into its very heart, de-urbanizing it, so to speak; agencies of social control because he thought parks would keep "the lawless classes" out of dram shops and off the streets, thereby reducing social disorder. But this interpretation overlooks the positive aspects of city life that saturate his writings, the "progress" it represented that he and his milieu found so beneficial. And it also ignores an assumption central to the nineteenth-century Romantic outlook he shared with many middle- and upper-class contemporaries: that exposure to nature and the natural world was beneficial—calming, soothing, morally uplifting—but that (and here he went beyond most contemporaries) since the countryside was unavailable to city dwellers unable to afford travel, which is to say, the great majority of city dwellers, nature must be brought to them. As to social control, his belief was that recreation, exercise, and contemplation of natural things would improve the physical and mental health of everyone, rich and poor alike, while exposure to "others," to social classes with which people did not ordinarily associate except as "inferiors" or "superiors," would ultimately enhance mutual understanding, returning to the city a semblance of the civility he experienced growing up in Hartford. It was not social control he sought, but social harmony. This may seem archaic and naive in the thoroughly uncivil twenty-first century, but in the late nineteenth, people like Olmsted who thought this way were pioneering advocates of social justice. They also understood that municipal appropriation when necessary of privately owned land and, of course, money (in the form of taxes) in order to build parks was a new but proper role for government. Today, they would be called liberals or progressives.

"What we want to gain [by creating parks] is tranquility and rest to the mind," he wrote in 1870, and that meant, as he insists over and again in these documents, gentle, subtle, easy transitions among their parts. This did not mean that a given park should have uniform terrain or should resemble another somewhere else, as if there were a universally applicable formula for tranquility and rest. It meant, rather, that since each park had its unique land configurations, soil qualities, climate, and exterior surroundings— was site specific, in today's terminology—its design would be determined by the limitations those conditions imposed and the opportunities they afforded. The graceful terrain of Prospect Park in Brooklyn, for example, was a world away from rugged Mount Royal Park in Montreal, where severe climate was another world away from Louisville's. But no matter how different one from another, all Olmsted's parks, indeed all his landscape projects regardless of purpose or size, were governed by an overarching "ideal," a holistic vision, to which everything must be subordinated, in which each boulder and tree, structure and stream, each meadow and hillock took its rightful place.

What impressed Olmsted most about a natural landscape was its "mass," the way in which the myriad colors and forms within its parameters seemed effortlessly to cohere. The same was true of a garden: no matter how beautiful an individual flower might be, its higher beauty came from taking its appointed place in a carefully orchestrated ensemble. So it should be with a small homestead, an estate, a park, or anything else a landscape designer took in hand. The goal must always be to find a concordance that would enable discreet and disparate entities to coalesce for the good of the whole as well as for each other.

So it is by no means inappropriate to consider Olmsted's landscape designs as physical exemplars of the social tranquility he believed would one day grace the nation he loved.

NOTES

1. Olmsted's words in this paragraph are from his 1872 report to the McLean Asylum quoted in Charles E. Beveridge and Paul Rocheleau, *Frederick Law Olmsted: Designing the American Landscape* (New York: Rizzoli, 1995), 134, and from a 1900 letter to "Folks at home" quoted in Laura Wood Roper, *FLO: A Biography of Frederick Law Olmsted* (Baltimore: Johns Hopkins University Press, 1973), 474.

2. On this issue see Francis R. Kowsky, *Country, Park & City: The Architecture and Life of Calvert Vaux* (New York: Oxford University Press, 1998), 96, 101, 164–165.

3. "Central Park, New York," *American Architect and Building News*, 2 (April 14, 1877), 120.

4. The quotations in this and the preceding paragraph are from Kowsky, *Country, Park & City*, 173–174.

5. See Lucy Lawliss, Caroline Loughlin, and Lauren Meier (eds.), *The Master List of Design Projects of the Olmsted Firm, 1857–1979* (Washington, D.C.: National Association for Olmsted Parks, 2008 rev. ed.), passim.

6. See William Alex and George B. Tatum, *Calvert Vaux: Architect and Planner* (New York: Ink, 1994), 199–201, for these renderings, and passim for other projects mentioned here.

7. Quoted in Beveridge and Rocheleau, *Frederick Law Olmsted*, 141.

8. Ibid., 136–148.

9. These photographs are reproduced in Lawliss et al., *Master List*, ii and xx.

I

YOUTHFUL
OBSERVATIONS

ONE

The People's Park at Birkenhead

(1851)

From April into October 1850, Olmsted took a "sabbatical" from his Staten Island farm to tour parts of England (and bits of Wales and Scotland), much of the time on foot, with his brother John Hull Olmsted and friend Charles Loring Brace. Studying agricultural practices, observing desperate poverty firsthand but also visiting museums and, through family connections, homes of the socially well placed, Olmsted was deeply moved by the graceful beauty of England's rural landscapes as well as the orderly cleanliness of its farms and villages, certainly in comparison with what he knew from home. But what struck him most was Birkenhead Park, the first public recreation ground he had ever seen, leading him later in his tour to visit others in Chester and London. His enthusiasm was almost unrestrained: "Is it not a grand good thing," he writes in this, his very first essay on a park, that Birkenhead "is entirely, unreservedly, and forever the People's own"? Olmsted drew two important conclusions from his English excursion: that he would join the ranks of Andrew Jackson Downing and others urging the creation of municipal recreation grounds in the United States, and that publicly owned parks were socially more beneficial than those held privately, even when opened to the populace.

Originally published as "The People's Park at Birkenhead, near Liverpool, by W., Staten Island, New York," The Horticulturist, *6*

(May 1851), and in longer form in Olmsted's Walks and Talks of an American Farmer in England, *2 vols. (1852). "W" stood for "Wayfarer," Olmsted's occasional pen name early in his career.*

Birkenhead is the most important suburb of Liverpool, having the same relation to it that Brooklyn has to New-York, or Charlestown to Boston. When the first line of Liverpool packets was established, there were not half a dozen houses here; it now has a population of many thousands, and is increasing with a rapidity hardly paralleled in the New World. This is much owing to the very liberal and enterprising management of the land-owners, which affords an example worthy of consideration in the vicinity of many of our own large towns. There are several public squares, and the streets and places are broad, and well paved and lighted. A considerable part of the town has been built with uniformity, and a reference to general effect, from the plans, and under the direction of a talented architect, Gillespie Graham, Esq., of Edinburgh.[1]

We received this information while crossing the Mersey in a ferryboat, from a fellow passenger, who, though a stranger, entered into conversation, and answered our inquiries, with frankness and courtesy. Near the landing we found, by his direction, a square of eight or ten acres, enclosed by an iron fence, and laid out with tasteful masses of shrubbery (not trees), and gravel walks. The houses about were detached, and though of the same general style, were sufficiently varied in details not to appear monotonous. These were all of stone.

We had left this, and were walking up a long, broad street, when the gentleman who had crossed the ferry with us, joined us again, and said that as we were strangers, we might like to look at the ruins of an abbey which were in the vicinity, and he had come after us; that if we pleased he might conduct us to it. What an odd way these Englishmen have of being "gruff and reserved to strangers," thought I.

Did you ever hear of Birkenhead Abbey?[2] I never had before. It has no celebrity, but coming upon it so fresh from the land of Youth as we did, so unexpecting of anything of the kind— though I have since seen far older ruins, and more renowned, I have never found anything so impressively aged.

At the Market place we went into a baker's shop, and while eating some buns, learned that the poorest flour in the market was American, and the best, French. French and English flour is sold in sacks, American in barrels. The baker asked us if American flour was *kiln dried*, and thought it must be greatly injured, if it was not, on that account. When we left, he obligingly directed us to several objects of interest in the vicinity, and showed us through the market. The building is very large, convenient, and fine. The roof, which is mostly of glass, is high and airy, and is supported by two rows of slender iron columns, giving to the interior the appearance of three light and elegant arcades. The contrivances to effect ventilation and cleanliness are very complete. It was built by the town, upon land given to it for the purpose, and cost $175,000.

The baker had begged of us not to leave Birkenhead without seeing their new Park, and at his suggestion we left our knapsacks with him, and proceeded to it. As we approached the entrance, we were met by women and girls, who, holding out a cup of milk, asked us—"Will you take a cup of milk, sirs! Good, cool, sweet, cow's milk, gentlemen, or right warm from the ass." And at the gate were a herd of donkeys, some with cans of milk strapped to them, others saddled and bridled, to be let for ladies and children to ride.

The gateway, which is about a mile and a half from the ferry, and quite back of the town, is a great massive block of handsome Ionic architecture, standing alone, and unsupported by anything else in the vicinity, and looking, as I think, heavy and awkward. There is a sort of grandeur about it that the English are fond of, but which, when it is entirely separate from all other architectural constructions, always strikes me unpleasantly. It seems intended as an impressive preface to a great display of art within. But here, as well as at Eaton Park,[3] and other places I have since seen, it is not followed up with great things—the grounds immediately within the grand entrance being very simple, and apparently rather overlooked by the gardener. There is a large archway for carriages, and two smaller ones for those on foot; on either side, and over these, are rooms, which probably serve as inconvenient lodges for the laborers. No porter appears, and the gates are freely open to the public.

Walking a short distance up an avenue, we passed through another light iron gate into a thick, luxuriant, and diversified garden. Five minutes of admiration, and a few more spent in studying the manner in which art had been employed to obtain from nature so much beauty, and I was ready to admit that in democratic America, there was nothing to be thought of as comparable with this People's Garden. Indeed, I was satisfied that gardening had here reached a perfection that I had never before dreamed of. I cannot attempt to describe the effect of so much taste and skill as had evidently been employed; I will only tell you, that we passed through winding paths, over acres and acres, with a constant varying surface, where on all sides were growing every variety of shrubs and flowers, with more than natural grace, all set in borders of greenest, closest turf, and all kept with most consummate neatness. At a distance of a quarter of a mile from the gate, we came to an open field of clean, bright, green-sward, closely mown, on which a large tent was pitched, and a party of boys in one part, and a party of gentlemen in another, were playing cricket. Beyond this was a large meadow with rich groups of trees, under which a flock of sheep were reposing, and girls and women with children were playing. While watching the cricketers, we were threatened with a shower, and hastened back to look for shelter, which we found in a pagoda, on an island approached by a Chinese bridge. It was soon filled, as were the other ornamental buildings, by a crowd of those who, like ourselves, had been overtaken in the grounds by the rain; and I was glad to observe that the privileges of the garden were enjoyed about equally by all classes. There were some who even were attended by servants, and sent at once for their carriages, but a large proportion were of the common ranks, and a few women with children, or suffering from ill health, were evidently the wives of very humble laborers. There were a number of strangers, and some we observed with note-books, that seemed to have come from a distance to study from the garden. The summer-houses, lodges, bridges, &c., were all well constructed, and of undecaying materials. One of the bridges which we crossed was of our countryman, Remington's patent, an extremely light and graceful erection.[4]

I obtained most of the following information from the head working gardener.

The site of the Park and Garden was ten years ago, a flat, sterile, clay farm. It was placed in the hands of Mr. Paxton[5] in June, 1844, by whom it was laid out in its present form by June of the following year. Carriage roads, thirty-four feet wide, with borders of ten feet, and walks varying in width, were first drawn and made. The excavation for a pond was also made, and the earth obtained from these sources used for making mounds and to vary the surface, which has been done with much *naturalness* and taste. The whole ground was thoroughly under-drained, the minor drains of stone, the main, of tile. By these sufficient water is obtained to fully supply the pond, or lake, as they call it, which is from twenty to forty feet wide, and about three feet deep, and meanders for a long distance through the garden. It is stocked with aquatic plants, gold fish and swans.

The roads are McAdamized.[6] On each side of the carriage way, and of all the walks, pipes for drainage are laid, which communicate with deep main drains that run under the edge of all the mounds or flower beds. The walks are laid first with six inches of fine broken stone, then three inches cinders, and the surface with six inches of fine rolled gravel. All the stones on the ground which were not used for these purposes, were laid in masses of rock-work, and mosses and rock-plants attached to them. The mounds were then planted with shrubs, and Heaths, and Ferns, and the beds with flowering plants. Between these, and the walks and drives, is everywhere a belt of turf, which, by the way, is kept close cut with short, broad scythes and shears, and swept with house-brooms, as we saw. Then the rural lodges, temple, pavilion, bridges, orchestra for a band of instrumental music, &c., were built. And so, in one year, the skeleton of this delightful garden was complete.

But this is but a small part. Besides the cricket and an archery ground, large valleys were made verdant, extensive drives arranged—plantations, clumps, and avenues of trees formed, and a large park laid out. And all this magnificent plea-sure-ground is entirely, unreservedly, and forever the People's own. The poorest British peasant is as free to enjoy it in all its parts, as the British Queen. More than that, the Baker of Birkenhead had the pride of an Owner in it.

Is it not a grand good thing? But you are inquiring who *paid* for it. The honest owners—the most wise and worthy town's people of Birkenhead—in the same way that the New-Yorkers pay for the Tombs,[7] and the Hospital, and the *cleaning* (as they amusingly say) of their streets.

Of the farm which was purchased, one hundred and twenty acres have been disposed of in the way I have described. The remaining sixty acres, encircling the Park and Garden, were reserved to be sold or rented, after being well graded, streeted and planted, for private building lots. Several fine mansions are already built on these (having private entrances to the park) and the rest now sell at $1.25 a square yard. The whole concern cost the town between five and six hundred thousand dollars. It gives employment at present, to ten gardeners and laborers in summer, and to five in winter.

The generous spirit and fearless enterprise, that has accomplished this, has not been otherwise forgetful of the health and comfort of the poor. Among other things, I remember, a public wash and bathing house for the town is provided. I should have mentioned also, in connection with the market, that in the outskirts of the town there is a range of stone slaughter-houses, with stables, yards, pens, supplies of hot and cold water, and other arrangements and conveniences, that enlightened regard for health and decency would suggest.

The consequence of all these sorts of things is, that all about, the town lands, which a few years ago were almost worthless wastes, have become of priceless value; where no sound was heard but the bleating of goats and braying of asses, complaining of their pasturage, there is now the hasty click and clatter of many hundred busy trowels and hammers. You may drive through wide and thronged streets of stately edifices, where were only a few scattered huts, surrounded by quagmires. Docks of unequaled size and grandeur are building, and a forest of masts grows along the shore; and there is no doubt that this young town is to be not only remarkable as a most agreeable and healthy place of residence, but that it will soon be distinguished for extensive and profitable commerce. It seems to me to be the only town I ever saw that has been really built at all in accordance with the advanced science, taste, and enterprising spirit that are supposed to distinguish the nineteenth century. I do not doubt it might be found to have plenty of exceptions to its general character, but I did not inquire for these, nor did I happen to observe them. Certainly, in what I have noticed, it is a model town, and may be held up as an example, not only to philanthropists and men of taste, but to speculators and men of business.

After leaving the Park, we ascended a hill, from the top of which we had a fine view of Liverpool and Birkenhead. Its sides were covered with villas, with little gardens about them. The architecture was generally less fantastic, and the style and materials of building more substantial than is usually employed in the same class of residences with us. Yet there was a good deal of the same *stuck up*, and uneasy pretentious air about them, that the suburban houses of our own city people so commonly have. Possibly this is the effect of association in my mind, of steady, reliable worth and friendship with plain or old fashioned dwellings, for I often find it difficult to discover in the buildings themselves, the elements of such expression. I am inclined to think it is more generally owing to some disunity in the design—often perhaps to a want of keeping between the mansion and its grounds or its situation. The architect and the gardener do not understand each other, and commonly the owner or resident is totally at variance in his tastes and intentions from both; or the man whose ideas the plan is made to serve, or who pays for it, has no true independent taste, but had fancies to be accommodated, which only follow confusedly after custom or fashion. It is a pity that every man's house cannot be really his own, and that he cannot make all that is true, beautiful, and good, in his own character, tastes, pursuits and history, manifest in it. But however fanciful and uncomfortable many of the villa houses about Liverpool and Birkenhead appear at first sight, the substantial and thorough manner in which most of them are built, will atone for many faults. The friendship of nature has been secured to them. Dampness, heat, cold will be welcome to do their best. Every day they will improve. In fifty or a hundred years, fashions may change, and they will appear, perhaps, quaint, possibly grotesque—at any rate, picturesque—but still strong, homelike, and hospitable. They have no shingles to rot, no glued, and puttied, and painted gim-crackery, to warp and crack, and molder, and can never look so shabby, and desolate, and dreary, as will ninetenths of the buildings of the same denomination now erecting about New-York, almost as soon as they lose the raw, cheerless, impostor-like airs which seem almost inseparable from their newness.

NOTES

1. James Gillespie Graham (1776–1855), a Scottish architect, designed the town of Birkenhead, located on the River Mersey, from 1825 to 1828.

2. Birkenhead Abbey was erected ca. 1250 for the Catholic Order of Benedict.

3. Eaton Park with its hall in Chester, England, was originally owned by the duke of Westminster.

4. Olmsted refers to John R. Remington (1817–53) who patented improvements for truss bridges.

5. Sir Joseph Paxton (1803–65), English landscape designer and architect, is best known for his Crystal Palace in Hyde Park, London, built for the Great (International) Exhibition of 1851.

6. John Loudon McAdam (1756–1836), Scottish engineer and road builder, improved drainage of thoroughfares by laying crushed stone mixed with gravel over a bed of larger stones. Others would later add tar to bind the materials.

7. The Tombs, a New York City prison, so called because its façade was based on an Egyptian mausoleum, was built from 1835 to 1838 according to plans by John Haviland (1792–1852). Olmsted may be referring to the New York City Lunatic Asylum (later Metropolitan Hospital), designed by Alexander Jackson Davis (1803–1892) in 1834–35.

TWO

The Phalanstery and the Phalansterians

(1852)

The North American Phalanx in Colt Necks Township, New Jersey, was a secular utopian community founded in 1841 upon the ideas of Frenchman Charles Fourier (1772–1837), who argued that cooperative living was more personally satisfying and economically productive than private enterprise. Cooperation would best be achieved, he believed, in somewhat isolated settlements called phalanxes in which approximately 1,600 people—the "associated"—would live in "grand hotels," or "phalansteries," sharing domestic chores while laboring together to generate income. The number of residents in the North American Phalanx never exceeded 150, and most were middle- and working-class Northeasterners. Disputes over the women's rights and abolitionist movements, a proposal to consider religious affiliation, and a costly 1854 fire brought the experiment to an end that year.

Olmsted was favorably enough impressed by what he saw to make the remarkable statement that if he had a sixteen-year-old son, he would prefer him to spend "the next four years of his life as a working member of the North American Phalanx than at Yale or Harvard" provided—and this was a big "provided" for Olmsted—the boy was studious and well informed, for his major reservation about the "associated" was their insufficient "attention to the intellectual" life.

This essay demonstrates Olmsted's own wide-ranging intellectual curiosity, in this case concerning the possibilities for human improvement, regardless of social class, through democratic cooperation.

Originally published in the New York Daily Tribune, *29 July 1852, as "The Phalanstery and the Phalansterians. By An Outsider.," a letter to the editor signed "An American Farmer" and dated 24 July 1852.*

I have just made a visit to the "North American Phalanx," Monmouth County, N.J. Many of the readers of *The Tribune*, however unwilling they may be to accept the views of its Editors on the subject of [the] Association, must have a curiosity to know how such ideas work in practice. It was such a motive induced me to accept an invitation from a member whose acquaintance I lately made, to visit this community, and I feel bound to give a candid relation of my observations. I confess to have paid but little attention to the subject previously and to have had no more knowledge or definite thoughts about it than any one must who has been in the habit of perusing *The Tribune* with much respect for the good intention and good sense of its editors, for several years.

There are six hundred acres of land in the domain of the Association, most of it of the ordinary quality of "Jersey land." About two hundred acres are under cultivation, much improved within a few years by dressing with marl, two beds of which, of superior quality, are on the property. A stream of water running through it, gives a small milling-power. The nearest tide-water is five miles distant, where steamboat communication may be had daily, but at irregular hours, with New-York, a poor sandy road to be traveled over between. The land cost twenty-five dollars an acre, and I believe I have stated all the material advantages of the location. The Association has a grist and a saw-mill driven with the aid of a steam-engine that they have added to the small water-power. No other branch of mechanical or manufacturing industry is carried on, and the labor of the members is mainly given to farming and market-gardening; and it is from the sale of agricultural products almost entirely that they must get their living and their profit.

The *Phalanstery* is much like the large hotel of a watering place or a sea shore house, made to accommodate 150 persons. There are chambers for single persons, and *suites* of rooms for families. There are also tenements detached from the main building, but having a covered way, that the members may reach it dry-shod in rainy weather—these are each occupied by a family. There are certain apartments also in the phalanstery, such as a reception room for visitors, a reading room, a dining hall; the kitchen, dairy and other domestic offices. A small steam-engine is employed for washing, mangling, churning, &c., and the arrangements of the domestic department are all admirably contrived for saving labor. I should guess roughly that one woman could do the work of ten, with the ordinary farm-house kitchen conveniences—in other words, as far [as] this goes, farmers would save their wives and *women folk* all but about one-tenth of their now necessary drudgery by living on the associated plan.

There is some pretty natural wood and a picturesque ravine near the house, but no garden or pleasure ground; indeed the *grounds* about the house are wholly neglected, and have a shabby and uninviting appearance. It is evident that the Association have neglected everything else in their endeavor to make the experiment successful, financially. They have worked hard and constantly for this, and though, from entire inexperience at the business of market-gardening, to which their attention was chiefly directed, they at first made numerous mistakes, similar to those playfully alluded to by Hawthorne at Blithedale,[1] and though they had a great many peculiar difficulties, they have been rewarded in finding it pay. Last year, after paying the members at a rate of wages for labor higher than that ordinarily given by farmers in this vicinity, the Association divided five per cent on the capital invested in the undertaking among the shareholders. When we consider how hard it is for farmers in general to make a decent living, we must acknowledge that they have proved a great advantage in the cooperative principle, as applied to agriculture.

That the financial success of the community is the legitimate result of the association of labor and capital, I am satisfied, and I should judge the peculiar description of husbandry to which its attention has been directed, was that in which it was least likely to have been profitably employed, because it is that in which labor saving implements and machinery can be employed with the least advantage. In addition to the profits divided last year, it should be mentioned that extensive orchards, as yet making scarcely any return, are growing.

The Refectory is a fine, spacious hall, with perhaps twenty tables, each long enough for a dozen persons to dine off. There are bills of fare changed every day in which the dishes provided for each meal are mentioned, with their cost—as at an eating-house. By buying at wholesale, and using all possible contrivances to lessen labor in preparing and cooking food, of course the cost of living is very low; but every little item counts. Thus: bread 1 cent, butter 1/2 cent, as well as roast-beef 3 cents, and ice-cream (a large ration of the richest "Philadelphia") 2 cents. During drought and short pasture the butter-cakes are graduated by the stamp a trifle smaller, which I mention as an indication of the systematic exactness to which the domestic economy of the establishment is brought. There are several summer or transient boarders at the establishment, and those are charged, in addition to the cost of the food they choose and a small rent for their bed-chamber, $2 a week for the profit of the Association. The waiters are mainly from among the most refined and pleasing young ladies of the Association. On taking a seat you are introduced to the lady who attends your table, and you feel yourself to be in the relation of guest, not of superior, to her. She takes part in the general conversation of the table, but comes and goes as there is need—is a very good waiter indeed, doing her duty with tact, sweetness and grace. "Why do so many of the best of your young people choose to be waiters, and so deprive themselves in a great measure of the social enjoyment of dining with their friends?" "They all dine together afterward, and, as they *are* among the best of us, it is a privilege to dine with them—of course to *wait* with them."

One great point they have succeeded in perfectly: in making labor honorable. Mere physical labor they have too much elevated I think, but at any rate the *lowest* and most menial and disagreeable duties of a civilized community are made really reputable and honorable, as well as generally easy and agreeable. A man who spent a large part of his time in smoking and reading newspapers, and chatting it away, or in merely recreative employments, would feel ashamed of himself here, would feel *small* and consider it a privilege to be allowed to black boots or sweep, or milk, a part of the time.

As to the people of the community in general, I have a strong respect for them as earnest, unselfish, hard-working livers in the faith of a higher life for man here below as well as hereafter "above." I think they are living devoutly and more in accordance with the principles of Christ *among themselves*, than any neighborhood of an equal number that I know of. There are fewer *odd* characters among them than I expected to see— generally there was much simplicity and self containedness:

they seem to care very little—too little—"for appearances," or what the world outside thought of them, and greatly to love one another. They are, so far as I could learn, strongly attached to the *Phalanx*, feel confident it is the right way to live, have *enjoyed* it and thus far fully realized their hopes in joining it. "I wouldn't leave for worlds"—"couldn't live, it seems to me, in any other way." "It is like the opening of heaven compared to what life was like before I came here," I heard from different individuals. One Episcopal clergyman who was formerly much respected and beloved and paid $1,000 a year for his services as Rector of a country church, and who, after a great struggle with the conviction that the morality and religion he was educated to preach, were not the morality and faith preached by Christ and designed by him for the conversion of the world from its ancient state of sin and misery, declares that he is satisfied that here is the true Church of Christ's gospel, and in this way it must be that the Kingdom must come. There is also a Unitarian clergyman who came hither by much the same road.

I cannot tell what sort of people the majority were when they came here, and thus find a difficulty in judging what the effect of the associative life has been upon them. Mostly New-Englanders, I should think, and working people; few or none independently wealthy. (The *stock* of the Phalanx is mostly held by New-York capitalists.) Whether any considerable number were actually day laborers, living from hand to mouth, uneducated and uncouth, I could not be satisfied. Some of the later additions plainly are so, many of the older ones might have been, and if so they have been a good deal refined and civilized by this life. If we compare their situation with an average of the agricultural class, laborers and all, even in the best of New-England, it is a most *blessed* advance. They are better in nearly all respects, and I don't see why, if such associations were common, and our lowest class—(I mean poorest and least comfortable, and least in the way of improvement, moral and mental) of laborers, could be drawn of their own will into them, why they should not be similarly advanced in every way. Put a *common place* man, of our poorest agricultural or manufacturing class into *such circumstances*, and it looks to me every way probable that he would be greatly elevated, be made a *new man* of in a few years. On the other hand, take the average of our people of *all* classes, and on the whole, it seems as if the influence of the system, if they would keep to it a little while, would be favorable. They would be likely to live more sensibly, happier, healthier and better. If you take our most religious and cultivated sensible people, then I think it would depend much on individual tastes and character. For most of these, particularly of English blood, it would require a change, a good deal of a struggle to come handsomely and profitably into it.

The long and the short of it is, I am more of a *Fourierite* than before I visited the experiment. The united household (and semi-conglomeration) of families even, works better than I was willing to believe possible. Nevertheless, I don't think I shall be a Fourierite for myself, but for many, for a large part of an American community (people), I think I may be. It wouldn't suit me, but many, I think, it would; and if I was obliged to live mainly by *manual* labor I am not sure but I should go in for it myself.

An *Associationist* I very decidedly am, more than I was before I went to the Phalanx. The advantages of cooperation are manifestly great, the saving of labor immense: the cheapening of food, rent, &c., enough to make starvation abundance. The advantages by making knowledge, intellectual and moral culture and aesthetic culture more easy—popular, that is, the advantages by *democratizing* religion, science, art, mental cultivation and social refinement, I am induced to think *might be* almost equally great among the *associated*. They are *not* at the N[orth] A[merican] Phalanx—and yet are to some degree. Those who came there refined, religious and highly intelligent, may have suffered. I saw no evidence that they had, but should have expected it, because they have given themselves up to too narrow ranges of thought, have worked too hard to make the Association succeed; sacrificed themselves, if so, for the benefit of the world's progress over them. It is not by any means yet a well organized and arranged establishment. They are constantly improving—seeing errors, and returning to do up matters which, in the haste of a struggle to get started, were overlooked. There is yet an immense deal, as they are aware, to be attended to and better arranged when they get time. They are in great need of mechanics, but I suspect it is an error of their theory that they are. What they need for improvement as a *community of moral creatures* is more attention to the intellectual. They want an *"Educational Series"* very much. A Frenchman acts as [a] teacher to the fry, but there is no proper nursing department, and the children, and not the children alone, are growing without proper discipline of mind. A rough lot one would expect them to make, but I must confess those who are breaking into manhood, and especially into womanhood, tell well for the system. They are young *ladies* and young *gentlemen* naturally, and without effort or disagreeable self consciousness. If I had a boy to educate, who at 16 had acquired at home habits of continued persevering application of mind in study, and who was tolerably stocked with facts and formulas, I would a good deal prefer that he should spend the next four years of his life as a working member of the North American Phalanx than at Yale or Harvard.

I have neglected to notice a number of points of the Phalanx that would be interesting, a good deal to praise, a good deal to reprove; but they do not bear upon the important questions which it is the purpose of the members to do something by their association to solve. If there are any slight errors in my statements, observations and conjectures, they will be excused as not materially affecting these. I have endeavored to notice what I thought most desirable for the public to know and reflect upon, and I cannot conclude without, as one of the public, expressing my gratitude to the members for the generous earnestness with which, for the public good, they are making their experiment. I pray for their success; but whether it comes as they anticipate or not, they will have their reward.

NOTE

1. *The Blithedale Romance* (1852), by Nathaniel Hawthorne (1804–64), was based on his experience of living briefly at Brook Farm (1841–47), a West Roxbury, Massachusetts, experiment incorporating Fourier's cooperative principles.

II

SMALL
RESIDENTIAL
SITES

THREE

Suburban Home Grounds

(1871)

Olmsted uses this review of Frank J. Scott's The Art of Beautifying
Suburban Home Grounds of Small Extent . . . *(New York: D.
Appleton & Company, 1870) to offer his own thoughts on the subject.
For a variety of historical and cultural reasons, he suggests, Americans think of the street-facing portions of their properties as decorative
embellishments of their houses to be viewed from their own or neighbors' windows and from the roadway but not to be used as outdoor
living rooms. Since their primary purpose is to display their own good
taste, owners consider it self-defeating to enclose their grounds with
perimeter plantings. This practice, he adds, is part of a more serious
problem: that Americans, especially women, no longer appreciate large
natural vistas and sweeping scenic overviews but focus instead on
particularly beautiful flowers, shrubs, and trees in isolation, thereby
reducing them to just another form of ornamentation.*

*Disagreeing with Scott's insistence that perimeter plantings not be
used in suburban settings, Olmsted contends that this remains an open
question, subject to circumstance, the need for privacy, for example,
particularly if grounds are indeed turned into outdoor living spaces,
which he urges. But he also implies that if grounds blend topographi-
cally with surrounding properties or have attractive vistas, visual
merging of the near and the distant—enhanced by the absence of perimeter plantings—might reinvigorate in Americans a sense of landscape*

wholeness, enabling them once again to appreciate the unity of the forest, so to speak, as well as the singularity of the trees.

Originally published in The Nation, *13 (October 26, 1871).*

Not one in a thousand, probably, of all those who, in this country, every year set about the preparation of a suburban home for their families, can readily obtain the aid of a landscape-gardener, properly so called. To those who cannot, Mr. Frank J. Scott, of Toledo, Ohio, undertakes to give elementary instruction in the art, which he defines to be that of "creating lovely examples of landscape in miniature," but which, in its application to such small spaces of ground as he has more particularly in view, might, perhaps, better be stated to be that of preparing agreeable *passages* of landscape scenery. This work is in two parts, the first relating to questions of site, extent, plan, and method; the second, to the special qualities for landscape planting of each of several hundred trees and shrubs. The two parts are of about equal bulk, and might very well have been bound apart; together, they form an inconveniently heavy volume. The advice given in the first part is copious and distinct, and may be understood and applied by most town-bred men. The principles of art are freshly, if incompletely, stated, and although a new and elaborate series of symbols is used, the numerous illustrative plans, upon which it is evident that much study has been spent, are intelligible and instructive.

In one respect, Mr. Scott abandons the usage of the established authorities, and adopts, to the fullest extent, what he regards as an improved, popular American practice. It has generally been thought desirable by the older landscape gardeners, in forming their plans, that certain objects standing outside the ground placed under their control should be given a greater apparent distance, or, perhaps, without entire concealment, should be rendered partially obscure from points of view within it. For this purpose, a plantation is generally laid out along the boundary which is designed eventually to establish a verdant middle distance in the landscape. Perhaps still more frequently, it has been desired to shut out completely objects which were originally in view, but which were discordant with more important landscape elements nearer the points of view, in which case plantations have been planned with the design of forming complete new backgrounds. Skillful use of boundary plantations for these purposes was originally made by Kent and his immediate associates and successors, but the practice being followed, in a mechanical way, by the famous Brown and other stupid pretenders, gave rise to "the belt," so unmercifully ridiculed by Uvedale Price in his prolonged discussion with Repton and others.[1] Mr. Scott uses no boundary plantations, and, unless to shut out some special deformity, would merge the surface of his grounds with whatever may lie beyond them. He would [do] so without a fence if he could, and, not being allowed to, would have it as nearly as possible transparent. It may be said for his plans that, in attempting to secure even miniature passages of landscape *of a complete character* within the usual limits of a suburban building lot, the inexperienced planter would be so likely to run into fussy conditions, that it would almost always be better for him to accept whatever objects there may be on or across the street or boundary as primary matters of interest, and that the main motive of his planting should be to gain elegance of foreground only. There is a sweet passage in the last work of Repton in which he justifies the pleasure he had taken in a design of this simple character. But Mr. Scott argues that the practice of planting closely along the boundary is a bad conventionalism, handed down from a period of "rude improvements and ruder men"; that it is a peculiarity of English gardening, which "it would be as unfortunate to follow as to imitiate the surly self-assertion of English traveling manners"; and, finally, that not to lay our private grounds open to the public gaze is ill-bred, inhospitable, unneighborly, and unchristian (pp. 51 and 61).

We are confident that Mr. Scott, in the passages to which we refer, has got upon a wrong road, and as he has, in general, evidently studied his way with care, we are anxious to see what has led him astray. On reflection, it appears to us that so far as there is a distinct American practice in the respect indicated, it has grown out of the fact that the motive of what Mr. Scott calls home grounds in this country has hitherto been, in most cases, almost exclusively a motive of decoration. They have been designed to be looked upon from a window, or from the street; much less generally than in Europe to be familiarly and frequently occupied and lived in. The difference in custom in this respect has been often remarked, and generally attributed to differences of climate. We are disposed, however, to think that it should be connected with a considerable series of well-marked distinctions, now passing away, with which climate has had little to do—with habits of more constant, more desultory, and, with individuals, more varied labor; with the habit of looking with suspicion upon anything tending to withdraw attention from productive occupations, unless it were to distinctly religious exercises; with the customs which have forced young people generally to seek social enjoyment much more apart from their parents than is thought necessary, desirable, or prudent, in old countries; and, in short, with [the] many direct results of the necessary privations and hardships of the pioneer period. It is not impossible, even in this country, with patience, ingenuity, and skill, to establish conditions under which, while engaged in many common domestic occupations, we may spend a good deal of time out of doors, but it is much more difficult than in the old countries, and while our emigrating fathers had their full stent [variation on "stint," or "acreage"] to keep the wolf and savage from their doors, it is not surprising that they did not undertake the task. Their houses were commonly built, at most, with but two doors, of which one opened upon a working yard, always more or less blocked up with logs saved for fuel or timber, and the larger implements of the farm, the other upon the trail, which afterwards became a high road or village street. After a certain period, some one in each neighborhood would acquire an enviable distinction by "slicking up" a place, and planting some slips of lilac or poplar, obtained from the older settlements, or perhaps direct from the mother country. The most available ground for such a purpose was just within the door opposite the working yard, where, accordingly, to protect the plants from cattle, a space would be fenced in. As a better class of houses were substituted for the original cabins, with increasing security and prosperity, front-door yards increased in number, until, at length, the distinction was reversed, and it became almost disreputable in many districts to live in a house without such an appendage. The notion of furnishing them with broad, clean, smooth floors of gravel, or carpets of fine, close turf, with sewing and reading seats; of coaxing nature to decorate their convenience, or protect them from sun and wind, or to give them any degree of seclusion or coziness; or of ever using them as *al-fresco* [open air] parlors, or tea-rooms, or workrooms, or kindergartens, was not at all entertained. Regarded simply as ornaments of the house front, or as badges of respectability, like chaises and green blinds, it would have been folly to hide them behind walls, hedges, or thickets.

Between home-grounds of this class, however enlarged and improved, and the characteristic miniature pleasure-grounds of the suburban villas of any part of Europe, there can be no comparison. The private planting of public roadsides, and the contribution of a small piece of decorated ground in front of every dwelling to public use, is an excellent custom; and, in contrast with it, the habit of regarding the highway as a strictly government or parish affair, and its improvement in any respect as no man's private concern, and the somewhat stern and often rude face which suburban homes often present to the street in Europe, seems churlish and clownish. But between this extreme and that of forbidding all family privacy out of doors, there is a wide range. Croquet is doing something to unsettle the traditional idea that the only use of a home-[ground is] to set off the house; but few among us as yet suspect how much time can be spent profitably, agreeably, and healthfully, or how large a share of our ordinary household duties, as well as our recreations, can be attended to in the open air, provided we have grounds suitably arranged and furnished.

There is reason for questioning whether women in this country are not gradually becoming disqualified for much enjoyment of nature. We have spent some months in a neighborhood so famed for its landscape beauty that it was, at the time, visited by hundreds of strangers. Notwithstanding the fact that there were the most inviting groves, ravines, and mountains on all sides, far and near, that the temperature was generally agreeably cool, and the walks in several directions not at all difficult, it was rare to meet women on foot a mile away from the houses at which they were staying; rare to meet them out of doors at all dressed otherwise than as for church or a shopping expedition in Broadway. In their driving and sailing, it was obviously the social opportunity, not the scenery, that was sought. A flower in the grass, a bunch of ash-keys, a birch trunk, the bark of which suggested the making of a house ornament, the most commonplace objects thus associated with indoor

life, would at once take, and completely withhold, attention
from the finest view. To have been once upon a certain road,
or to a certain point, was a reason for not going there again.
We have seen also, recently, seven carloads of people wait at
Suspension Bridge,[2] the greater part [of] all the time in their
seats, for half an hour of a fine autumn afternoon, but two of
the whole number, and these men, taking the trouble to step
the length of the train ahead, where, instead of the gloom of
the station-house, there was a view that would repay a voyage
across the Atlantic. To be sure, the greater number had been
over the road, and had seen it before, from the car-windows,
as they passed the bridge. Not one in a hundred of the women
who can command a carriage in the Central Park has ever
been in the Ramble; not one in a thousand has cared to walk
in it twice. This lack of interest in nature is not often found
in Europe except among the lowest peasantry. The vulgarest
Englishwomen make at least an effort to appear superior to it,
and they cannot do this without benefiting their children. At
places of resort in Great Britain and Germany which may be
compared with that we have referred to, go where we would,
within a good half-day's walk, we have always found scores of
women and girls, many of them showing by their attitude and
occupation that they were not only really enjoying but studying nature with earnestness and deliberation. If there is such a
defect, and it is growing upon us, how is it to be accounted for?
We are inclined to think that the too exclusively indoor life,
with intervals of church, lecture-room, and street, to which
the better part of our women have been hitherto led, tends
to disqualify them for observing truly, and consequently for
enjoying, the beauty of nature on a large scale. With constant
training of his faculties, no artist feels that he can appreciate
or fully enjoy a landscape the first time or the first hour that he
looks upon it.

Our American homes are, in some respects, the best for women in the world, but they are far from faultless, and they do not, in all respects, compare favorably, class for class, with those of the Old Country; and the weakest point of our suburban and rural homes is their lack of open-air family apartments, adapted to the climate and other conditions of our country— pieces of ground designed not so much to form pretty pictures from the windows, and thus add to our wall decorations, or from the street, and thus add to our cheap and showy house-fronts, but to be enjoyed from their own interior; to be occupied and lived in as an integral part of the home, as the grounds of Old Country homes so much more commonly are. In suburban building-lots of the ordinary dimensions, the space between the building line, established by a good custom, if not by law, and the street is not often a suitable one to be used for this purpose, while the limited space in the rear of the house is commonly required for other necessary purposes. Mr. Scott urges that building-lots should generally be laid off twice the depth they usually are; but his plans are adapted to the customary conditions, and the question of attempting to secure family privacy out of doors by means of close plantations, under these artificial conditions, may, as we have already admitted, be considered as an open one. We simply protest against the principle involved in his argument. His work is intended and adapted to have a large influence in cultivating out-of-door habits and a love of nature, and the apparently unqualified support given in such passages as we have cited of a common prejudice against out-of-door domestic privacy is the more to be regretted.

In the second part, some seven hundred species and varieties of trees and shrubs are enumerated, and, as far as practicable, their landscape qualities indicated. The report made in regard to many of the acquisitions of the last twenty years is the best that we have seen; and it is gratifying to observe that, in numerous instances, it is based on observations of specimens found in our public grounds. In regard to many novelties, the mature character of which in this climate cannot be known for some years to come, we are glad to notice a commendable and unusual caution observed. The foliage of many of the new conifers, which is most attractive while they are in the sapling stage, changes character so greatly when they begin to bear seed, as to render them quite valueless for home plantations. With regard to shrubs, Mr. Scott truly says that if half a dozen of the commonest of the old kinds are thrown out of the long and bewildering series named in the catalogues of the great foreign nurseries, we shall find it difficult to select as many that will be their equals in beauty of form, foliage, or bloom. But it should be known also that, notwithstanding the number of high-priced and far-fetched novelties now offered, for some of the bushes that are of the highest value for landscape planting, we shall ask both our own and the foreign dealers in vain. We must look them up, as Mr. Scott shows that he has done, in our woodland pastures and along our neglected roadsides.

Of each part of Mr. Scott's work it may be said that it is the most valuable of its class that has been published in America since Mr. Downing's "Landscape Gardening."[3]

NOTES

1. Olmsted mentions four highly influential English landscape designers and writers: William Kent (1685–1748), also a major Palladian Revival architect, who helped pioneer "naturalistic" English gardens; Lancelot "Capability" Brown (1715–83), a prolific practitioner of the "picturesque" whom Olmsted labels a "stupid pretender," presumably for relying on "the belt," that is, perimeter plantings to block exterior views and enhance the seclusion of private parks in which he specialized; Uvedale Price (1747–1829), a widely read theoretician of "picturesque" design; and Humphry Repton (1752–1818), an "eclectically picturesque" disciple of Brown but capable of producing more

modest work than his mentor, hence Olmsted's reference to Repton's "sweet passage" about "a design of . . . simple character" in his last book, *Fragments on the Theory and Practice of Landscape Gardening* (1816).

2. Olmsted refers to the Niagara Falls Suspension Bridge built in the early 1850s according to designs by John A. Roebling (1806–69) that segregated carriage and pedestrian traffic on its lower deck from rail traffic on the upper. Beginning with childhood family excursions, Olmsted continued to visit Niagara Falls and nearby Buffalo, New York, for professional reasons, most recently in May 1871 to examine the grounds he and Calvert Vaux were preparing for the Buffalo State Hospital for the Insane, which was designed and constructed from 1869 to 1880 by his frequent collaborator, Henry Hobson Richardson (1838–86).

3. Alexander Jackson Downing (1815–52), *A Treatise on the Theory and Practice of Landscape Gardening, Adapted to North America; with a View to the Improvement of Country Residences*, was published in 1841. The author under review, Frank Jesup Scott (1828–1919), was a Toledo, Ohio, architect who dedicated his book to Downing, with whom he had studied landscape design.

FOUR

Plan for a Small Homestead

(1888)

Olmsted has his client say that "people find their love of Nature most gratified when they have a trim lawn and a display of flowers and delicacies . . . in front of their houses. [But] I find Nature touches me most when I see it in a large way . . . that gives me a sense of its infinitude." This in a nutshell is the essence of Olmsted's design philosophy, hinted at in Document 3 of 1871 but well established in word and deed during the subsequent seventeen years.

The challenge here is to reconcile a small, irregularly shaped, steeply graded, almost unmarketable urban site with poor soil—a realtor's nightmare—with its inspiring views, and Olmsted lays out with great precision how to do it. In addition to his provocative suggestions about how best to organize, integrate, yet keep discrete the utilitarian and recreational subdivisions of a difficult-to-arrange small lot, two other conclusions about Olmsted emerge from this essay: One is that he was in fact quite interested in small residential holdings, which is not generally recognized. The other is, and is here well illustrated, that his knowledge of horticulture—of what plant forms are best deployed under given climatic and topographical conditions, and to what aesthetic effects they are best put not only in their immediate locations but also in relation to both middle and far distances—is encyclopedic.

Originally published in Garden and Forest, *1 (May 2, 1888).*

Conditions and Requirements

The site is upon the south face of a bluff, the surface of which is so steep that the rectangular street system of the city, to the east and south, had not been extended over it. The diagonal streets, *M* and *N*, have been lately introduced and building lots laid off on them, as shown in Figure 1. The triangular space between *L* and *M* Streets is a public property containing the graves of some of the first settlers of the region. Its northern and western parts are rocky and partly covered by a growth of native Thorns and Junipers, east of which there are Willows and other planted trees. At *A* there is a meeting-house and parsonage. Arabic figures show elevations above city datum.

The lot to be improved is that marked *IX*. The usual conveniences of a suburban cottage home are required, and it is desired that it should be made more than usually easy and convenient for members of the household, one of whom is a chronic invalid, to sit much and be cheerfully occupied in out-of-door air and sunlight. A small fruit and vegetable garden is wanted and a stable for a single horse and a cow, with carriage room and lodgings for a man. Water for the house, garden and stable is to be supplied by pipes. There is a sewer in *M* Street.

The problem is to meet the requirements thus stated so snugly that the labor of one man will be sufficient, under ordinary circumstances, to keep the place in good order and provide such gratification of taste as with good gardening management the circumstances will allow.

The north-west corner of the lot is 21 feet higher than the south-east corner, the slope being steeper in the upper and lower parts than in the middle. There is a small outcrop of a ledge of limestone about 30 feet from the south end, and the ground near it is rugged and somewhat gullied. *M* Street, which has a rapid descent to the eastward, opposite the lot, was brought to its grade by an excavation on the north side and by

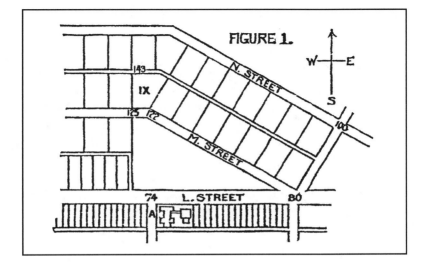

FIGURE 1.

banking out on its south side, the bank being supported by a retaining wall. The excavation has left a raw bank two to five feet high on the street face of the lot.

Looking from the middle part of the lot over the roof of the parsonage a glimpse is had of a river, beyond which, in low bottom land, there is a body of timber, chiefly Cottonwood, over which, miles away, low, pastured hills appear in pleasing undulations.

The narrower frontage of lot *IX*, its irregular outlines, its steepness, its crumpled surface, the raw, caving bank of its street face and its apparent rockiness and barrenness, had made it slower of sale than any other on the hill streets, and it was, accordingly, bought at so low a price by its present owner that he is not unwilling to pay liberally for improvements that will give him such accommodations upon it as he calls for. From the adjoining lots and those higher up the hill to the north the view which has been referred to, over the roof of the parsonage, is liable to be curtained off by trees to grow, or houses to be built, on the south side of them. Either this liability has been over-looked or the view has been considered of little value by those who have bought them. "Most people," says the owner of lot *IX*, "find their love of Nature most gratified when they have a trim lawn and a display of flowers and delicacies of vegetation upon it in front of their houses. I find Nature touches me most when I see it in a large way; in a way that gives me a sense of its infinitude. I like to see a natural horizon against the sky, and I think that the advantage we shall have here in that respect will fully compensate us for the want of a fine lawn-like front, provided the place can be made reasonably convenient." Fortunately his wife is essentially like-minded. "I am a Western woman," she says, "and would not like to live in a place that I could not see out of without looking into the windows of my neighbors."

Controlling Landscape Considerations

The only valuable landscape resource of the property lies in the distant view eastward from it. Looking at this from the house place, it can evidently be improved by placing in its fore-ground a body of vigorous, dark foliage, in contrast with which the light gray and yellowish greens of the woods of the river bottom will appear of a more delicate and tender quality, and the grassy hills beyond more mysteriously indistinct, far away, unsubstantial and dreamy. Such a foreground can be formed within the limits of lot *IX*, and, strictly speaking, the forming of it will be the only landscape improvement that can be made on the place. It is, however, to be considered, that when the mid-dle of the lot is occupied by a house but small and detached spaces will remain to be furnished with verdure or foliage, and that anything to be put upon these spaces will come under direct and close scrutiny. Hence nothing should be planted in them that during a severe drought or an intense winter or in any other probable contingency is likely to become more than momentarily shabby. Further, it is to be considered, that when the eye is withdrawn from a scene the charm of which lies in its extent and the softness and indefiniteness, through distance, of its detail, the natural beauty in which the most pleasure is likely to be taken will be of a somewhat complementary or antithetical character. But to secure such beauty it is not necessary to provide a series of objects the interest of which will lie in features and details to be seen separately, and which would be most enjoyed if each was placed on a separate pedestal, with others near it of contrasting qualities of detail, each on its own separate pedestal. It may be accomplished by so bringing together materials of varied graceful forms and pleasing tints that they will intimately mingle, and this with such intricate play of light and shade, that, though the whole body of them is under close observation, the eye is not drawn to dwell upon, nor the mind to be occupied, with details. In a small place much cut up, as this must be, a comparative subordination, even to obscurity, of details, occurring as thus proposed, and not as an effect of distance, is much more conducive to a quiescent and cheerfully musing state of mind than the presentation of objects of specific admiration.

Anatomical Plan

The important common rooms of the family and the best chambers are to be on the southern side of the house, in order that the view over the river, the south-western breeze and the western twilight, may be enjoyed from their windows. (See Figure 2.) It follows that the kitchen and the main entrance door to the house are to be on its north and east sides. Were it not for excessive steepness, the best approach to the house would be on a nearly straight course between its east side and the nearest point on *M* Street—*i. e.*, the south-east corner of the lot; this partly because it would be least costly and most convenient, and partly because it would make the smallest disturbance of the space immediately before the more important windows of the house. But to get an approach of the least practicable steepness the place will be entered at the highest point on M Street—*i. e.*, the south-west corner; then a quick turn will be taken to the right, in order to avoid the ledge, then, after passing the ledge, another to the left. On this course a grade of one in twelve and a half can be had. (The grade on the shortest course would be one in seven.) Opposite the entrance to the house there is to be a nearly level space where carriages can rest.

The caving bank made by the cut for grade of *M* Street requires a retaining wall four feet high along the front of the lot. This will allow a low ridge, nearly level along the top, to be formed between the wheelway and the street, making the wheelway safer and a less relatively important circumstance to the eye.

Even in the part of the lot chosen, as being the least steep, for the house, a suitable plateau for it to stand upon can only be obtained by an embankment on the south and an excavation on the north. The embankment is to be kept from sliding down hill by a wall ten feet in front of the wall of the house. This retaining wall is to be built of stained and crannied refuse blocks of limestone which have been formerly thrown out from the surface in opening quarries on the back of the bluff. They are to be laid without mortar and with a spreading base and irregular batter. Where the ledge can be exposed they will rest upon it, and the undressed rock will form a part of the face of the wall. A railing two and a half feet high is to be carried on the top of the retaining wall, and the space (*b*) between this and the

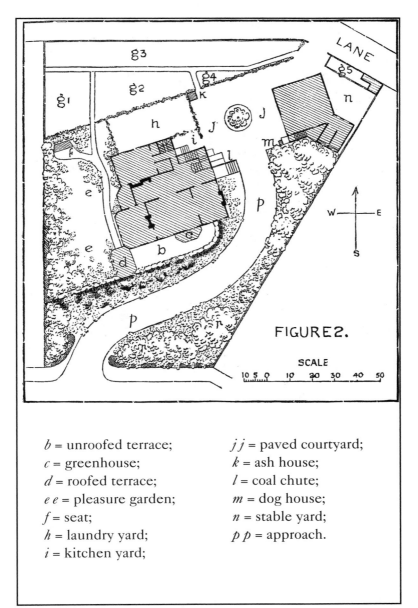

FIGURE 2.

b = unroofed terrace;
c = greenhouse;
d = roofed terrace;
e e = pleasure garden;
f = seat;
h = laundry yard;
i = kitchen yard;
j j = paved courtyard;
k = ash house;
l = coal chute;
m = dog house;
n = stable yard;
p p = approach.

wall of the house will be an open terrace upon which will open half-glazed French windows on the south of the library, parlor and dining-room. At *c* (Figure 2) there is to be a little room for plants in winter, the sashes of which are to be removed in summer, when the space is to be shaded by a sliding awning. At *d* a roof covers a space large enough for a tea table or work table, with a circle of chairs about it, out of the house proper, forming a garden room. This roof is to be sustained by slender columns and lattice-work, and lattice-work is to be carried over it and the whole to be overgrown with vines (Honeysuckle on one side, Wisteria on the other, the two mingling above). The space *ee* is reserved for a tiny pleasure garden, to be entered from the house and to be considered much as if, in summer, it were a part of it carpeted with turf and embellished with foliage and flowers. At *f* there is to be a retired seat for reading and intimate conversation, and east of this an entrance to the service gardens, to be described later. The laundry yard, *h*, and the kitchen yard, *i*, are to be screened by high lattices covered by Virginia Creeper. The court yard, *jj*, is to be smoothly paved with asphalt blocks or fire brick, which it will be easy to thoroughly hose and swab every day. In one corner of it is a brick ash house, *k*; in another a gangway to the cellar and a chute for coal, *l*; in another a dog house, *m*. The stable and carriage house are entered from the court yard, but hay will be taken into the loft from a wagon standing in the passage to the back lane. At *n* is the stable yard.

Landscape Gardening

The soil to be stripped from the sites of the house, terrace, stable, road and walks, will be sufficient, when added to that on the ground elsewhere, to give full two feet of soil wherever needed for turf or planting.

Trenches, nowhere less than two feet deep, are to be made on each side of the approach road south of the terrace and to be filled with highly enriched soil, the surface of which is to slope upward with a slight concavity as it recedes from the approach. The base of the wall is to merge irregularly into this slope. The space between the terrace and the street is so divided by the approach, and, in the main, is so steep and dry, that no part of it can be well kept in turf, nor can trees be planted in it, because they would soon grow to obstruct the southward view from the house and terrace. The steep dry ground and the rock and rough wall of this space are to be veiled with vines rooting in the trenches. The best vine for the purpose is the common old clear green Japan Honeysuckle (*Lonicera Halliana*). In this sheltered situation it will be verdant most, if not all, of the winter, and blooming, not too flauntingly, all of the summer. It can be trained not only over the rough sloping wall of the terrace, but also over the railing above it, and here be kept closely trimmed, so as to appear almost hedge-like. Also it may be trained up the columns of the shelter and along its roof; the odor from its bloom will be pleasing on the terrace, and will be perceptible, not oppressively, at the windows of the second story. Other vegetation is to be introduced sparingly to mingle with it, the wild Rose and Clematis of the neighborhood; the Akebia vine, double flowering Brambles, and, in crevices of the wall, *Rhus aromatica*, dwarf Brambles, *Cotoneaster microphylla*, Indian Fig, Aster, and Golden Rod, but none of these in conspicuous bodies, for the space is not too large to be occupied predominatingly by a mass of foliage of a nearly uniform character. Near the south-west corner of the pleasure garden, *Forsythia suspensa* is to fall over the wall, and, also, as a drapery in the extreme corner (because the odor to those near the bloom of it is not pleasant), Matrimony vine (*Lycium vul-*

gare). Upon the walls of the house east of the terrace, Japanese Ivy (*Ampelopsis veitchii*) is to be grown, and before it a bush of the fiery Thorn (*Crataegus pyracantha*). For the ground on the street side of the approach, *pp*, smooth-leaved shrub evergreens would be chosen were they likely to thrive. But both the limestone soil and the situation [are] unfavorable to them. Next, a dark compact mass of round-headed Conifers would best serve the purpose of a foreground to the distant view, but there are none that can be depended on to thrive long in the situation that could be kept within the required bounds except by giving them a stubbed and clumsy form by the use of the knife. The best available material for a strong, low mass, with such deep shadows on the side toward the terrace as it is desirable to secure, and which is most sure to thrive permanently in the rather dry and hot situation, will be found in the more horizontally branching of the Thorn trees (*Crataegus*), which grow naturally in several varieties on other parts of the hill. Their heads may be easily kept low enough, especially in the case of the Cockspur (*C. crus-galli*), to leave the view open from the terrace without taking lumpy forms. But as a thicket of these spreading thorn bushes, fifty feet long, so near the eye, might be a little stiff and monotonous, a few shrubs are to be blended with them, some of which will send straggling sprays above the mass and others give delicacy, grace and liveliness, both of color and texture, to its face. Common Privet, red-twigged Dogwood, common and purple Barberry, *Deutzia scabra*, Spice-bush and Snowberry may be used for the purpose. American Elms have already been planted on the lot adjoining on the east. The Wahoo Elm (*Ulmus alata*) and the Nettle tree (*Celtis occidentalis*) are to be planted in the space between the approach and the boundary. They will grow broodingly over the road, not too high, and mass homogeneously with the larger growing Elms beyond. Near the stable two Pecans (*Carya olivaeformis*) are to be planted. The three trees last named all grow in the neighboring country and are particularly neat and free from insect pests. A loose hedge of common Privet having the effect of a natural thicket is to grow along the boundary. No other shrub grows as well here under trees.

As the pleasure garden is to be very small, to be closely associated with the best rooms, and to be not only looked at but used, it must be so prepared that no excessive labor will be needed (as in watering, mowing, sweeping and rolling), to keep it in superlatively neat, fresh and inviting condition. No large trees are to be grown upon or near it by which it would be overshadowed and its moisture and fertility drawn upon to the injury of the finer plantings. It must be easy of use by ladies when they are shod and dressed for the house and not for the street. Its surface is to be studiously modeled with undulations such as might be formed where a strong stream is turned aside abruptly into a deep and narrow passage with considerable descent. It will be hollowing near the house and the walk, and will curl and swell, like heavy canvas slightly lifted by the wind, in the outer parts. Wherever it is to be left in turf the undulations are to be so gentle that close mowing, rolling and sweeping will be easily practicable. The upper and outer parts are to be occupied by bushy foliage compassing about all the turf; high growing shrubs next [to] the fences and walls; lower shrubs before them; trailers and low herbaceous plants before all. But there must be exceptions enough to this order to avoid formality, a few choice plants of each class standing out singly. The bushes are to be planted thickly, not simply to obtain a good early effect, but because they will grow better and with a more suitable character in tolerably close companionship. As the good sense of the lady who is to be mistress of this garden ranges more widely than is common beyond indoor matters of taste, it may be hoped that due thinnings will be made from year to year and that the usual mutilation of bushes under the name of pruning will be prevented.

The following little trees and bushes may be used for the higher range: The common, trustworthy sorts of Lilac, Bush-honeysuckle, Mock-orange, Forsythia, Weigelia, the Buffalo-berry (*Shepardia*), common Barberry, the Cornelian Cherry and the red twigged Dogwood. In the second tier, Missouri Currant, Clethra, Calycanthus, Jersey Tea, Japanese Quince, Japanese Mahonia, Spiraeas, and the Mezereon Daphne.

In the third tier, *Deutzia gracilis*, Oregon Grape, flowering Almond (white and red), *Spiraea thunbergii* and *S. japonica*, Waxberry, *Daphne cneorum*, small-leaved Cotoneaster, and the Goatsbeard Spiraea. The Virginia Creeper is to be planted against the walls of the house, Chinese Wisterias near the garden room. Oleanders, Rhododendrons, Figs, Azaleas and Bamboos, grown in tubs, are to be set upon the terrace in summer. They are to be kept in a cold pit during the winter.

The service garden (*g* 1–5, Fig. 2) will have a slope of one to five inclining to the south. It is intended only for such supplies to the house as cannot always be obtained in the public market in the fresh condition desirable, and is divided as follows :

*g*1. Roses and other plants to provide cut flowers and foliage for interior house decoration;

*g*2. Small fruits;

*g*3. Radishes, salad plants, Asparagus, Peas, etc.;

*g*4. Mint, Parsley, Sage, and other flavoring and garnishing plants for the kitchen;

*g*5. Cold-frame, wintering-pit, hot-beds, compost-bin, manure-tank, garden-shed and tool-closet.

FIVE

Terrace and Veranda—Back and Front
(1888)

A reader of Document 4 complained to Garden and Forest *that Olmsted's "Small Homestead" would be insufficiently shaded, but worse, it had no front door, an act of impropriety, he thought. After Olmsted replied "with pleasure" that the house was indeed sufficiently shaded and cooled by awnings, openings, and plantings, he went on to offer a brief history of "front" and "back," concluding that these terms are "no more applicable to a well designed house in America than anywhere else" because "with us a country house, and often a suburban house, will best have three fronts": one with the finest view, another overlooking the garden, and a third for entry. But he does not insist that every house requires all three; one front might well serve more than one purpose. Nor does he argue that the entry side should necessarily be the most attractive. His point is that everything depends on what "circumstances admit": near and distant vistas, the best place for a garden, ease of vehicular access and to outdoor living rooms, where to place the more unsightly aspects of residential life: the kitchen, waste disposal, storage and carriage sheds, and so on. Let the site, its surroundings, and the family's manner of living determine what goes where, Olmsted is saying; let there be no hard and fast rules.*

Originally published in Garden and Forest, *1 (June 6, 1888).*

The following queries suggested by the "Plan for a Small Suburban Homestead," in the issue of *Garden and Forest* for May 2d, have been referred to me.

"On the south side, where, in a typical American house, there would be a shady veranda, instead of it there is what is called a terrace—an uncovered platform—upon which the sun must fall and be reflected with burning heat and blinding light into the adjoining rooms. The house has no front door. To enter it from the street, visitors must go round by the back yard, close by the stable. What can be said for such arrangements except that they are striking from their originality or their foreign character? If a speaker chose to turn his back upon his audience he would offend a sense of propriety. Is there no question of propriety about the front and back of a house?"

I reply with pleasure to these inquiries.

A well-shaded apartment having been provided, outside the walls, at the south-west corner of the house, much better adapted for the seating of a family circle than an ordinary veranda, the platform called a terrace will serve desirable purposes that a veranda in the same situation would not. The family rooms giving upon it can be opened to sunshine, as it is best that all rooms should be occasionally, summer and winter. The sun can be excluded from them when it is better that it should be (leaving the air free course through the windows), by adjustable awnings. Interesting forms of decorative sub-tropical vegetation can be fittingly set upon such a terrace in immediate connection with the principal family rooms, as they could not be in the shade of a veranda. There are several months in the year when the terrace could be occupied for one or two hours of most days as a work-room for ladies or as an airing place for an infant or a convalescent, when it would be imprudent to sit in the shade out-of-doors, or to walk on damp turf.

As to a common sense of propriety and respectability in matters of the front and back of houses, let us consider how what may pass for such a sense has probably originated.

A feudal chief wishing to lodge a body of his vassals at a particular point, before unsettled, of his domain, would provide rows of huts set closely together on each side of a common passage or street. They would have the characteristics of such huts as are to be seen now by the score, for example, at Paso del Norte on our southern frontier; a single room for a family, a door on the street side, a door on the other side, no windows, a little corral into which goats, swine and fowls are driven through the hut at nightfall.[1]

As civilization advanced the manorial lords would find it to their profit to extend these villages, build larger dwellings, and, after a long interval, give them a little window on each side of the street door. Later, the roof would be pitched steeper and a sleeping-loft added. Then, on the street side, the walls would be built higher so that there could be upper rooms, also with windows, the roof still carried down to the first story on the opposite side.

At this stage of the evolution certain landlords might come to regard certain of their villages as a part of their lordly array; to conduct guests through their streets and to take pride in their cottages as they would be seen from the streets. It follows that new cottages would be built a little set off from the street and would be given a street door-yard; their street walls would be whitewashed and tenants would be encouraged to decorate the street yards with flowering plants and to line the ways from the street to the street doors with rows of box or shells or white stones. The other side of the house would still preserve the original hovel character; would have no windows, and the door would open upon a dunghill and rough shelters for the increasing personal wealth of the tenant in goats, pigs, donkeys, geese and fowls.

It can hardly be necessary to pursue the process of development nearer to "the typical American house."

Why is it that we so often see the family rooms of a house in the country on the least valuable part of the site of a homestead; the kitchen, wash room, drying yard and out-houses on the best part of it? Why is it that if one asks at a Seaside Hotel, where he can see the ocean, he is told to go out back of the stable? The answer is that it is because of a lingering superstition—a spurious semi-religious sentiment—which had its origin when one side of most houses—the side facing a public road—was the human side, the other the side of pigs and goats and geese, filth, darkness and concealment.

The front, *the* back, are terms no more applicable to a well designed house in America than anywhere else. Our Capitol and our White House have two fronts. Our beloved house at Mt. Vernon has two fronts. The old Hosack house at Hyde Park on the Hudson, the finest country-seat in its natural elements in America, has four fronts,[2] as have most palaces and many other monumental buildings, as those of our Interior and Post Office Departments. (But this is a plan hardly ever to be recommended except where there is to be a spacious interior court, as in many French and Spanish country houses.)

Generally with us a country house, and often a suburban house, will best have three fronts. Except as regard for winter shelter or summer breeze may overrule, one of these will be on the side looking from which there is the most pleasing natural scenery, and here will be the more important family rooms (as at Mt. Vernon and at the White House). If the outlook from them has a fine distant background (as at Mt. Vernon and the White House), then the nearer premises should be treated partly with a purpose to provide a place of common, quiet, domestic occupation, to be used in connection with the parlor or library, and partly with the aim of fitting the landscape with a foreground nicely conforming to, and helping the effect of, the middle distance and the background. It is desirable for neither of these purposes that there should be a sweep of gravel on that side of the house upon which horses may be driven or be kept standing, nor that there should be a public entrance to the house there. Usually a lawn, framed and sparingly furnished with masses of shrubbery that will not grow so high as to hide the distant view, will be best. But if the natural surface of the ground is rapidly declining from the house, especially if it is in the form of a broken and one-sided declivity, having a dislocating effect in connection with the distant view, then a level platform before the house, its further edge having a parapet, balustrade or hedge, will be desirable, both in order to give an effect of security and quiet to the immediate border of the house, and to make a strong foreground line by which the distance will be softened and refined.

Another side of the house will be its garden front, chosen because (of the three remaining sides) it offers the best conditions for a garden, properly so called. Another will be the entrance front, the treatment of which will be large in scale and less fine than either of the others. But here, if possible, there should be umbrageous trees. There will remain that part of the house containing the kitchen and laundry, from which will extend yards and sheds and spaces where wagons can stand and turn when bringing supplies or taking off wastes. Beyond them, perhaps, a carriage-house, stable and smaller out-houses. This should be the side on which the outlook is of the least value, and on which the natural circumstances favor convenient but not conspicuous lines of approach.

When such a complete arrangement, as has been thus suggested, is impracticable, the same general principles may be adopted as far as circumstances admit. It rarely occurs in any interesting place that the principal entrance can be best made on the more attractive side of a house. It often occurs, as in the finest places at Newport and Long Branch, that the best location for the stables, stable yard and laundry yard is on the street side of the house, and that the approach to its principal entrance passes near these, bringing them, exteriorly, under close view.

NOTES

1. So named in 1536 by Spaniards entering the area, El Paso del Norte (Northern Pass) is a region straddling El Paso County, Texas, and the State of Chihuahua, Mexico.

2. Dr. David Hosack, botanist, medical doctor, and Columbia University professor, purchased the Hyde Park, New York, residence of Dr. Samuel Bard (for whom Bard College is named) in 1828 and employed Andre Parmentier (1780–1830), a Brooklyn landscape gardener and nurseryman, to design and develop the estate.

III

CITIES

SIX

Chicago in Distress
(1871)

This may well be one of the most level-headed, unhysterical analyses of the 1871 Chicago fire written in its immediate aftermath, an example as well of Olmsted's excellent reportorial skills. In it, he examines the climatic, topographical, and architectural milieus contributing to the fire's rapid spread and awful destructiveness, the herculean relief efforts well underway at the time of his writing, and the unselfishness with which Chicago's residents helped each other out. Olmsted is not shy about criticizing shoddy and ill-considered building practices he believed made the fire more damaging than it might otherwise have been, and is especially critical of political corruption that left important buildings like the Court House unnecessarily vulnerable, his worst example being the collapse of the pumping station that rendered portions of the city waterless at its moment of greatest need. Nowhere does he offer the bromide that in the end everything will be all right, but he does suggest that careful study by Chicago's "best and most conservative minds" will produce reforms—"firmer steps"—that will better enable the city to cope with its uncertain future.

Originally published in The Nation, *13 (November 9, 1871).*

I have had an opportunity of looking at Chicago at the beginning of the fourth week after the fire, and, as you requested, will give you a few notes of my observation.

Chicago had a central quarter, compactly built, mostly of brick, stone, and iron, and distinguished by numerous very large and tall structures, comparable to, but often more ostentatious than, Stewart's store[1] in New York. They were mostly lined, to the fourth, fifth, or sixth floor, with pine-wood shelves, on which, or in pine-wood cases, a fresh stock of—larger at the moment than ever before—dry goods, or other inflammable materials, was set up, with plentiful air-space for rapid combustion. This central quarter occupied a mile and a half square of land. On one side of it was the lake; on the other three sides, for the distance of a mile, the building, though irregular, was largely of detached houses, some of the villa class, with small planted grounds about them, and luxuriously furnished, but generally comfortable dwellings, of moderate size, set closely together. There were also numerous churches and tall school buildings, and some large factories. At a distance of two miles from the center, and beyond, houses were much scattered, and within a mile of the political boundary there was much open prairie, sparsely dotted with cabins and a few larger buildings. It will be seen that a much larger part of the town proper was burned than a stranger would be led to suppose by the published maps.

The fire started half a mile southwest, which was directly to windward, of the central quarter, rapidly carried its heights, and swept down from them upon the comparatively suburban northern quarter, clearing it to the outskirts, where the few scattered houses remaining were protected by a dense grove of trees. The field of ruin is a mile in width, bounded by the lake on one side and mainly by a branch of the river on the other, and four miles in length, thus being as large as the half of New York City from the Battery to the Central Park, or as the whole of the peninsula of Boston. The houses burned set ten feet apart would form a row over a hundred miles in length. I judge that more than a third of the roof-space and fully half the floor-space of the city, the population of which was 330,000, was destroyed.

Familiar with these facts and comparisons before I came here, and having already seen many who had left the city since the fire, I now feel myself to have been able but slightly to appreciate the magnitude of its calamity. Besides the extent of the ruins, what is most remarkable is the completeness with which the fire did its work, as shown by the prostration of the ruins and the extraordinary absence of smoke-stains, brands [partially burned pieces of wood], and all *débris*, except stone, brick, and iron, bleached to an ashy pallor. The distinguishing smell of the ruins is that of charred earth. In not more than a dozen cases have the four walls of any of the great blocks, or of any buildings, been left standing together. It is the exception to find even a single corner or chimney holding together to a height of more than twenty feet. It has been possible, from the top of an omnibus, to see men standing on the ground three miles away across what was the densest, loftiest, and most substantial part of the city.

Generally, the walls seem to have crumbled in from top to bottom, nothing remaining but a broad low heap of rubbish in the cellar—so low as to be overlooked from the pavement. Granite, all sandstones and all limestones, whenever fully exposed to the southwest, are generally flaked and scaled, and blocks, sometimes two and three feet thick, are cracked through and through. Marble and other limestones, where especially exposed, as in doors and window-dressings, especially if in thin slabs, have often fallen to powder. Walls of the bituminous limestone, of which there were but few, instead of melting away, as was reported, seem to have stood rather better than others; I cannot tell why. Iron railings and lamp-posts, detached from buildings, are often drooping, and, in thinner parts, seem sometimes to have been fused. Iron columns and floor-beams are often bent to a half-circle. The wooden (Nicholson) asphalt-and-tar-concrete pavements remain essentially unharmed, except where red-hot material or burning liquids have lain upon them. Street rails on wood are generally in good order; on McAdam, as far as I have seen, more often badly warped.[2]

Where houses stood detached, and especially where they were surrounded by tall trees, there is less evidence of intense heat, charred wood and smoke-stains being seen in the ruins. I had heard it surmised that, by furnishing numerous small brands, the planted trees of the North Division would have helped to scatter the fire, but I find them generally standing to the smallest twigs, so inclined and stiffened, however, as to show perfectly the action upon them of the wind at the moment of death. It is evident that they would have been an efficient protection to the houses they surrounded had the buildings to windward been a little less tall, or the gale a degree less furious. For the wind appears not only to have been strong, but gusty and whirling. There is evidence of concentrated slants, eddies, and back-sets. This partly explains the small salvage. Many, a moment after they had been out to observe the flames in the distance, and had judged that they had still a chance to save their houses, were suddenly driven by a fierce heat, borne down upon them apparently from above, to flee, leaving even their choicest property, though previously packed and ready to be carried by hand. The radiated heat from the larger buildings was so strong that it scorched men ten rods away across the wind. Families were driven from one place of refuge to another—in several cases, to my knowledge, four times, and, finally, a few into the lake; many thousands into the open country. Some were floated or swam across the river.

Burning fragments of wooden parapets, sheets of roofing metal, signs, and scuttle-doors were carried great distances, and, with blazing felt, tarred paper, and canvas, and myriads of smaller sparks, sometimes swept down upon the fugitives with a terrific roar. Very sensible men have declared that they were fully impressed at such a time with the conviction that it was the burning of the world. Loose horses and cows, as well as people of all conditions on foot and in wagons, were hurrying half-blinded through the streets together, and it often happened that husbands and wives, parents and children, even mothers and infants, were forced apart and lost to each other. Sudden desolation thus added to the previous horrors, made some frantic who would otherwise have maintained composure. In general, however, the people, especially the households of the north side, appear to have manifested a greater degree of self-possession and of considerate thoughtfulness one for another, under these circumstances, than can be easily believed. Almost every one holds the remembrance of some instance of quiet heroism, often flavored with humor. The remains, of only about one hundred human bodies have thus far been recognized in the ruins, and the coroner and others are of the opinion that not more than two hundred lives were lost.[3] That the number should be so small can only be accounted for by the fact that there was an active volunteer rear-guard of cool-headed Christians, who often entered and searched houses to which they were strangers, dragging out their inmates sometimes by main force, and often when some, caught unawares, were bewildered, fainting, or suffocating. One still sees burned garments and singed beards.

Of course, a state of mind approaching insanity followed with many. After the lost had been found, as in most cases they soon were—children especially having been almost invariably taken up, tenderly cared for, and advertised by strangers—and after food and rest had been had, there was a reaction from desperation. For a time men were unreasonably cheerful and hopeful; now, this stage appears to have passed. In its place there is sternness; but so narrow is the division between this and another mood, that in the midst of a sentence a change of quality in the voice occurs, and you see that eyes have moistened. I had partly expected to find a feverish, reckless spirit, and among the less disciplined classes an unusual current setting towards turbulence, lawlessness, and artificial jollity, such as held in San Francisco for a long time after the great fire there—such as often seizes seamen after a wreck. On the contrary, Chicago is the soberest and the most clear-headed city I ever saw. I have observed but two men the worse for liquor; I have not once been asked for any alms, nor have I heard a hand-organ. The clearing of the wreck goes ahead in a driving but steady, well-ordered way. I have seen two hundred brick walls rising, ten thousand temporary houses of boards, and fifty thousand piles of materials lifting from the ruins; but, on Sunday, although there were other reports, in a walk of several miles among the ashes, I saw no hand-work going on, except that in two half-made cabins German women were holding boards while their husbands nailed them to the framing. It is obvious that the New England man is taking the helm.

There are respectable citizens who hold to the opinion that the fire was started and spread systematically by incendiaries, and I have seen one, lately from Paris, who is sure that it was part of a general war upon property. Numerous alleged facts are cited to sustain this view, but I believe them generally to be delusions growing out of the common excitement, or accidental coincidences. It is certain that the origin, progress, and all the unusual general phenomena of the fire can be reasonably accounted for in other ways.

You will have heard bad symptoms reported among the workingmen since the fire, but, on the whole, their conduct seems to have been as satisfactory as could have been reasonably expected. An unusual proportion of them are Germans, Swedes, and Norwegians, and, what is of great consequence, they were the owners of a lot and cottage. There has been an advance of about twenty per cent, in wages, and this has occurred without strikes or any general ill-feeling. Laborers now command $2 a day, carpenters and masons $4 to $5. Good mechanics are wanted, and many hundred more than are now here will be required in the spring.

The responsibility of leading affairs is felt to be too great to be trifled with. Even in politics this is true; perhaps, on the principle of locking the stable-door after the horse is stolen. City officers are to be elected next week, and citizens who have heretofore been unable to spare time for public from their private business, are exhibiting some concern about the character of the candidates. The old knots of dirty, overdressed men waiting for something to turn up seem to have had enough, and have disappeared. I have seen no soldiers, nor the slightest occasion for them. The police, as usual, except those regulating the passage of the crossings, seem to have nothing on their minds but a lazy looking forward to the arrival of their reliefs.

Although few of those who were men of substance yet know where they stand, and the work of general permanent reconstruction must, from loss of land titles and other reasons, be postponed till next summer, there has been no delay in deciding upon and starting efficient temporary arrangements for nearly all the old business of the city, except that of the courts. The shipping, railways, telegraphs, are all doing more work than before the fire, and will probably continue to. The city is again supplied with water, most of it with gas; it is as well sewered and paved as before. Omnibuses and street-cars are running on all the old lines; newspapers are published, schools are open and full, and half the numerous churches of the past are working more than double tides—the sensible, economical Roman Catholic custom of successive congregations and relays of clergymen having been adopted; while every day in the week the most effective preaching of the Gospel, in the form of bread, beef, and blankets, is uttered from each. Theaters, concerts, and lectures are advertised, and a new public library is started in the basement of a Baptist meeting-house. Three hundred of the burnt-out business concerns advertise themselves in new quarters, and new stocks of goods are constantly seen coming from the Eastern railway stations. In but few respects will the market a week hence be much worse, either to buy or sell in, than before. There is no difficulty in handling the crops, and, fortunately, they are large and excellent. Chicago, in short, is under jury-masts, and yet carries her ensign union down, but she answers her helm, lays her course, is making fair headway, and her crew, though on short allowance and sore tried, is thoroughly sober and knows its stations.[4]

You ask whether it is in the power of man adequately to guard against such calamities—whether other great cities are as much exposed as was Chicago? All the circumstances are not established with sufficient accuracy for a final answer, and one cannot, in the present condition of affairs, make full enquiries of men who must be best informed; but to such preliminary discussion as is in order, I can offer a certain contribution.

The prevailing drought was, I think, a less important element of the fire in Chicago—whatever may have been the case as to those other almost more terrific fires which occurred simultaneously in Wisconsin and Michigan—than is generally assumed; yet doubtless it was of some consequence. As to the degree of it, I learn that there had been no heavy rain since the 3d of July, and, during this period of three months, it is stated by Dr. Rauch, the Sanitary Superintendent,[5] the total rain-fall had been but two and a half inches. The mean annual rain-fall at Chicago is thirty-one inches. With regard to the cause of the drought, it is to be considered that millions of acres of land hereabouts, on which trees were scarce, have been settled within thirty years by people whose habits had been formed in regions where woods abound. They have used much timber for building, for fencing, railroads, and fuel. They have grown none. They are planting none to speak of. The same is true of nearly all parts of our country in which a great destruction of forests has occurred or is occurring. If the reduction of foliage in any considerable geographical division of the world tends to make its seasons capricious, as there is much evidence, the evil both of destructive droughts and devastating floods is very likely to extend and increase until we have a government service which we dare trust with extensive remedial measures. It is not a matter which commerce can be expected to regulate.

I can obtain no scientifically definite statement of the force of the wind. Several whom I have questioned recollect that they found it difficult, sometimes for a moment impossible, to make head against it; but I think that no year passes that some of our cities do not experience as strong a gale, and that every city in the country must expect to find equal dryness coinciding with equal force of wind as often, at least, as once in twenty years.

The origin of the fire was probably a commonplace accident. The fire started in a wooden building, and moved rapidly from one to another, close at hand, until the extended surface of quickly-burning material heated a very large volume of the atmosphere, giving rise to local currents, which, driving brands upon the heated roofs and cornices of the tall buildings to leeward, set them on fire, and through the rapid combustion of their contents, loosely piled tier upon tier, developed a degree of heat so intense that ordinary means of resistance to it proved of no avail. Under an old law, wooden buildings had been forbidden to be erected in or moved to the locality where the fire started. In 1867, upon the motion of men who wished to dispose of buildings they had contracted to move out of the more compact part of the city, the Common Council consented to a modification of this law. The Board of Health at the time urged the danger of doing so, and was told to mind its business. Underwriters, merchants, and capitalists were silent.

Chicago had a weakness for "big things," and liked to think that it was outbuilding New York. It did a great deal of commercial advertising in its house-tops. The faults of construction as well as of art in its great showy buildings must have been numerous. Their walls were thin, and were often overweighted with gross and coarse misornamentation. Some ostensibly stone fronts had huge overhanging wooden or sheet-metal cornices fastened directly to their roof timbers, with wooden parapets above them. Flat roofs covered with tarred felt and pebbles were common. In most cases, I am told by observers, the fire entered the great buildings by their roof timbers, even common sheet-metal seeming to offer but slight and very temporary protection to the wood on which it rested. Plain brick walls or walls of brick with solid stone quoins and window-dressings evidently resisted the fire much better than stone-faced walls with a thin backing of brick.

There has been no court-martial called for the trial of the fire service of the city. I understand that it was under the same board with the police. Most of the so-called police force of Chicago whom I had seen before the fire appeared in dirty, half-buttoned uniforms, and were either leaning against a door-post in conversation with equally disreputable-looking friends, and incessantly spitting on the sidewalk, or were moving with a gait and carriage which can be described by no word but loafing.

No one can be sure that with reasonably solid brick walls, reasonably good construction, and honest architecture, this fire could, once under strong headway, with the wind that was blowing, have been stopped at any point in its career, even by good generalship, directing a thoroughly well-drilled and disciplined soldierly force of firemen and police. But that the heat thrown forward would have been less intense, the advance of the fire less rapid, the destruction of buildings less complete, the salvage of their contents greater, and the loss of life smaller, may be assumed with confidence.

The walls least dilapidated are those of the Post-Office. They are of brick faced with stone, and two to three feet thick. It is stated that the fire entered by the upper windward windows, which, strangely, were not protected by iron shutters. The interior is thoroughly burned out. The windward side of the exterior is scaled and seared with heat, but the leeward side is scarcely injured at all; the glass even remains in the windows, and the sidewalks, rails, and lamp-posts are essentially unimpaired. It appears to me that this one building stood for a time a perfect dam to the fiery torrent. It was far from fireproof; but had there been a dozen other as well-built walls standing in line across the wind, and had there been no excessively weak roofs and cornices to leeward of them, I should suppose that half of all that was lost might have been saved.

The two most important buildings in the city were the Court-House, which was also the City Hall, and the pumping-house of the Water-Works. The Court-House was a costly structure with a stone exterior, ostensibly fireproof, standing in the midst of a public square. No respectable structure in the same situation would have been seriously injured. Large additions had been made to it two years ago, and the design for them is said to have been bargained for under such conditions that no respectable architect could have been employed. The result, architecturally, was at all events very bad. There is much more beauty in the walls now, where they have been chipped and crumbled by the fire, than ever before. It has also been publicly charged that some of the legislators of the city were interested in the building contracts, and that much money was made on them. The first fall of snow after the roof was put on caused it to fall in, and other parts of the structure were so thoroughly shattered that it was feared that the whole would come down. A proposition to tear it down and rebuild it was seriously entertained, but, as one of the gentlemen who decided the question told me, in view of what it had already cost, the taxpayers would not have stood it, and it was determined to patch it up. On the top of it, a tall wooden, tin-clad cupola was set. The fire, true to its mission of instructive punishment, made a long leap forward to seize upon this; it soon fell in; and, before the nearest adjoining commercial blocks to windward had even taken fire, it had been completely burnt out with all its invaluable contents.

I have neither seen the Water-Works nor the justly distinguished engineer[6] who is regarded as responsible for their construction, and who may be depended on to give the reason of their unfortunate break-down with the utmost accuracy and candor. The roof of the pumping-house, of metal, I believe, is publicly stated to have been upheld by wooden timbering, which was charred by heat from firebrands which had fallen above. Breaking down, it broke some part of the pumping-engine, and thus the city was left without water. The main battle, such as it was, had been before this fought and lost, but that much might still have been saved had the flow of water continued, a single experience will sufficiently indicate.

A friend who had, with other treasures, a choice library of several thousand volumes, tells me that he had thought much of the danger of fire, and was prepared to meet it. His house stood apart from all others, and was surrounded by trees. He had a strong force of instructed assistants, with private hydrants, hose, wet carpets, and buckets, well distributed. He had horses and wagons ready, but to the last was confident in his means of resistance. All houses to windward of him had nearly burned down, and he had extinguished every spark that had fallen upon his own, when the water failed. Five minutes afterwards his roofs and walls were on fire in a dozen places, and he had all he could do to save the lives of his household.

Considering the circumstances under which the arrangements for relief were formed, they appear to be admirably good. In the midst of the most pressing demands of their private affairs, men of great good sense and well informed have taken time to devise and bring others into a comprehensive and sufficient organization, acting under well-guarded laws. Chicago, when all did well, exceeded all in her manner of providing for the sick and wounded, prisoners and refugees as well as friends; and now the bread she then floated is truly returning to her under natural laws; for men and women more fit to be trusted in every way than those to whom the control of the contributions for relief have at length, after, it is said, a hard struggle with political speculators, been given, could hardly be found in any other city. The most scrupulous caution is taken to guard against waste or imposition, and to avoid encouraging improvidence, indolence, or a disposition to mendicant habits. Among hundreds of women drawing rations, I saw few who did not appear to have been decent, tidy, motherly persons— nearly all were European born.

The most costly and best form of charity has been that of supplying, either as a loan or as a gift, a limited amount of building materials with printed plans for a rough cabin of two rooms to be made of it, together with a stove, mattresses, and blankets, to men having families, and able by their work to support them. This has already been done in 6,000 cases. Great eagerness is shown to obtain this favor, especially by those laboring men who were burned out from houses of their own, and who can thus at once re-occupy their own land. The thankfulness expressed by these men—thankfulness, as the Mayor says,[7] "to all the world"—is sometimes very touching. The cost of the cabins, lined with heavy paper and supplied with a chimney, is, according to size, from $90 to $120. Besides the shelter thus provided, the public squares are filled with temporary barracks, and the whole number of those who have been housed by means of contributions received is, I believe, about 35,000. Wherever it is possible, persons not of families able to at least partly support themselves by labor, are helped to leave the city. The number of those to whom aid is thought needful to be administered has been rapidly reduced, every care being taken to obtain work for them and to avoid feeding those who avoid work. It is now a little over 60,000. With the coming on of winter, work will fail, and the number needing assistance increase. The funds thus far promised are not enough to meet the requirements of the barest humanity, and, especially if the winter should be severe, larger contributions than there is now reason to expect will be sorely needed.

Arrangements are made for searching out and privately and delicately administering to such sufferers as will not ask or be publicly known to receive charity. It is easy to see that the number of such must be very large. It was a maxim in Chicago that a fool could hardly invest in city real estate so badly that, if he could manage to hold it for five years, its advance would fail to give him more than ten percent interest, while there was a chance for a small fortune. Acting on this view, most young professional men and men on small salaries, if they had families, bought a lot and built a small house for themselves, confident that by hook or by crook they should save enough to pay the interest as it fell due on the necessary mortgage, together with the cost of insurance. To accomplish this they lived pinchingly, and their houses and lots were their only reserves. In thousands of cases, they have lost their houses, their insurance, and their situations all at one blow. Fifty of the insurance companies doing business here have suspended payment, seven of them being Chicago companies, whose directors were men of local influence and often employers.

The Sanitary Department has a list, known to be as yet incomplete, of 180 regular physicians who were burned out. Many, if not most of these lost house and furniture, as well as office, instruments, and books, and the families in which they practiced are dispersed. Judge Wilson reckons the number of lawyers, mostly young men, whose libraries were burned at five hundred. Many of both classes, for some days after the fire, took their places in the lines in order to get the rations of biscuits served out by the relief agents.

But even the condition of young men with families who have lost everything is hardly as sad as that of many of the older citizens, much overworked men who had fairly earned leisure and affluence. Owing to peculiar commercial conditions here, the number of such who have lost everything is larger than it would be in an older city. Cautious men averse to the general habits of speculation were most disposed to invest in buildings, and patriotic men, who had grown up with the city, and who had the most interest and pride in it, were most apt to insure in the local companies.

Amidst all the material prosperity of Chicago, there had always been a few of her citizens who had really bonded themselves to have no share in it, in devotion to higher pursuits. As examples of these, the Kinnicut brothers,[8] as both are dead, may perhaps be named. There were others, their instructors, leaders, supporters, and followers, who, like them, had traveled frugally and far, studied devotedly, and who, aided by a few worthy men of greater wealth, were laying the foundations of a true seat and school of art, science, and learning. Several special collections had already been gathered which money can never replace. These, with libraries, many series of notes, the work of half a lifetime, and some unpublished books, more or less nearly complete, are lost; and most of those who had supplied the funds to sustain these most interesting and important bases of the higher civilization for the great Northwest, are thrown back to struggle again for the decent maintenance of their families.

But great as is this loss, it will be consciously felt by comparatively few. Even more appalling, in view of the long years of weary labor of many educated men involved, is the destruction of important papers, contracts, agreements, and accounts, notes of surveys, and records of deeds and mortgages. It is estimated that nine-tenths of the papers held by attorneys were kept in various patent safes on upper floors, and were destroyed. The same is true of those held by surveyors, real-estate agents, etc. The city and county records were, I believe, in vaults built, like those of the Custom-House and Post-Office, on stone slabs, supported on iron columns, which, soon yielding to the heat, tumbled them into a pit of fire, and all were lost. How the city is to recover from this blow no one can yet see, but the difficulty is engaging the study of its best and most conservative minds; and that in some way it will recover, and that it will presently advance even with greater rapidity, but with far firmer steps, than ever before, those most staggered and cast down by it have not a shadow of doubt.

NOTES

1. Albert Turney Stewart's first department store of 1846, lavish enough to be called "the Marble Palace," was surpassed in elegance, size, and height by its 1862 successor farther uptown.

2. Samuel Nicholson (dates unknown) was granted patents in 1867 and 1868 for a road paving system in which wooden blocks or planks covered by tar paper or asphalt served as a foundation for a layer of larger wooden blocks and gravel covered with melted tar. John Loudon McAdam (1756–1836), Scottish engineer and road builder, pressed a mixture of crushed stone and gravel over larger stones in a convex configuration to facilitate drainage. Subsequent road builders added tar or other water-resistant materials, but the name "macadam" remained.

3. The fire raged from October 8 to 10, after which 125 bodies were recovered, although estimates of fatalities ranged up to 300. Approximately 90,000 of the city's 300,000 residents were left homeless, 17,500 buildings were destroyed, and some $225 million in property value was lost (or at least $4 billion in today's dollars depending on the method of calculation).

4. A jury mast is a distress signal; an ensign union, an identifying flag.

5. Dr. John H. Rauch (dates unknown) was sanitary superintendent for the Chicago Board of Health.

6. The pumping station (1866) and water tower (1869) were designed by William W. Boyington (1818–98), a prominent local architect before and after the fire.

7. The mayor at the time was Roswell B. Mason (1805–92).

8. Olmsted was likely referring to Robert Kennicott (1835–66), naturalist, Alaska explorer, and founder and director of the Chicago Academy of Sciences. He had a younger brother the editor could not identify.

SEVEN

The Future Of New-York

(1879)

After outlining what he thinks enables a city to become a metropolis, Olmsted argues that while New York is undoubtedly the most important commercial center in the United States, it is not, and is unlikely to become, a true metropolis. The problem is the grid street system that organizes much of Manhattan into blocks two hundred feet deep by several hundred feet long (depending on how far apart the north-south avenues are spaced), which are divided into narrow lots. Cultivated "men who have accumulated means elsewhere, and who wish to engage in other than purely money-making occupations"—patrons of the arts, he means, who turn cities into metropolises—will not move to New York because building sites are too cramped for gracious living and too uniform for individual self-expression.

Olmsted's bête noire is the 1811 Commissioners' Plan that overlaid a grid on Manhattan Island from 1st to 155th streets regardless of terrain, and was later extended farther north. Believing it subverted variety in both building design and street patterns by ignoring topographical differences, he was also convinced it was the grid's narrow lots—not foreseen in the Commissioners' Plan, however—that encouraged developers to throw up airless, dark, unhealthy tenements in which the poor were packed. Steep grades that could have been reduced by curving thoroughfares, and inadequate display of prominent public and private edifices that could have been remediated by foreground plazas or street termination at their doors, further pro-voked Olmsted's disdain.

However humane his sensibility, Olmsted exaggerated somewhat, and was hasty with his predictions. Changes in city law brought air and light into party wall tenements, however imperfectly, beginning the very year of his essay. The typical building lot was a hundred feet deep by twenty-five feet wide, not fifteen or less as he implies, and it is not uncommon to combine two or more to accommodate large struc-tures. Dwellings typically extend sixty-five to seventy-five feet inward from the sidewalk on either side of the block, leaving fifty or more feet between them, collectively forming a long open rectangle. Unscrupu-lous speculators sometimes erected a third row of houses in that inte-rior space, but not in neighborhoods attracting the wealthier residents Olmsted feared would shun Manhattan. The reality is that they did indeed flock to New York, which did indeed become a metropolis.

Originally published in the New-York Daily Tribune, *December 28, 1879.*

Aids and Checks to Progress

If a wise despot had undertaken to organize the business of this continent, he would have begun by selecting for his head-quarters a point where advantages for direct dealing with all parts of it were combined with advantages for direct dealing with all parts of Europe. He would then have established a series of great and small trading posts, determining their posi-tions by regard, first, to the local resources of various parts of the country, and secondly, to facilities of transportation. Each of these would be an agency of exchange for a district, but, the several districts not being strictly defined, there would, as trade developed and individual enterprise came more and more into play, be much competition between different agencies, and by greater economy of management one would often draw away trade from and prosper to the disadvantage of, another. But except in a limited and superficial way, abnormal to the system, the interests of the central and of the local agencies would be identical, and the relation between them not one of rivalry but of cooperative and reciprocal service. The business of the general agency would be proportionate to the business of the country; its local profits to the profits of trade generally. Whatever it gained would as a rule be a gain to every community on the continent.

The general agency would, unless special obstacles interposed, soon come to be the best place for comparing, testing, appraising and interchanging information and ideas on all concerns common to the New World and the Old. It would therefore take the foremost place in affairs of fashion and luxury. It would be the headquarters of dramatic and musical enterprises. It would be a center of interest in matters of science and art. It would be the readiest point for making collections and for comparing and testing values for a great variety of affairs not usually classed as commercial. All this would cause people to resort to it, either as occasional visitors, or with a view to residence, more than to any other place on the continent. It would thus become the best market for high ability in crafts of refinement. It would be the best "shopping place." As the resources of the continent were more and more fully exploited, it would thus tend to become a metropolis. Special advantages of climate, topography or of personal leadership and particular enterprise might give a local agency a leadership in some particular field; but the tendency, as a matter of continental economy, to concentrate leadership in general, even social leadership, at the trade center, could be permanently overcome only by local conditions which would make life in it decidedly less secure, healthy, peaceful, cleanly and economical than elsewhere. Considerable natural disadvantages in this respect, even, might be gradually overcome.

The Great Peter of Russia and his successors, in fact, proceeded much in this way which has been supposed. The position which he selected for a general center of exchange for Eastern Europe and Western Asia was in many respects unpromising; the harbor shallow and nearly half the year closed by ice, the land marshy and malarious, natural scenery tame and sad, and the climate most inclement. Nevertheless St. Petersburg has been made not only the center of commercial exchanges, but the chief seat of learning, science and art, and of all intellectual and social activities, for a vast population of more varied and antagonistic races, creeds, tastes and customs than that of America.

Commercial Position of New-York

New-York has long been the general center of commercial exchanges for the continent. There is not the least likelihood that any other city will supersede it. Even if any other had somewhat superior local advantages for the purpose, it is not desirable in the general interests of commerce at this stage that a change should be made. The cost of the rearrangement would be too great. Such transfer of particular branches of business to other growing towns, as now occurs, is simply a modification of commercial organization by which the mutual business of New-York and the country at large is to be done with more profit on the whole to both. St. Louis, Cincinnati and Chicago are in rivalry with one another but never except in a temporary and superficial way, with New-York. Boston, Philadelphia and

Baltimore are more plainly in competition with New-York; yet in the main they likewise so far cooperate with her that New-York gains more than she loses by every advance that is made by either of them.

But New-York is yet hardly ready to assume the full duty and take the full profits of a metropolis. In some respects Boston leads New-York, Philadelphia in others; in still others Cincinnati at least aims to do so. And in many respects New-York is not as yet nearly as well equipped as many cities of Europe of less than half her population and commercial prosperity. Treasures of art and the results of popular familiarity with treasures of art must be gained slowly, and New-York can in a long time only partially overcome its inevitable disadvantages in this respect. Yet, as to the higher results of human labor, in general attractiveness to cultivated minds and as a place of luxury, New-York has probably been gaining of late, even during the hard times, more rapidly than any other city in the world. She has gained, for instance, the Natural History Museum, the Art Museum, the Lenox Library, the Cathedral, the railways to and the great plant for healthful recreation at Coney Island.[1] She is decidedly richer and more attractive in libraries, churches, clubs and hotels. The display of her shops is very greatly finer than it was a few years ago. Shops more attractive in general effect are now hardly to be found in any older city. Great advances have been made also by half a dozen of her business concerns which are all large employers of the finer artisans and artificers: wood carvers, workers in metal, enamels, glass and precious stones, decorative painters. Better workmanship can now be had here in almost anything than was available five years ago. Take pottery, wood-engraving, upholstery, gas-fixtures, furniture, for example; in all these we could now make a better show than we did in the Centennial Exhibition.[2] Without doubt that exhibition did much for New-York; possibly more than for Philadelphia. It is, at least, certain that New-York has since had better workmen, better designers, better tools and a more highly educated market; and all these things have distinctly advanced her metropolitan position.

Unfortunate Plan of the City

Next to the direct results of a slipshod, temporizing government of amateurs, the great disadvantage under which New-York labors is one growing out of the senseless manner in which its streets have been laid out. No city is more unfortunately planned with reference to metropolitan attractiveness. True, it may be said that large parts of many old world cities have not been planned at all, but their accidental defects are compensated by their accidental advantages. The tenement-house, which is the product of uniform 200-feet-wide [Olmsted might better have said "deep"] blocks is beginning to be recognized as the primary cause of whatever is peculiarly disgraceful in New-York City politics, through the demoralization which it works in the more incapable class of working-people. It is a calamity more to be deplored than the yellow fever at New-Orleans,[3] because more impregnable; more than the fogs of London, the cold of St. Petersburg, or the malaria of Rome, because more constant in its tyranny.

On the other hand, the first-class brown-stone, high-stoop, fashionable modern dwelling house is really a confession that it is impossible to build a convenient and tasteful residence in New-York, adapted to the ordinary civilized requirements of a single family, except at a cost which even rich men find generally prohibitory.

Dr. Bellows[4] once described the typical New-York private house as "a slice of house fifteen feet wide, slid into a block, with seven long flights of stairs between the place where the cook works and sleeps"; and really, the family is now fortunate which gets twenty feet and which has more than two rooms out of three of tolerable proportions with windows looking into the open air.

There are actually houses of less than fifteen feet wide, to which men, who anywhere else in the world would be in comfortable circumstances, are obliged to condemn their families. A gentleman of rare attainments and in every way a most valuable addition to any community, whose private professional library and collections must have cost him $10,000, has been obliged to compress his family into a five-floored stack, the party walls of which are but twelve feet apart.

In none of those older towns in which domestic convenience has been systematically sacrificed to considerations of military expediency is a man of like value condemned to such a preposterous form of habitation. Its plan is more nearly that of a light house built upon a wave-lashed rock, than of a civilized family home. New-York has need of great attractions to draw people into quarters of this kind from such houses as they could better afford in any other American city.

The Same Defects Up-Town

But what is worst in the lookout for New-York is that the elevated roads and the up-town movement lead as yet to nothing better; for even at Yorkville, Harlem and Manhattanville,[5] five or six miles away from the center of population, there are new houses of the ridiculous jammed-up pattern, as dark and noisome in their middle parts and as inconvenient throughout as if they were parts of a besieged fortress.

Nay, there is a prospect of even worse to come, for on the slopes south of Manhattanville there are new streets, some of them paved and flagged, which, out of respect to the popular prejudice in favor of continuing the regular system, are laid out on just the worst course possible, so that in passing through them you must mount an inclination of one in six, eight or ten. What this means may be guessed by thinking of the steeper grades in the lower part of the city. That of Fifth-ave, north of Thirty-fourth-st., for instance, is one in twenty-five, and it brings every omnibus and most hackney coaches from a trot to a walk. Every ton of coal dragged up such a street, every load of garbage gathered and taken from it, is to cost three or four times as much in horsepower as it would in the lower part of the town, and yet in the lower part of the town we cannot afford to prevent great mounds of garbage from lying before our doors for weeks at a time. Its daily removal is found to be too costly.

Small families who do not wish to entertain many friends may find some relief in the better of the new apartment houses. But still, what these offer, as compared with what is offered in other cities, is of most extravagant cost. They are no places for children, and to any really good arrangement of apartments the 200-foot block still bars the way. Apartment houses in the old countries, of corresponding luxury in other respects, have much more spacious courts. The court, instead of being regarded as a backyard and every inch given to it and every dollar laid out upon it begrudged, often gives the noblest and usually the pleasantest fronts to the house. What are advertised as apartment houses for people in New-York of more moderate means, such as must be looked to by teachers, artists, artisans, writers, and nearly all the rank and file of the superior life of a metropolis, are as yet only a more decent sort of tenement-house, nearly half their rooms being without direct light and ventilation. The same classes that are compelled to live in them in New-York would regard them as intolerable in Philadelphia, or in London, Paris or Vienna.

Many attempts have been made to subdivide the block so that comfortable small houses which would come in competition with the tenement-houses might be built. The result in the best cases is that family privacy and general decency in fact and appearance are attained at an outlay which in any other large city would be thought preposterous. A better arrangement than any which has been tried is probably that proposed by Mr. Potter,[6] which consists essentially in subdividing the block by a series of lanes running from street to street; but capitalists as yet draw back from it.

Origin of the Evil

How did the city come to be saddled with this misfortune? Probably by a process of degeneration. In the old city of Amsterdam, after which it was first named, many houses are still to be found which approach in proportions the fashionable New-York house. But from the beginning these had one great advantage. At their back, running lengthwise through the middle of the block, there was a canal. Into this the closet and kitchen drains had direct discharge. Dust, ashes and garbage could be shot down to the lower floor and then passed directly into boats and floated off to farms in the suburbs. At the base of the house, on the street, there was a narrow brick terrace, and outside the front door a little open-air sitting-room, and everything on that side was kept as neat as a pin. The streets of old Amsterdam were, indeed, as much celebrated in the seventeenth century for their cleanliness as those of New-Amsterdam have since ever been for their filthiness.

New-York is in short a Dutch town with its canals and cleanliness omitted and its streets straightened and magnified. Long after the present street plan was adopted it was the custom of its citizens to throw their slops and garbage out of the front door, and droves of hogs got their living in the gutters. Out of this state of things New-York streets have been slowly improved to their present condition and New-York houses have come to be more inconvenient, uncomfortable and unhealthy, for the money and labor spent upon them, than those of any other American city.

But when we speculate upon the future of New-York as a metropolis we must not think of it as confined by arbitrary political boundaries. As a metropolis, Newark, Newport and Bridgeport, as well as Brooklyn, Yonkers and Jersey City, are essential parts of it. For all scholarly and scientific purposes Yale College with its thousand students is already annexed to New-York, and is possibly today a more actively important element of its intellectual life than either or all of the four colleges which stand within its political limits.[7]

In fact, the railway, the telegraph and the telephone make a few miles more or less of so little consequence that a large part of the ideas of a city, which have been transmitted to us from the period when cities were walled about and necessarily compact and crowded, must be put away.

Concentration and Dispersion

There is now a marked tendency in most large and thriving towns in two opposite directions—one to concentration for business and social purposes, the other to dispersion for domestic purposes. The first leads toward more compact and higher building in business quarters, the other toward broader, lower and more open building in residence quarters. The old-fashioned "country houses" of city people are growing more and more out of vogue, but residences in a greater or less degree combining urban and rural advantages, neither solitary on the one hand nor a mere slice of a block on the other, wherever they can be had in healthy and pleasing localities, with quick and frequent transit to business, social, artistic, literary and scholarly centers, are gaining favor. They are springing up in hundreds of charming neighborhoods about London and Paris; Boston and our Western cities are largely formed of them. They are as yet less used by New-Yorkers than by the people of any other large town. The reason is simply that hitherto there have been no thoroughly healthy suburban neighborhoods suf-ficiently accessible about New-York. In time such neighbor-hoods will be formed. Whenever they are, the metropolitan advantages of New-York and the profits of its local trade must be greatly increased by constantly increasing accessions to its population of men who have accumulated means elsewhere, and who wish to engage in other than purely money-making occupations. Such men, living under favorable circumstances and with capital and energies economically directed to mat-ters of general interest, are the most valuable constituents of a city; and it is by their numbers, wealth and influence, more than anything else, that a city takes the rank in the world of a metropolis.

NOTES

1. Calvert Vaux and J. Wrey Mould designed the first stages of the Ameri-can Museum of Natural History (1872–77) and the Metropolitan Museum of Art (1874–80); Richard Morris Hunt designed the library (1870–77)—later incorporated into the New York Public Library—for James Lenox (1800–80), philanthropist son of a wealthy Scottish merchant; James Renwick designed St. Patrick's Cathedral, its archbishop's residence, and its rectory between 1878 and 1888.

2. The Centennial Exposition celebrating U.S. independence was held in Philadelphia in 1876.

3. The most recent of several yellow fever epidemics in New Orleans occurred in 1878.

4. Henry W. Bellows (1814–82) was a founder of the U.S. Sanitary Commission, where he met Olmsted, and was later a prominent Unitarian minister in New York City.

5. At one time independent villages, Manhattanville, Yorkville, and Harlem are not administratively independent nor precisely defined districts of Manhattan. Despite differences of opinion regarding all three, Manhattanville today more or less comprises the area bordered by 121st and 135th streets, the Hudson River, and St. Nicholas Park; Harlem, the area between the East and Hudson rivers from 159th Street to 110th Street west and north of Central Park (which includes Manhattanville) but south to 96th Street to its east; and Yorkville, the East Side area bounded by 79th and 96th streets, Lexington Avenue, and the East River.

6. Edward T. Potter (1831–1904) made this proposal in a series of six essays entitled "Urban Housing in New York," which ran in *American Architect and Buildings News* from March 1878 to September 1879.

7. Not counting two theological seminaries, there were actually six "colleges" in New York City in 1879: the College of the City of New York, Manhattanville and St. John's colleges, and Columbia, New York, and Fordham universities.

EIGHT

"A Healthy Change in the Tone of the Human Heart"

(1886)

Olmsted agrees with John Ruskin that something of a sea change in matters of taste, especially concerning landscape, occurred during the nineteenth century. Once preferring orderliness, that is, nature cleaned up and "improved" by human intervention, "the most cultivated of men" are today drawn to "natural scenery which is indefinite, blending, evasive" in its "breadth, sedateness, [and] serenity."

American cities, Olmsted believes, have great "treasures of scenery" within or adjoining their jurisdictions, which, were they not regularly appropriated for speculative or "industrial" purposes, could be purchased at reasonable prices for public benefit. Some cities had done so, and Olmsted gives credit where it is due, but most had ignored, neglected, or destroyed their scenic resources, and he names several. Olmsted is not lobbying here solely for large public parks, arguing that even small spaces—one in Providence, Rhode Island, for example, not more than a hundred feet square—may be "a choice refreshment to a city" if it offers a pleasing vista, and he especially regrets that so many cities have ignored the scenic possibilities of rivers, lakes, and the sea. What he is lobbying for is recognition by cities of the regenerative power of nature, and asks them to consider this question: "Is the regard paid to . . . natural scenery by the city less an evidence of growing civilization than . . . the granite statues on its court-house or in its soldiers' monument?" To him, the answer was obvious.

Originally published in The Century Illustrated Monthly Magazine, *32 (October 1886).*

This is the term used by a great writer to describe what indolent people would be apt to call a difference of taste, the difference between the "taste" that led to the building of the Parthenon and that evinced in the building of the cathedrals, and, again, between the public taste of the period of cathedral-building and the time of the building of—what shall be said?—our soldiers' monuments? our patent iron bridges?

In the fifteenth century, Mr. [John] Ruskin tells us, the most cultivated of men found delight in scenes of which the chief characteristics were trimness, orderliness, framedness, surface fineness—sources of gratification that could be so only through a conspicuous manifestation of human painstaking. The water in which they took pleasure was water flowing in a channel paved at the bottom, walled at the sides, rimmed at the surface, and bordered by parallel floral fringes, specimen trees, or hedges. The rocks they enjoyed were any but crannied, craggy, mossy, and weather-stained rocks. They liked best to look on forest trees when they had been trimmed, shorn, and disposed in rows by the side of the road. They disliked all that we mean by depth, intricacy, mystery, in scenery. They liked clear outlines, fences, walls, defining circumstances, scenes fretted with bits of bright color, turf patched with flower-beds, nature dressed on the principles of our drawing-room and garden decorative art. They fairly hated the site of the disorderly, unconfinable sea, with its fluctuating lights and shadows and fugitive hues. The civilization of our time, Mr. Ruskin thinks, finds a greater pleasure in rivers than in canals; it enjoys the sea, it enjoys the distinctive qualities of mountains, crags, rocks; it is pleasantly affected by all that in natural scenery which is indefinite, blending, evasive. It is less agreeably moved by trees when standing out with marked singularity of form or color than when the distinctive qualities of one are partly merged by those of others, in groups and masses, as in natural woodsides. It takes pleasure in breadth, sedateness, serenity of landscape. If modern art has any advantage over that of the middle ages, it is through its awakening to the value of these aspects of nature and [its] less[er] respect for the more material wealth of man's manifest creation.

This doctrine is not Mr. Ruskin's alone. Scholars in general have substantially taken the same view from the time of [Joseph] Addison and Horace Walpole down.[1] Mr. Ruskin has but presented it more fully and accurately than others. But if we accept it, what are we to think of the neglect that is apparent at many of our centers to civilization to preserve, develop, and make richly available their chief local resources of this form of wealth? Let me refer to a few examples.

At our national capital, while we are every year adding to its outfit new decorations in marble and bronze, formal plantations, specimen trees, and floral and bushy millinery, we leave the charmingly wooded glen of Rock Creek in private hands, subject any day to be laid waste. Once gone, the wealth of the nation could not buy for Washington half the value of landscape beauty that would thus have been lost.[2]

Again, one of our Northern cities has always had lying at its feet a passage of scenery in which, with some protection and aid to nature, and a little provision of convenience, there might be more of grandeur, picturesqueness, and poetic charm than it is possible that this city shall ever otherwise be able to possess, though it should increase a hundred-fold in population and wealth, and command the talents of greater artists than any now living. No effort is made to hold the opportunity. No thought is given to it. The real estate in which it lies, as yet mainly if not wholly unproductive, is from year to year bought and sold as private property with regard alone to its possible future value for some industrial purpose to which thousands of acres near by can easily be as well adapted. There is a river running through it, but its chief interest to "the human heart" does not lie in the water. The water is of no small value, yet it might be wholly drawn off to turn wheels and all that I have said remain true.

We have another fine city, a city of some repute for its poets, its architecture, sculpture, music, gardening, its galleries and its schools of art. Liberal, provident, thrifty, clean, it sits at the head of a harbor giving directly on the sea. The harbor had made the city. Various islands and headlands make the harbor. The islands and headlands are thus the life of the city. Following Mr. Ruskin, one would suppose that whatever of beauty lies in them would long since have engaged all the art-sense of its people. But, in fact, hitherto, a stranger wishing to look down the harbor toward the sea could not find a foot of ground along the shore prepared for the purpose. Once the islands were bodies of foliage. Seen one against another and grouping with woody headlands, they formed scenery of grace and amenity, cheerful, genial, hospitable. But long ago they were despoiled for petty private gains, and the harbor made artificially bald, raw, bleak, prosaic, inhospitable. Each island now stands by itself, as sharply defined in all its outlines as the most medieval mind could desire. Several of them are the property of the city and are in use for excellent purposes. It would not lessen but enhance their value for these purposes to dress them again with all the graces of naturally disposed foliage; and under a well-prepared system, patiently followed, it would cost little more every year to do this than is spent for an hour's exhibition of fireworks. The harbor is often more crowded than any other on the coast with pleasure-seeking yachts and yacht-lets; all that has been stated is perfectly plain; but the opportunity remains not only unused, but, so far as publicly appears, unconsidered—a matter of no account.

One of the most impressive (and by its impressiveness most recreative, and [by] its recreativeness most valuable) city grounds that I have known, I strayed into by accident, never having heard of it before. This was thirty years ago, and I have not heard of it since; but the impression it made was so strong that being asked for a note on this topic, it is instantly and vividly recalled. The entire value of this city property lay in its situation. Otherwise it was barbarous—barbarous in its squirming gravel-walks, its dilapidated essays of puerile decoration, its shabby gentility; its hogs and its hoodlums. But far below flowed a great river, and one looked beyond the river downward upon the unbroken surface of an unlimited forest; looked upon it as one looks from a height upon the sea.

No matter what is beyond, an expanse of water, as you say, can never fail to have a refreshing counter interest to the inner parts of a city; it supplies a tonic change at times even from the finest churches, libraries, picture galleries, conservatories, gardens, soldiers' monuments, parks, and landward outskirts. What is easier than to provide a grateful convenience for such refreshment? Yet if one wants it at Troy, Albany, Newburgh, Springfield, Hartford, Middletown, New London, Trenton, Norfolk, Louisville, St. Louis, Memphis, Vicksburg, what is offered? What was lost for Brooklyn when the brow of its heights was wholly given up to paved streets and private occupation! What resources is Burlington wasting?

The wayfarer in Lynchburg may come to know by a chance glimpse at a street-corner that the city holds one of the greatest treasures of scenery at its command; but if he would see more of it, he must ask leave to climb a church-steeple, or, what is better, plod off by a dusty road to a point beyond the city's squalid outskirts, where the James river will give him an undisturbed space for western contemplation. Many [other] illustrations of the general fact might be given.

But one who believes that Ruskin is describing tendencies of civilized moment rather than stages attained, as he looks over our land, is not left cheerless. Years ago a traveler arriving in Buffalo asked in vain where he could go to look out on the lake. "The lake?" he would be answered in the spirit of the middle ages; "nobody here wants to look at the lake; we hate the lake." And he might find that two large public squares had been laid out, furnished and planted, leaving a block between them and the edge of a bluff to be so built as to shut off all views from the squares toward the lake and toward sunset. But lately land has been bought and prepared, and is much resorted to, expressly for the enjoyment of this view. The new public property also commands a river effect such as can be seen, I believe, nowhere else—a certain quivering of the surface and rare tone of color, the result of the crowding upward of the lake waters as they enter the deep portal of the Niagara. Is the regard paid to these elements of natural scenery by the city less an evidence of growing civilization than is given in the granite statues on its court-house or in its soldiers' monument? San Francisco holds a grand outlook upon the Pacific; New Haven has acquired a noble eminence overlooking the Sound. Be it remembered, also, that at Chicago and at Detroit, at Halifax and at Bridgeport, sites have been secured at which the public interest in great, simple, undecorated waters may be worthily cared for.

Between the two neighboring cities of St. Paul and Minneapolis the Mississippi flows majestically. Its banks are bold and nobly wooded, a virgin American forest. Mr. Horace Cleveland,[3] a veteran artist, a kinsman of the President's, is urging upon the people of these two cities that they secure the opportunity thus offered for a public ground common to both with which no other city recreation-ground could be brought in comparison. If Mr. Ruskin be right, it speaks well for the health of these two wonderfully growing communities that the suggestion has been gravely received and is earnestly debated.

A small space, it should not be forgotten, may serve to present a choice refreshment to a city, provided the circumstances are favorable for an extended outlook upon natural elements of scenery. This is seen at Durham Terrace at Montreal, the inward as well as the riverward characteristic scenes of which Mr. [William Dean] Howells has described in "Their Wedding Journey."[4] Another illustration of the fact may be found in a queer little half-public place, half-domestic back-yard, from which the river may be overlooked if anyone cares for it, at Hudson, New York. Yet another may be come upon at Providence, a public balcony, not more than a hundred feet square, thrown out from a hill-side street. A trifling affair, but a trifle that expresses much of public civilization.

For low-lying towns upon the sea or lake coasts, promenade piers will generally offer the best means to the purpose. A simple promenade pier built with tree-trunks from neighboring woods, nicely hewn, nicely adzed, nicely notched, nicely pinned, without a bolt or strap of iron, with no paint or applied "gingerbread," built by a village bee, would be a work worthy to be celebrated in a wood-cut poem of the century.

NOTES

1. Joseph Addison (1672–1719), English politician and essayist, was cofounder with Richard Steele (1672–1729), Irish politician and playwright, of *The Spectator*, a witty journal of ideas, intended to inform sophisticated English readers about issues of the day. During the 1740s, Horace Walpole (1717–97), Member of Parliament and art historian, transformed his estate, Strawberry

Hill, in Twickenham near London, into the first English example of Gothic Revival.

2. Administered by the National Park Service, Rock Creek Park was established by an act of Congress in September 1890.

3. Horace William Shaler Cleveland (1814–1900) was one of the premier American landscape architects of the nineteenth century.

4. Howell's first novel, written in 1872.

Olmsted and Vaux, Greensward Plan for Central Park, 1858. Courtesy New York City Department of Parks and Recreation.

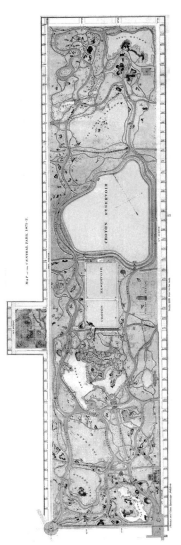

Olmsted and Vaux, Plan of Central Park as Built, 1872. Courtesy Central Park Conservancy.

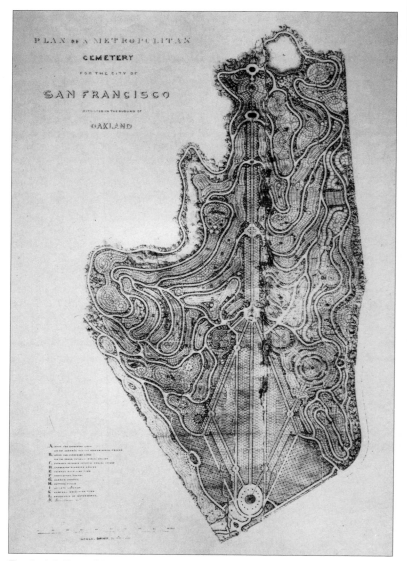

Frederick Law Olmsted, Plan for a Metropolitan Cemetery for the City
of San Francisco (Mountain View Cemetery, Oakland, California), 1865.
Courtesy of the National Park Service, Frederick Law Olmsted National Historic Site.

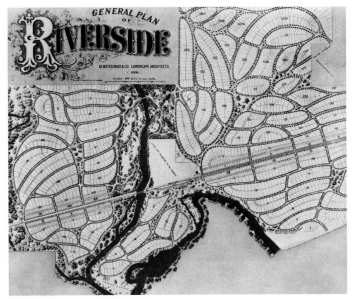

Olmsted, Vaux & Co., General Plan of Riverside, Illinois, 1869.

Courtesy of the National Park Service, Frederick Law Olmsted National Historic Site.

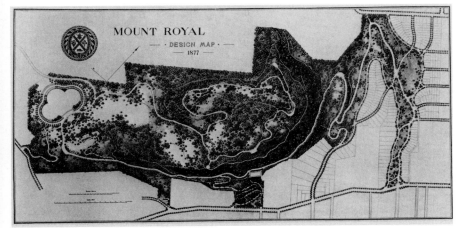

Frederick Law Olmsted, Plan of Mount Royal park, Montreal, 1872.

Courtesy of the National Park Service, Frederick Law Olmsted National Historic Site.

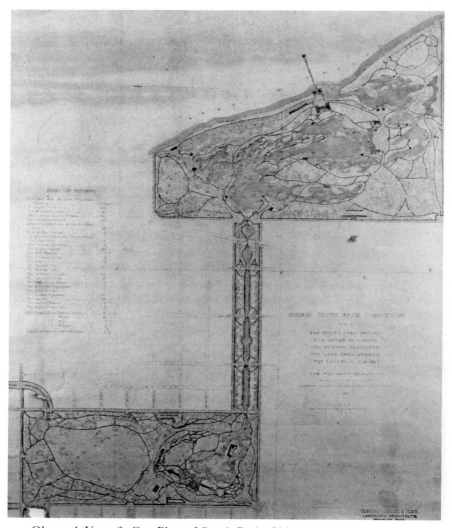

Olmsted, Vaux & Co., Plan of South Park, Chicago, 1871. Courtesy of the National Park Service, Frederick Law Olmsted National Historic Site.

Olmsted, Vaux & Co., Plan for Prospect Park, Brooklyn, 1871. Courtesy of
the National Park Service, Frederick Law Olmsted National Historic Site.

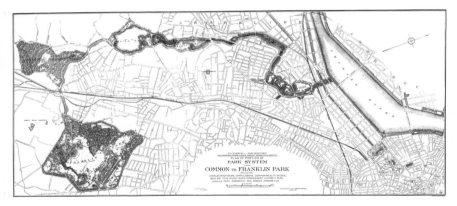

Frederick Law Olmsted, Plan of Portion of (Boston) Park System from
Common to Franklin Park, 1884. Courtesy of the National Park Service, Frederick
Law Olmsted National Historic Site.

Landscaping at the 1893 World's Columbian Exposition, Chicago (see Document 11). Photo by Charles Dudley Arnold taken from west side of the Lagoon showing (left to right) the Merchant Tailors Building, Brazilian Pavilion, Café de Marine, Fisheries Building, the Japanese Ho-o-den pavilions on the Wooded Island, and the U.S. Government Building. Courtesy Avery Architectural Library, Columbia University, New York.

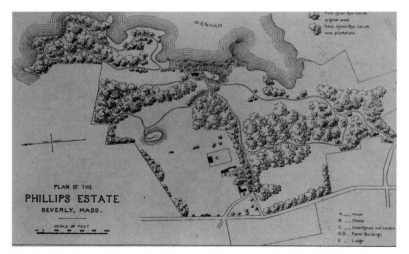

Frederick Law Olmsted, Moraine Farm, the J. C. Phillips Estate, Beverly, Mass., 1880. Courtesy Avery Architectual Library, Columbia University, New York.

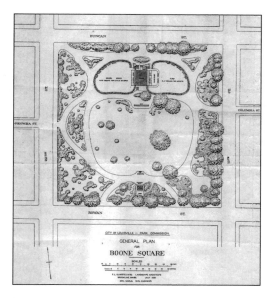

Frederick Law
Olmsted, General
Plan of Boone
Square (Children's
Playground),
Louisville,
Kentucky, 1880.
Courtesy Louisville
Olmsted Parks
Conservancy.

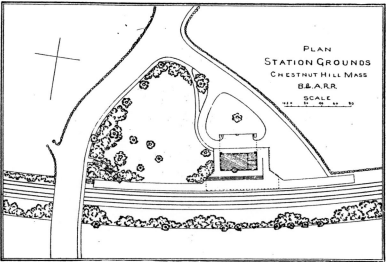

Frederick Law Olmsted, Plan of Boston & Albany Railroad Station
Grounds at Chestnut Hill, Massachusetts, 1883–44. From *Garden and Forest*
2 (April 3, 1889).

Front view of Fairsted, the Frederick Law Olmsted House, Brookline, Massachusetts, ca. 1900. Courtesy of the National Park Service, Frederick Law Olmsted National Historic Site.

Rear view of Fairsted, the Frederick Law Olmsted House, Brookline, Massachusetts, ca. 1900. Courtesy of the National Park Service, Frederick Law Olmsted National Historic Site.

IV

LANDSCAPE GARDENING

NINE

On Landscape Gardening

(1876)

Olmsted focuses here on two issues he thinks fundamental to the nature, the very definition, of what in 1876 was increasingly being called "landscape architecture." The first—the relationship between architects and landscape gardeners (his preferred term)—and the second— the growing emphasis on plant "classification and nomenclature," in particular on "tropical botany and exotic horticulture"—are in his mind intimately connected.

As he sees it, the relationship between architecture and landscape design on any given project requires a delicate balancing act. Too often the one is subordinated to the other, sometimes because of professional arrogance, on other occasions because of one practitioner's uncertainty about the other's role. To remedy this, Olmsted calls for the architect and the landscape gardener to develop a thorough understanding of what the other does and to "work with reference to the same general idea," each "subordinating his art to it."

He also worries that "overlong absorption" by landscape gardeners in the study of plant types and their deployment will create a kind of professional solipsism, a losing sight of the big picture, which is "the subordination of all materials used to a general ideal of simplicity, tranquility, and repose." His thinking on these matters anticipates by generations what would later be termed overspecialization—"tunnel vision"—an inability to envision the proper relationship of parts to their larger whole.

Originally published as "Mr. Olmsted on Landscape Gardening," a letter to the editor of The Garden, *10 (August 12, 1876).*

I am gratified to have the good opinion which led you to think me the author of an article in the "Gardeners' Monthly," quoted in *The Garden* of July 1, and which you pleasantly make the occasion for showing how you and I, from our different points of view, may observe a subject of common interest.[1] You rightly assume that I have been placed by circumstances in a position to regard the relation between the professions of landscape gardening and architecture with more than usual interest. I must confess, however, that as far as this relation has a bearing on the question of professional education, I yet stand a little too much in a waiting and enquiring attitude to write upon it with satisfaction. Still if you care to know my view of the subject, you are entitled to have an authentic report of it, and so far as I can give you this, I will do so with pleasure. It has long been a practice to introduce temples, pagodas, pavilions, "ruins," bridges, arches, obelisks, and other monuments, in works of landscape gardening, not alone where they were required by considerations of health and convenience, but with a view to give interest, character, and finish to the scenes in which they appear. In the war on this practice which you are leading, I claim to be with you. With, perhaps, a single justifiable exception, no architectural object has ever yet been introduced in any work of landscape gardening with my consent which was not first devised with a view to some other purpose than of display or effect in the landscape. But what

are the grounds of objection to the practice? To find and sub-
stantiate them, I think it is necessary to see, more clearly than
most intelligent men seem ready to do, in what the essence of
landscape gardening consists. [John C.] Loudon, after making
an extended study of the manner in which the term is used
by a series of authors, says of a simple example: "All the parts
unite in forming a whole which the eye can comprehend at
once and examine without distraction. Were this principle not
prevalent, the groups of trees, the lake, and the building would
only please when considered separately, and the result would
be as poor a production as a machine, the wheels of which are
accurately finished and nicely polished, but which do not act in
concert so as to effect the intended movement."[2]

The objection, then, to monumental and architectural
objects in works of landscape gardening is this, that, as a rule,
they are not adapted to contribute to any concerted effect, but
are likely to demand attention to themselves in particular, dis-
tracting the mind from the contemplation of the landscape as
such, and disturbing its suggestions to the imagination. But
the object of producing an effect on the imagination being
to make the life of man more agreeable, war on architectural
objects may be carried too far whenever the objects which it
removes are likely to add more to the satisfaction of life than
they deducted from it by their injury to the landscape. Where
the number or extent of artificial objects thus called for is large
as compared with the ground to be operated upon, landscape
gardening, properly speaking, is out of place; gardening material should then be made to support, strengthen, and aggran-
dize architectural design. But there are intermediate cases
where the landscape gardener, as such, will neither retire from
the field nor refuse to yield anything of landscape effect to
convenience. If, in laying out a ground which is to be used by
a hundred thousand people of all classes, we seek to have no

more numerous or more substantial artificial structures than we should if it were to be used only by a quiet, private family and its guests, we shall overreach ourselves. It is better that the ultimate special requirements of the situation should be foreseen from the outset, that provisions for them should be ample, that the necessary structures, however inconspicuously they may be placed, should be substantial, and their real character not only undisguised but artistically manifested, and that, finally, they should become as far as possible (preserving the above conditions) modest, harmonious, and consistent elements of a general landscape design, in which no more ambitious landscape motives are to be admitted than will allow them to be so assimilated. In such cases it is obvious that the architect would work with reference to the same general idea as the gardener, and should take pride and pleasure in subordinating his art to it. It follows that no architect is perfectly fit for the duty who cannot enter heartily into the spirit of a general design embodying landscape considerations; considerations, for example, of the modeling of ground-surface and of the disposition of foliage, as to density and color and shade and sky-line. It is to be said that architects are often shamefully ignorant in this respect, and I have no doubt that they are sometimes somewhat conceited and presumptuous in their ignorance. But we do not, as a rule, find that men trained as shoemakers have a propensity to chequer their hats with leather, nor men trained as hatters to slash their boots with felt; and I do not believe that it is a necessary result of properly educating an architect that he should be irresistibly disposed to patch a lawn with bricks and mortar. Whenever such a mania manifests itself, we may be sure it signifies too crude, not too refined a professional training.

But our present business is rather with the question of the education of landscape gardeners than of architects. Let me ask then, if it be a just cause of reproach to an architect that he cannot comprehend, and therefore cannot avoid overdoing his proper part in a landscape design, whether it is not equally true that the landscape gardener, who cannot upon occasion work hand-in-hand with the architect cheerfully, loyally, and with fore-reaching sympathy, is unqualified for his duty? Practical occasion for this close alliance of the two professions is not uncommon; indeed, in the greater number of cases where either is called in, there is to be a building or group of buildings, the site, aspect, elevation and outline of which cannot be properly determined without an understanding as to how the adjoining grounds are to be managed; as to where an approach is to be laid, as to where trees are to close the view and lawns open it, as to where the surface is to be gentle and quiet, and as to where it is to be abrupt, broken, and picturesque. On the other hand, it is equally impossible to properly design the walks and drives, the slopes, lawns and foliage, without regard to the position, the height, the breadth, the openings, the skylines, and even the decorative details of the buildings. There is then, properly, no distinctive field of general design for each profession; there is only a distinctive field of operations under the general design, the landscape gardener being responsible in the outlying parts of that of which the special field of the architect is the center. The house comes first, because shelter is the first necessity, and it is only with increasing wealth and refinement that the garden part grows out of it. In the familiar aphorism of Lord Bacon, the art of pleasure-gardening is thus regarded as a higher development of the art of architecture;[3] and, in fact, if we look to the origin of the word we shall find that an art worker in soils and living plants is as accurately an architect as one who is confined to brick and mortar. But you suggest that if the landscape gardener interests himself in architecture and other fine arts, it will be likely to overmuch distract his mind from another class of interests which, if not essentially, are yet closely connected with landscape gardening, such, for example, as those of tropical botany and exotic horticulture. The range of study which is called for in these is already so greatly extended that simply to call by name the various plants that are to be found under glass in England, a man must have gone through an amount of special mental discipline which would have been appalling to a gardener of fifty years ago. And yet this range is rapidly enlarging, and no one can guess where it will end. If, then, a young man, in addition to the study necessary to the practice of landscape gardening pure and simple, is to make himself master of tropical botany and exotic horticulture, and [perfectly] adept in all other branches of botany, I question if there will not come in time another danger to the art of more gravity than that which I am disposed to apprehend exists in its disalliance with architecture.

To recognize what I mean, please ask yourself what is the one sure product which any professional education in landscape gardening must be adapted to cultivate? It surely is that of a special sensibility to the characteristic charms of broad, simple, quiet landscape compositions, united with a power of analyzing these charms, and of conceiving how they may be reproduced through other compositions adapted to different topographical circumstances and different requirements of convenience; and this united again with a power of organizing and directing means through which, after many years, these conceptions may be realized. In order to acquire such a wide range of information and of skill as will before long evidently be required of a gardener professing to be equipped at all points, a man of ordinary abilities must begin young, and must for some years be thoroughly absorbed in his work. This cannot occur without a strong tendency to establish a propensity to regard trees and plants from mental points of view in which the special qualities of each are to be of interest only as they favorably affect broad harmonies of landscape. It appears to me that the likeness of the materials and processes of botanical and exotic gardening to those of landscape gardening instead of being an advantage in this respect, really establishes an insidious danger greater than that which you apprehend from an interest in an art dealing with such different materials and processes as that of architecture. It is a matter of history that the revolution in which landscape gardening originated was practically led more than by any other man by one (his monument should be in Westminster Abbey) who was educated as a coach painter, grew from that to be an historical painter, from that again wandered as a student of the fine arts in general into Italy, and finally on his return started in business as an architect before making his first imperfect essay in landscape gardening.[4] How we should now rank his more mature work, and that of his contemporaries, few of whom were gardeners bred from youth, is an interesting question, for the profitable study of which there may yet be opportunity in England. How we should rank it as an arboretum, how we should rank it with regard to brilliancy of coloring, how as a living museum of botany, how as an exhibition of the fashionable plants of the day, there can be no doubt; but I mean what should we think of it as a work of art? what would be its influence on the imagination? We know that in its day it compelled the unbounded admiration of the most cultivated people, not only of England but of all Europe, and we may presume that if it lacked the incident and varied interest of modern work, it was not without some impressive poetical qualities. We may be sure, I think, that the profession of landscape gardening has not since been gaining as steadily in power to affect the imagination as it has gained in working material and in science. It is possible that it has lost something; and if so, I should judge from descriptions, and from a few old engravings, that it was in the qualities of breadth, consistency of expression, subordination of all materials used to a general ideal [of] simplicity, tranquility, and repose. I do not want to give undue importance to this suggestion, but it is obvious that defects with reference to these qualities are precisely what should be expected to result from an overlong absorption of mind in questions of classification and nomenclature, from an excess of interest in conservatory, winter garden, terrace garden, and bedding-out effects, and from the resulting necessity of a forced retreat from the border grounds of allied arts and professions.

My *alter ego*, if you please, of the "Gardeners' Monthly" apparently regards the title of landscape architect as one in which an assumption of superiority is affected toward those who beforetime have been called landscape gardeners. I do not see the assumption, but to remove the suspicion, however it arises, in at least one case, I will mention that the word architect, as applied to the manager of a public work, of which landscape gardening should be the chief element, was here in America adopted directly from the French, and was first fastened upon the occupant of such an office, who was not an architect in the English usage of the term, in disregard of his repeated remonstrances.[5] As it is not wholly without an etymological propriety, as it has a certain special value in addressing a public which, in my humble judgment, is too much rather than too little inclined to regard landscape considerations as one thing and architectural considerations as quite another, and as it has now been fairly accepted as an intelligible term on this side of the water, I will submit to whatever reproach must follow on the other in subscribing myself, in all goodwill,

Frederick Law Olmsted, Landscape Architect

NOTES

1. Rye, New York, landscape gardener B. S. Olmsted published "Who Shall Lay Out Our Ornamental Grounds?" in *Gardener's Monthly and Horticulturist*, 18 (June 1876). In his July 1, 1876, essay, "Landscape Gardeners of the Future" in *The Garden*, editor William Robinson confused B. S. with F. L. Olmsted, hence the latter's response reprinted here.

2. Olmsted quotes from John C. Loudon, *An Encyclopaedia of Gardening*, 4th ed. (1826).

3. Olmsted refers to Francis Bacon (1561–1626), "Of Gardens" (1625), published that year in the third edition of his *Essays*.

4. Olmsted refers to William Kent (1684–1748), English landscape gardener, architect, and painter, who in large measure led "the revolution" in which naturalistic or picturesque compositions supplanted more formal, symmetrical, and orthogonal approaches to garden layout.

5. Traditionally, the English used "architect" to mean a craftsperson who erected a structure, that is, an implementer, while the French used the word to mean someone who practiced the art of architecture, that is, a designer. In 1858, Olmsted was named "Architect-in-Chief" of Central Park, a title to which he objected because he was not an architect; nor did he approve of "landscape architect" because he thought it did not recognize the singularity of his work by making it appear to be an offshoot of architecture. Signing this essay "Landscape Architect" was therefore his tongue-in-cheek way of insisting that he was not a mere craftsperson and that his profession was not lesser than that of architects.

TEN

Landscape Gardening

(1878)

Taking issue with the popular notion that landscapes are always "distinguished by a certain degree of breadth and distance of view," that is, by sweeping vistas, Olmsted argues that landscaping should more properly be understood as the "subordination of various details to a characteristic effect of the scene as a whole" regardless of scale or locale. He illustrates his point by proposing two quite different treatments of the same "common village dooryard." Everything must be done, he says, with "an ideal in view" and "each element introduced a consistent pursuit of that ideal." When this happens even the "common village dooryard" takes on the characteristics of poetry and music, becoming art, and as such "will often be found to have a persistent influence which may be called its charm—a charm possibly of such power as to appreciably affect the development of the character and shape the course of life" itself. This is a large claim, but in making it forthrightly, Olmsted states as clearly here as anywhere else in his writings, albeit by indirection, why he is a landscape gardener.

Originally published in Johnson's New Universal Cyclopaedia: A Scientific and Popular Treasury of Useful Knowledge, *v. 2 (1877).*

Landscape gardening is a branch of horticulture, the highest results of which may be attained by processes of a comparatively simple character—simpler, for instance, than those of kitchen or of floral gardening. Failure of success in it being oftener due to a halting purpose than to lack of science, of means, or of skill, this article will be chiefly given to establishing the definition and limitation of the general end proper to the art; some indications being incidentally presented of the manner in which, under the requirement of different individual tastes and different local conditions, it may be judiciously pursued.

There are two other branches of horticulture, which in ordinary practice are often so much confounded with that of landscape gardening that the reader may find it convenient to have them set apart from it at the outset. One of them is the cultivation of plants with special regard to an interest in their distinctive individual qualities. The other is the cultivation of plants (trees, shrubs, perennials, and annuals) with a view to the production of effects on the principles commonly studied in the arrangement of precious stones, enamel, and gold in an elaborate piece of jewelry, or of flowers when sorted by colors and arranged for the decoration of a head-dress, a dinner-table, or a terrace. Whether, in any undertaking, one of these two leading motives or that of landscape gardening be adopted, it may be presumed that the result will satisfy that motive in proportion as it shall be followed to the end with singleness of purpose. We now turn, therefore, from the two which have been defined to consider what, in distinction from them, the leading motive of landscape gardening may be.

Derivatively, the word "landscape" is thought to apply only to such a scene as enables the observer to comprehend the shape of the earth's surface far before him, or, as we say in common idiom, "to get the lie of the land," the land's shape.

Consistently with this view, it will be found, on comparing a variety of scenes, that those which would be most unhesitatingly classed as landscapes are distinguished by a certain degree of breadth and distance of view. Looking at the face of a thick wood near at hand or of a precipitous rock, we do not use the term. Pursuing the comparison farther, it will be found that in each of those scenes to which the word more aptly applies there is a more marked subordination of various details to a characteristic effect of the scene as a whole. As Lowell says, "A real landscape never presents itself to us as a disjointed succession of isolated particulars; we take it in with one sweep of the eyes—its light, its shadow, its melting gradations of distance."[1] But there are many situations in which plant-beauty is desired where the area to be operated upon is so limited, or so shaped and circumstanced, that the depth and breadth of a landscape scene must be considered impracticable of attainment. In America gardening is required for the decoration of places of this class many thousand times for one in which such restraining conditions are not encountered; and the question may be asked whether they must all be excluded from the field of landscape gardening, and if not, what, in these cases, can be the significance of the prefix "landscape"? As a general rule, probably, so many purposes require to be served, and so many diverse conditions to be reconciled, that the only rule of art that can be consistently applied is that of architecture, which would prescribe that every plant, as well as every molding, shall bear its part in the "adornment of a service." To this end, parterre and specimen gardening are more available than landscape gardening. But it may happen that where, with due regard to considerations of health and convenience, there would be scant space for more than two or three middle-sized trees to grow, there will yet be room for a great deal of careful study, and, with careful study, of success in producing effects the value of which has nothing in common with either of the objects of horticulture thus far defined.

As an example, suppose a common village dooryard, in which are found, as too often there may be, a dozen trees of different sorts planted twenty years before, and that, by good chance, among them there is one, standing a little way from the center, of that royal variety of European linden called *Alba pendula*. Trampled under by its coarser and greedier fellows, and half starved, youth and a good constitution may yet have left it in such condition that, all the rest being rooted out, sunlight given it on all sides, shortened in, balanced, cleaned, watered, drained, stimulated, fed, guarded from insidious enemies, its twigs will grow long, delicate, and pliant; its branches low and trailing, its bark become like a soft, finely-grained leather, its upper leaf-surface like silk, and its lower leaf-surface of such texture and tint that, with the faintest sunlight and the softest summer breeze, a constant wavering sheen, as of a damask hanging, will be flowing over the whole body of its foliage. While it regains its birthright in this respect it will also acquire, with fullness of form and moderate play of contour, a stateliness of carriage unusual in a tree of its age and stature. If landscape gardening is for the time to take its order from this princess of the fields, and all within the little court made becoming with her state, the original level surface of the ground need be but slightly modified, yet it may perceptibly fall away from near her, dipping in a long and very gentle wave to rise again with a varying double curve on all sides. There cannot, then, be too much pains taken to spread over it a velvet carpet of perfect turf, uniform in color and quality. Looking upon this from the house, it should seem to be margined on all sides by a rich, thick bank, generally low in front and rising as it recedes, of shrubs and flowering plants; the preparation for which may have required for years a clean-lined border, curve playing into curve, all the way round. A very few plants of delicate and refined character may stand out in advance, but such interruptions of the quiet of the turf must be made very cautiously. Of furniture or artificial ornaments there must be none, or next to none, for even bodily comfort may willingly defer a little to the dainty genius of the place. They may well walk, for instance, a few steps farther who would take a lounging seat, put up their feet, and knock the ashes from their pipes. Yet a single Chinese garden-stool of a softly mottled turquoise-blue will have a good effect if set where a flickering light will fall upon it on the shady side of the tree. The rear rank of shrubs will need to stand so far back that there will be no room to cultivate a suitable hedge against the street. The fence will then best be a wall of cut stone, with decorated gate-piers; or with a base of stone it may be of deftly-wrought iron touched with gilt. By no means a casting with clumsy and overdone effort at feeble ornament—much better a wooden construction of less cost, in which there is a reflection, with variety, of the style of the house if that is of wood also, or if it is not, then something like a banister-rail of turned work, but with no obviously weak parts. The gateway being formed in a symmetrical recess of the fence nearly opposite the tree, the house-door being on the side, the approach to it will bend, with a moderate double curve, in such a way as to seem to give place to the tree, and at the same time allow the greatest expanse of unbroken lawn-surface. Near the gateway, and again near the corner farthest from it, there may be a small tree or a cluster of small trees or large shrubs, forming low, broad heads (dogwood grown in tree-form, sassafras kept low, or, to save time, the neat white mulberry), the tops of which, playing into that of the loftier linden on the right, will in time give to those sitting at the bay-window of the living-room a flowing sky-line, depressed and apparently receding along the middle. If there is a tall building over the way with signs, or which otherwise offends, and the sidewalk space outside admits, we will plant upon it two trees only, adjusting them, as to both kind and position, so that they will almost repeat the depressed line of the nearer foliage, at no greater distance than is necessary to obscure the building. Quite hidden it need not be, lest, also, there should be some of the sky lost, banishment from the lower fields of the sky being a punishment that we should strive not to need. But let us hope that at the worst we have but our neighbor's stable opposite, and that the tops of more distant trees may be seen over it; we shall then still be glad to have the chance of bringing up two trees, set somewhat farther apart than before, on the roadside, as their effect will be to make an enlarged consistency of character, to close in and gather together all that makes up the home-scene, and to aid the turf in relieving it of a tendency to pettiness and excitement which lies in and under the shrubbery.

Let a different theme be sung on the same ground. Suppose that it is an aged beech that we have found, badly used in its middle age as the linden in its youth—storm-bent, lop-limbed, and one-sided, its veteran trunk furrowed, scarred, patched, scaly, and spreading far out to its knotted roots, that heave all the ground about like taut-set cables. If we had wanted a fine-dressy place, this interesting object would have been cut away though it were the last tree within a mile. Accepting it, nothing would be more common, and nothing less like landscape gardening, than to attempt to make a smooth and even surface under it. Let it be acknowledged that fitness and propriety require that there should be some place before the house of repose for the eye, and that nowhere in the little property, to all parts of which we may wish at times to lead our friends in fine attire, can we risk danger of a dusty or a muddy surface. Starting from the corner nearest the tree, and running broader and deeper after it has passed it and before the house, there shall be a swale (a gentle water-way) of cleanly turf (best kept so by the cropping of a tethered cosset and a little play now and then of a grasshook [a sickle], but if this is unhandy we will admit the hand lawn-mower). Now, to carry this fine turf right up over the exposed roots of the beech would be the height of landscape gardening indelicacy; to let it come near, but cut a clean circle out about the tree, would be a landscape gardening barbarism. What is required is a very nice management, under which the turf in rising from the lower and presumably more humid ground shall become gradually thinner and looser, and at length darned with moss, and finally patched with plants that on the linden's lawn would be a sin—tufts of clover and locks and mats of loosestrife, liverwort, and dogtooth-violets; even plantain and sorrel may timidly appear. The surface of the ground will continue rising, but with a broken swell towards the tree, and, in deference to its bent form, hold rising for a space on the other side; but nowhere will its superior roots be fully covered.

Suppose that we are to come to this house, as it is likely we may, three times out of four from the side opposite to where the beech stands; our path then shall strike in, well over on that opposite side and diagonally to the line of the road; there will be a little branch from it leading towards and lost near the tree (the children's path), while the main stem bends short away toward a broad bowery porch facing the road at the corner nearest the gate. The path must needs be smooth for ease of foot and welcomeness, but if its edges chance to be trodden out a little, we will not be in haste to fully repair them. Slanting and sagging off from a ringbolt in the porch there is to be a hammock slung, its farther lanyard caught with two half-hitches on an old stub well up on the trunk of the beech. A strong, brown, seafaring hammock. There shall be a seat, too, under the tree of stout stuff, deep, high-backed, armed, and, whether of rustic-work or plank, fitted by jointing (not held together by nails, bolts, or screws). It may even be rough-hewn, and the more checked, weatherworn, and gray it becomes, without dilapidation or discomfort to the sitter, the better; here you may draw your matches and clean out your pipe, and welcome. We will have nothing in front to prevent a hedge, but must that mean a poor pretense of a wall in leafage? Perhaps it must have that character for a few years till it has become thick and strong enough at bottom, and always it may be a moderately trim affair on the roadside, otherwise we should be trespassers on our neighbors' rights. But its bushes shall not be all of one sort, and in good time they shall be bushes in earnest, leaping up with loose and feathery tops, six, eight, and sometimes ten feet high. And they shall leap out also towards us. Yet from the house half their height shall be lost behind an under and out-growth of brake and bindweed, dog-rose and golden-rod, asters, gentians, buttercups, poppies, and irises. Here and there a spray of low brambles shall be thrown out before all, and the dead gray canes of last year shall not be every one removed. There will be coves and capes and islands of chickweed, catnip, cinquefoil, wild strawberry, hepatica, forget-me-not, and lilies-of-the-valley, and, still farther out, shoals under the turf, where crocuses and daffodils are waiting to gladden the children and welcome the bluebird in the spring. But near the gate the hedge shall be a little overrun and the gateposts overhung and lost in sweet clematis; nay, as the gate must be set-in a little, because the path enters sidewise, there shall be a strong bit of lattice over it, and from the other side a honeysuckle shall reinforce the clematis; and if it whirls off also into the thorn tree that is to grow beyond, the thorn tree will be none the worse to be held to a lowly attitude, bowing stiffly towards the beech. Inside the gate, by the pathside, and again down by the porch, there may be cockscombs, marigolds, pinks, and pansies. But nothing of plants tied to the stake, or of plants the names of which, before they can command due interest, must be set before us on enameled cards, as properly in a botanic garden or museum. Above all, no priggish little spruces and arborvitaes, whether native or from Satsuma;[2] if the neighbors harbor them, any common woodside or fence-row bushes of the vicinity may be set near the edge of the property to put them out of sight; nannyberry, hazel, shadbush, dogwood, even elder, or if an evergreen (conifer) will befit the place, a stout, short, shock-headed mountain-pine, with two or three low savins and a prostrate juniper at their feet. Finally, let the roadside be managed as before. Then, if the gate be left open not much will be lost by it; not all the world will so much as look in, and some who do will afterwards choose to keep the other side of the way, as it is better they should. Yet from the porch, the window beyond, or the old seat under the tree there will be nothing under view that is raw or rude or vulgar; on the contrary, there will be a scene of much refinement as well as of much beauty, and those who live in the house, especially if they have a way of getting their work or their books out under the beech, will find, as the sun goes round and the clouds drift over, that taking it altogether there is a quality more lovable in it than is to be found in all the glasshouses, all the ribbon borders, all the crown jewels of the world.

The same will be equally true of the result of the very different kind of gardening design first supposed. We come thus to the question, What is the distinctive quality of this beauty? In each case there has been an ideal in view, and in each element introduced a consistent pursuit of that ideal, but it is not in this fact of consistency that we find the beauty. We term it landscape beauty, although there is none of the expanse which is the first distinguishing quality of a landscape. This brings us to the consideration that from the point of view of art or of the science of the imagination we may ask for something more in a landscape than breadth, depth, composition, and consistency. A traveler, suddenly turning his eyes upon a landscape that is new to him, and which cannot be directly associated with any former experience, may find himself touched as if by a deep sympathy, so that in an instant his eyes moisten. After long and intimate acquaintance with such a landscape it will often be found to have a persistent influence which may be called its charm—a charm possibly of such power as to appreciably affect the development of the character and shape the course of life. Landscapes of particular types associate naturally and agreeably with certain events. Their fitness in this respect is due to the fact that, through some subtle action on the imagination, they affect the same or kindred sensibilities. If in these dooryards there is something to which every element contributes, comparable in this respect to a poetic or a musical theme, as well, in the one case, of elegance and neatness, carried perhaps to the point of quaint primness, as in the other of homely comfort and good-nature, carried close to the point of careless habits, then the design and process by which it has been attained may lay some slight claim to be considered as a work of art, and the highest art-significance of the term landscape may properly be used to distinguish its character in this respect.

In the possibility, not of making a perfect copy of any charming natural landscape, or of any parts or elements of it, but of leading to the production, where it does not exist, under required conditions and restrictions, of some degree of the poetic beauty of all natural landscapes, we shall thus find not only the special function and the justification of the term landscape gardening, but also the first object of study for the landscape gardener, and the standard by which alone his work is to be fairly judged.

There are those who will question the propriety of regarding the production of the poetic beauty of natural landscape as the end of landscape gardening, on the ground that the very term "natural beauty" means beauty not of man's design, and that the best result of all man's labor will be but a poor counterfeit, in which it is vain to look for the poetry of nature. Much has been written to this effect; with what truth to the nature of man it will be well cautiously to consider.

It is to be remembered, however, with reference to landscape effect, that nature acts both happily and unhappily. A man may take measures to secure the happy action and to guard against the unhappy action in this respect with no more effrontery than with respect to the production of food or protection from lightning, storm, frost, or malaria. He need not take the chance that a certain thick growth of saplings will be so thinned by the operation of what are called natural causes that a few of them may yet have a chance to become vigorous, long-lived, umbrageous trees. Knowing how much more valuable a very few of these will be in the situation, with the adjoining turf holding green under their canopy, than the thousands that for long years may otherwise occupy it, struggling with one another and barring out the light which is the life of all beneath them he may make sure of what is best with axe and billhook. The ultimate result is not less natural or beautiful when he has done so than it would have been if at the same time the same trees had been eaten out by worms or taken away, as trees sometimes are, by an epidemic disease.

On the other hand, there are several considerations, neglect of which is apt to cause too much to be asked of landscape gardening, and sometimes perhaps too much to be professed and attempted. The common comparison of the work of a landscape gardener with that of a landscape painter, for example, easily becomes a very unjust one. The artist in landscape gardening can never have, like the landscape painter, a clean canvas to work upon. Always there will be conditions of local topography, soil, and climate by which his operations must be limited. He cannot whenever it suits him introduce the ocean or a snow-capped mountain into his background. He cannot illuminate his picture with constant sunshine nor soften it by a perpetual Indian summer. Commonly, he is allowed only to modify the elements of scenery, or perhaps to bring about unity and distinctness of expression and suggestion in a locality where elements of beautiful landscape already abound, but are partly obscured or seen in awkward, confusing, and contradicting associations. This is especially likely to be the case in undulating and partially wooded localities, such as in America are oftenest chosen for rural homes. Again, the artist in landscape gardening cannot determine precisely the form and color of the details of his work, because each species of plant will grow up with features which cannot be exactly foreknown in its seed or sapling condition. Thus, he can see his designed and imaginary landscape only as one may see an existing and tangible landscape with half-closed eyes, its finer details not being wholly lost, yet nowhere perfectly definable. Still, again, it is to be remembered that works in landscape gardening have, as a general rule, to be seen from many points of view. The trees which form the background, still oftener those which form the middle distance, of one view must be in the foreground of another. Thus, the working out of one motive must be limited by the necessities of the working out of others on the same ground, and to a greater or lesser degree of the same materials. Finally, the conditions of health and convenience in connection with a dwelling are incompatible with various forms of captivating landscape beauty. A house may be placed in a lovely situation, therefore, and the end of long and costly labors of improvement about it prove comparatively dull, formal, and uninteresting.

What is lost is a part of the price of health and convenience of dwelling. The landscape gardener may have made the best of the case under the conditions prescribed to him.

It has been said that landscapes of a particular type associate naturally and agreeably with certain events. It is to be added that the merit of landscape gardening consists largely in the degree in which their designer has been inspired by a spirit congenial to elements of locality and occasion which are not, strictly speaking, gardening elements. The grounds for an ordinary modest home, for instance, may desirably be designed to give the house, gardens, and offices an aspect of retirement and seclusion, as if these had nestled cozily down together among the trees in escape from the outside world. The grounds of a great public building—a monument of architecture—will, on the other hand, be desirably as large in scale, as open, simple, and broad in spaces of turf and masses of foliage, as convenience of approach will allow, and every tree arranged in subordination to, and support of, the building. The grounds of a church and of an inn, of a cottage and of an arsenal, of a burying-place and of a place of amusement, will thus differ, in each case correspondingly to their primary purpose. Realizing this, it will be recognized that the choice of the site, of the elevation, aspect, entrances, and outlooks of a building [cannot] be judiciously determined except in connection with a study of the leading features of a plan, of its approaches, and grounds. Also, that in the design of roads, walks, lakes, and bridges, of the method of dealing with various natural circumstances, as standing wood, rocks, and water; in a determination of what is possible and desirable in respect to drainage, water-supply, distant prospects to be opened or shut out, the avoidance of malaria and other evils—all these and many other duties are necessarily intimately associated with those of gardening (or the cultivation of plants) with a view to landscape effects.

NOTES

1. Slightly modified in wording from James Russell Lowell's essay "Spencer," *The North American Review*, 120 (April 1875).

2. A Japanese province on Kyushu Island.

ELEVEN

The Landscape Architecture of the World's Columbian Exposition

(1893)

Landscaping the Chicago World's Fair was one of the most difficult challenges Olmsted ever faced. The site was huge and the soil conditions terrible, the weather unpredictable and the climate harsh, the design time frighteningly short and the demands of interested parties immensely disparate, so that his vision of broad, open, restful grounds intended as a foil to the visual stimulation of monumental buildings and as a respite from the intense energy of large crowds was severely compromised.

In the end Olmsted, ever optimistic, concluded that while the completed fairgrounds were less than successful, the collaboration of thousands of planners, administrators, and laborers was nothing short of remarkable, an achievement "possible only in a country which was, in a high degree socially, as well as politically, a republic."

This essay is valuable for illustrating the enormous complexities involved in such a large project and the manner in which Olmsted handled them. Improvisation and careful planning were forced into uneasy partnership, as were broad vision and ad hoc demands. Yet Olmsted seems to have maintained his equanimity, not to mention flexibility, fully understanding that the multiplicity of agendas at play— some complementary but others contradictory to his own—was only natural in an undertaking of this size.

If the two preceding documents on landscape gardening are largely concerned with definition and theory, this one reveals a nitty-gritty, worm's-eye view of what his work entailed.

Originally published in The Inland Architect and News Record, *22 (September 1893), this lecture was delivered to the annual convention of the American Institute of Architects meeting under the auspices of the ad hoc World Congress of Architects at the World's Columbian Exposition, Chicago, August 2, 1893.*

This paper has been written at the request of the [American] Institute [of Architects] with the object of briefly accounting for such part of the preparation of the Exposition of 1893 as has come within the responsibility of the landscape architects, and as a contribution in this respect to a record of its genesis and development as a work of design. No comprehensive definition of the responsibility of the landscape architects has been recorded, and as to what is implied by the name of their office, different understandings are had. For this reason, something needs first to be said in explanation of the view which will herein be taken.

In the *Quarterly Review* of 1820, page 303, there is an article written by Sir Walter Scott, from which it appears that this master of words did not approve of the term "landscape gardening," which was then coming into popular use. His objection to it was that it tended to confusion between two classes of purposes, or motives of art, which could not well be blended together.[1] To make this objection clear, it may be observed that the word garden comes to us from the same root with girdle, girth, garth [a close or yard] and others to be found in every European tongue, all of which imply something limited, restrained and separated from what exists beyond or about it, or that is the cause of such limitation, restriction or separation. From remote times the word in its various forms, English, Spanish, French, Italian, Scandinavian, has carried with it this idea of limitation and exclusion. We yet speak of "garden flowers," meaning certain flowers exclusive of others. Taking up a book with the title "A Garden of Verse," we should understand it to be a selection of verse. Being told at a farmhouse that one of the family of the house is "in the garden," no countryman would think that this meant either simply out-of-doors or in a stable yard, or an orchard, or a common cultivated field: a grove, a park, or a pasture. The word implies reference to a limited, defined and exclusive space, and it may be used in this way antithetically to the word landscape, the application of which is so comprehensive that it may take in houses, lawns, gardens, orchards, meadows, mountains, and even the sky, with the stars to the remotest nebulae.

The word landscape is often used by accurate writers interchangeably with the word scenery, as, for example, by [the Reverend William] Gilpin in his series of works on the "Scenery of Great Britain"; also by [Philip Gilbert] Hamerton in a recent treatise on "Landscape" written from the point of view of a landscape painter.

A distinction implied by the word landscape unfitting it to be compounded with the word garden is indicated by Hamerton when he says that: "Much of the comprehensiveness of natural scenery depends upon the degree in which mass appears to predominate over detail. In perfectly clear weather a mountain does not look nearly so grand as when . . . its nearer details are only partially revealed amid broad spaces of shade. So it appears with other elements of landscape, they lose in comprehensiveness as the details become more visible."[2] Thus, for the enjoyment of landscape beauty, we are to regard the detail of what we see mainly as it affects the character and expression of masses, these masses being considered as elements of composition and perspective. On the other hand, for the enjoyment of garden beauty as such, we must scrutinize objects of detail discriminatingly. We must see roses as roses, not as flecks of white or red modifying masses of green.

Lastly, to understand aright the term "landscape architect," we must bear in mind that the word architecture is not limited in application to works of building. The Almighty is referred to as the "Architect of the Universe." Plutarch writes of the architecture of a poem, meaning the plotting of it. "The architect of his own fortune" is an old proverbial term yet commonly used in our newspapers, and is applicable as well to a banker or a miner as to one whose fortune has been made by directing works of building.

In view of the considerations thus presented, when the office of Landscape Architects to the Exposition was created, what in the absence of specific instructions, was to be understood as the leading duty of that office? The answer assumed by those to whom the title was applied was that their leading duty must be to reconcile the requirements of the problem which the directors had before them in respect to buildings and means of access to, and means of communication between, buildings, with the requirements of pleasing scenery, and of scenery which would be pleasing, not because of the specific beauty of its detail, but because of the subordination and contribution of its detail to effective composition of masses as seen in perspective.

Adopting such a view, the first thing to be noted in an account of the landscape architecture of the Exposition is this: Immediately after the settlement in the directory of the question of its own organization and rules, the question of a choice of sites came up, and it soon appeared that the debate of it was likely to be inconveniently prolonged. Thereupon, the suggestion was made that expert counsel upon it might be desirable, and an inquiry was addressed to our office as to the terms upon which such counsel could be had. Upon receipt of our reply by telegraph, we were asked to come to Chicago as soon as practicable. We did so by the next train, and upon arrival were presently taken to examine in succession seven proposed sites; three on the lake and four inland.

The country immediately about Chicago is flat and mainly treeless, except that in a few places there are small areas of dense woods. Its sub-soil generally, and its surface soil largely, is a tenacious brick-clay. The climate in the spring is severe under successive alterations of southerly and northerly winds. The latter sweeping over the icy lake from the semi-arctic regions north of Lake Superior, the demand upon energy of vegetation is apt to be peculiarly trying. Accordingly the choice of a suitable site was necessarily to be a choice of difficulties. Of the seven sites to which our attention was called, there was not one the scenery of which would recommend it if it had been near Boston, New York or Philadelphia. After our first general review of the premises, we adopted the opinion that nothing was to be found on any of the inland sites that could be weighed against the advantages, in respect to scenery, of the lake shore. Next, as to sites on the shore, we concluded that, provided suitable means of transportation for goods and passengers between the town and the place could be secured, the northernmost of those proposed would be the best. By comparison with the most nearly competing site, it would require less outlay to prepare the ground and establish suitable means of interior transportation, water supply, drainage and sewerage; the great marine commerce of Chicago would be passing in review before it at a suitable distance for spectacular effect; an arrangement of buildings simpler and much grander than elsewhere would be practicable; and the buildings would have a much better setting and framing of foliage provided by standing woods, fairly vigorous and of sufficient height to serve as a continuous background.

But a committee of the directory, taking up the question of transportation between this site and the central parts of the town, advised us that the railroad companies concerned could not be induced to make the outlay of capital required for such arrangements of transportation as we thought needful. Thereupon, we fell back on the southernmost of the sites proposed on the lake, which went by the name of Jackson Park.

Our report favoring this place excited much remonstrance. Opposition to it was concentrated in favor of an inland site near by, known as Washington Park, the advantages of which were thought to be so great and so obvious that a leading member of the National Commission[3] assured us that after an inspection of the two sites in question, not one vote in ten could be got for our proposition. In the few days that intervened before the commission met, we gave the reasons of our choice as well as we could in private conversation, but I do not think we accomplished much. In the end the commission accepted our advice, not because a majority of its members understood the grounds of it, but because they could not be led to believe that we should have given this advice without having, as experts, sound reasons for doing it. The result was due to respect for professional judgment. Comparing this experience with some of my earlier professional life, I can but think that it manifests an advance in civilization.

Unquestionably, to common observation, the place was forbidding. At different periods in the past sand bars had been formed in the lake a few hundred feet from and parallel with the shore. The landward one of these, gradually rising, would at length attain an elevation above the surface of the water.

There would then be within this bar a pool accurately definable as a lagoon. Gradually, in this case, lagoons thus formed had been filled nearly to the brim with sand drifting from the outer bar, and had been turned into marshes. Thus nine-tenths of the surface of the site, or, in fact, all of it that had not been artificially made otherwise, consisted of three ridges of beach sand, the swales between which were more or less occupied by boggy, herbaceous vegetation. Upon the innermost two of the ridges vegetable mold had gathered and trees had sprung up in scattered groups. The most important of these trees were oaks. The situation being extremely bleak, the soil subject to be[ing] flooded, and the sandy sub-soil water-soaked, these had had an extremely slow growth. The largest were about forty feet in height. They were very feeble and many of them dilapidated through loss of limbs broken off by gales from the lake.

A more serious difficulty than any involved in this consideration was found in the circumstance that the level of water in the lake, and consequently in the marshes, was fluctuating, and this not only from day to day, as would be determined by winds at a distance drawing it off or backing it up, but its average level varied from year to year. An engineer who had been in charge of operations upon the lake shore, and who had occasion to study the matter with accuracy, advised us that the probabilities were that in 1893 the average elevation of the surface of the lake would be four feet higher than it was at the time we were studying the plan, or than it had been during the year before. It will be readily understood how difficult it became to forecast landscape effects in a region of low shores, without knowing within four feet what the level of the water was to be by which these shores were to be washed.

The Jackson Park site had, twenty years before, been selected as a site to be reserved for a public park. If a search had been made for the least parklike ground within miles of the city, nothing better meeting the requirement could have been found. It will, then, naturally be asked: Why was such a place fixed upon for a park? I have not the specific knowledge required for an answer, but I may mention that it is a common thing with town governments when they find bodies of land which, because of their special topographical condition, are not favorable to the ends of dealers in building lots, to regard them as natural reservations for pleasure grounds; to label them accordingly on their maps, and to refrain from ordering streets to be laid out across them. This is not peculiarly a western custom. The sites for the Central Park, for the Morningside Park, for the Riverside Park, for the Mount Morris Park, for Tompkins Square, and, no doubt, for other public grounds in the city of New York, were thus selected. So was the site of the public ground in Boston, officially called the Fens, but popularly known as the Back Bay Park. Sites having been thus obtained, landscape architects are asked to contrive how pleasure grounds can be made of them. It has been so, I believe, in London, conspicuously in the case of Battersea Park. And it may be remembered that the opportunity of making the Tuileries Garden in Paris occurred because, while the city had been building out about the place, the necessary ground had been held in reserve, while the clay which it contained was being removed to be used for making roofing tile. In the [next] Millenium it may be hoped that landscape architects will be employed to select land with regard to the specific purpose for which it is to be used. When that is the case, the making of a park will be less costly than it is at present.

At the time the land and water of Jackson Park had been taken for a public park, I was in partnership with Mr. Calvert Vaux, and we were asked to devise a plan for making it available for a public pleasure ground, together with the site now known as Washington Park and the strip of land between them known as the Midway.[4]

As the starting point for the development of the proposition which we then made, the suggestion was adopted that dredging boats might be employed, to begin at the lake and first reopen the old lagoons, taking the excavated material to be lifted out of their bottoms to form the basis of the higher, more undulating and varying banks resting on the old sand bars; next, to move through the Midway and so on to the inland park site, everywhere lifting out the material needing to be removed in order to open a channel in which they could float, and so shifting this material to one side or the other as to provide the base of varying shores, these shores to be afterward covered with soil and landscape masses of vegetation.

When Jackson Park was chosen as the site for the World's Fair the general landscape design of no part of the plan of which the expedient I have described was the germ, had been carried out. In the Washington Park part of the scheme a good deal had been done following the leading outlines of the plan, but with a modeling of surfaces and a choice of material and disposition of foliage looking to condition of detail rather than of masses, and with entire disregard of the elements of mystery through effects of aerial perspective and the complicated play of light and shadow, and of reflected tints, in extended composition.

In the nominal carrying out of plans in the preparation of which I have had part, there have often been sacrifices of the designs of these plans which have been mortifying and disappointing. In no other case, however, had the disappointment been so great as this. Nowhere else had the opportunity for forming agreeable scenery been so lost. But in the lagoon district what little had been done had not been done unwisely.

Coming to consider what might yet be done with this same lagoon district suitably for the purposes of the Exposition, the question at once came up how far the general theory of the old plan for a public pleasure ground to be formed upon it could be made available to the specific purpose of the Exposition.

As a result of this consideration, we came to the conclusion that the element of the waterways in the original plan being carried out, retaining walls being built in various places for holding up the excavated material to be piled upon the shores, so that in these places terraces would be formed, the necessary buildings of the Fair could be advantageously distributed upon the surrounding sandy ridges.

Before making their formal report favoring the choice of Jackson Park for the site of the Exposition, the landscape architects took counsel with Messrs. Burnham & Root,[5] presenting their views of the manner in which, this site being adopted, it should be used, and obtaining confirmation of them, more especially with reference to the expediency of distributing the needed large buildings upon the sandy ridges and of spreading out these ridges suitably for the purpose by retaining walls to be backed by the excavated material from the lagoons. It may be observed that to accomplish this purpose in various localities where otherwise lagoons with shores of a natural character would become unsuitable for boats, it was thought best to give them the character of canals; that is to say, to make them formal and give their banks, which would necessarily be walls, an architectural character in harmony with the buildings to which, in a near perspective view, they would form foregrounds.

Mr. Burnham in his report of operations, addressed to the president of the Exposition, on October 24, 1892, thus describes the process of forming the first complete graphic sketch illustrative of the design.[6]

After consideration of sketches made on the ground . . . a crude plot, on a large scale, of the whole scheme was rapidly drawn on brown paper, mostly with a pencil in the hand of Mr. Root, whose architectural prescience and coordinating talent was of invaluable service to the result. The plot, formed in the manner described, contemplated the following as leading features of design: That there should be a great architectural court with a body of water therein; that this court should serve as a suitably dignified and impressive entrance hall to the Exposition, and that visitors arriving by train or boat should all pass through it; that there should be a formal canal leading northward from this court to a series of broader waters of a lagoon character, by which nearly the entire site would be penetrated, so that the principal Exposition buildings would each have a water as well as a land frontage, and would be approachable by boats; that near the middle of this lagoon system there should be an island, about fifteen acres in area, in which there would be clusters of the largest trees growing upon the site; that this island should be free from conspicuous buildings and that it should have a generally secluded, natural sylvan aspect, the existing clusters of trees serving as centers for such broad and simple larger masses of foliage as it would be practicable to establish in a year's time by plantations of young trees and bushes. Because the water in the lagoons would be subject to considerable fluctuations, it was proposed that its shores should be occupied by a selection of such aquatic plants as would endure occasional submergence and yet survive an occasional withdrawal of water from their roots. Time pressing, the pencil, large-scale, brown-paper plot above described with a brief written specification, almost equally sketchy, was submitted to the corporation and, after due consideration, on December 1, 1890, was adopted as the plan of the Exposition.

The question may be asked: In what degree at this early period was the result forecast which has since been attained in respect to the effect of boats, bridges and water fowl and overhanging foliage on the lagoons? The answer is that it was quite fully anticipated in a general way. The effect of the boats and water fowl as incidents of movement and life; the bridges with respect to their shadows and reflections, their effect in extending apparent perspectives and in connecting terraces and buildings, tying them together and thus increasing unity of composition, all this was quite fully taken into account from the very first, and the style of boats best adapted to the purpose became, at once, a topic of much anxiety and study.

The next important step in the progress of the enterprise to which reference is here necessary, was that taken by Mr. Burnham which resulted in the meeting at Chicago of the advisory board of architects; with Mr. Hunt as its chairman.[7] The landscape architects were made members of this board, and their general plan came up for critical review. Many suggestions for its amendment were made by the building architects, but in nearly all cases counter suggestions were offered by others of them, and the balances of advantages being weighed, the result was at length a cordial and unqualified approval of the plan as originally presented, and this was duly expressed by a resolution and report to the commission.

The general plan was, however, afterward modified in certain particulars. These particulars were the abandonment of a proposed outer harbor for which the landing pier now seen was substituted; the introduction of the Peristyle, and of the Colonnade at the end of the south transept of the main court. All of these changes resulted from suggestions of the building architects, cordially welcomed by the landscape architects.

The general plan was later modified in one matter, to its great injury. Two of our firm had visited the last World's Fair in Paris, while it was in preparation, under the guidance of its landscape architect. The third of our number, Mr. Codman, had passed several months in Paris while the Fair was in progress.[8] We all thought, and Mr. Codman was particularly strong in the conviction, that it was an unfortunate circumstance that visitors so generally entered the Paris Exposition at points and by ways not adapted either to give them a grand impression, or to provide a convenient point of dispersal for systematic observation. This in Paris grew largely out of the situation of the Exposition. There was no similar difficulty in the Chicago situation, and the very first step in our revision of the old park plan in adaptation to the requirements of the Fair was to fix upon a focal point of interest to be regarded as the center of design, and to so place this center that conveyances of all kinds, by land and by water, the railways and the boats, both those of the interior and those of the exterior, should conveniently discharge visitors into it and receive visitors from it. That it should thus be made a place of general exchange, a place for obtaining information and guidance, as well as a place of departures and returns, a spacious court was designed; the Administration building was placed in this court;[9] the buildings likely to be most frequented were placed so that they would open from it; the intramural railway was to have its principal station in it; the whole interior water system was planned with a view to easy connection with and through it by the small boats. All railways and all steamboats were to conveniently receive and discharge passengers through it. A union station was provided for with the latter object in view. We intended that the Administration building, which stands in this court, and this railway station, should contain the principal provision of guides and wheelchairs, and the central office of a system of offices of "public comfort," to be in telephonic communication with it. We did all in our power to have this arrangement carried out. The failure to carry it out has added, in my opinion, to the cost of the Exposition, and deducted much from its value. In reporting to you professionally, I have thought it necessary to say this, not in the least in a complaining way, but that it may go on record for the benefit of those who may have to deal hereafter with a similar problem. You will ask why we were unsuccessful? I do not fully know. I can only answer that our failure took the form of a failure of prolonged negotiations with the Illinois Central Railway.

At the period when the general plan was formed it was impossible to have building masses definitely in view except in the case of a few of the larger ones. Our instructions as to these were that a classification similar to that of the last Paris Exposition was to be contemplated, but that the buildings required under the classification would be a third larger than the corresponding buildings in Paris. We presumed that additional buildings would be wanted and that they would be of smaller but of varying size. For these presumed, but as yet undetermined, smaller buildings, we held three large spaces in reserve. First, for such as would be wanted for the livestock exhibits, an area at the south end; second, for the distinctive office and "headquarters" buildings of the national and state committees, an area at the north end; third, for miscellaneous exhibition buildings of a smaller class, the strip of land called the Midway. We calculated that restaurants would be established in the great Exposition buildings, and that the terraces of some of these buildings would be occupied to a considerable extent with refreshment tables and chairs, under awnings. We did not suppose that there would be many small buildings scattered about between the main great buildings, nor do I think that it was at the outset contemplated by those in direction that there would be. Afterward they were seen to be financially desirable. Also, it is to be noted that it was our original intention and that this intention was fully set forth, to have what has since been called the Wooded Island, occupying a central position, held free from buildings and from all objects that would prevent it from presenting, in connection with the adjoining waters, a broad space, characterized by calmness and naturalness, to serve as a foil to the artificial grandeur and sumptuousness of the other parts of the scenery. After a time demands came for the use of the island for a great variety of purposes, and at length we became convinced that it would be impossible to successfully resist these demands. When we reluctantly reached this conclusion, the question with us was which of all the propositions urged, if adopted, will have the least obtrusive and disquieting result? Probably we were fortunate in securing the occupation of the island only by the temple and garden of the Japanese, and for the display of horticultural exhibits. Nevertheless, we consider that these introductions have much injured the island for the purpose which in our primary design it was intended to serve. If they could have been avoided, I am sure that the Exposition would have made a much more agreeable general impression on visitors of cultivated sensibility to the influence of scenery.

With regard to the subsequent occupation of ground by smaller structures, especially such as are of the class called pavilions and concession buildings, many of these have been inserted without consulting us; places being often given them in which they intercepted vistas and disturbed spaces intended to serve for the relief of the eye from the too nearly constant demands upon attention of the Exposition buildings. As a caution to those who will manage the next affair of a similar class it is best to record the opinion that the effect of these little structures among the larger has been bad. I can best show our judgment of it by saying that it had been our original intention to use on the grounds a great deal more of gardening decoration in various forms than we have. We had, at considerable expense, provided materials for the purpose, largely in the form of plants propagated and kept last winter under glass. But at last when the time approached for making the intended use of this material, the spaces of the Exposition grounds not occupied by the larger building masses and trees appeared to us to be everywhere already a great deal too much divided and disturbed by little features intended to be more or less of a decorative character. So much was this the case that, after consideration, and with reluctance, we concluded that our intended floral decorations would add so much disquiet to the already excessive disquiet of the scenery, and so detract from the effect of the more massive elements, that they must be abandoned.

One other modification of the original plan must be referred to. The administration at one time contemplated the introduction of a branch railway by which Illinois Central trains would be taken from the Midway to the station upon the Main Court through the Fair ground. To give room for this branch road we were required to change the position assigned to the Horticultural building;[10] reduce the breadth of the lagoon and modify the outlines of the island. Afterward the railway project was abandoned, but in the meantime work had been done compelling adherence to the unfortunate revision of the shores. It will readily be seen that the cramping of the water at this point has been a considerable loss, and that had the advances and recesses of the foliage masses opposite the Horticultural building been much greater than they are, a more picturesque effect would have been obtained.

Passing from matters of design to matters of construction: as to the more bulky preliminary operations of dredging and subgrading, they were mostly affairs of large contracts, and, while we were constantly consulted, the preparation of details and the superintendence of the contractor's work was made by the director of works mainly the duty of the engineer corps. The same was the case in a still greater degree with respect to the often extremely difficult and delicate matters of drainage, sewerage and water supply throughout the grounds. It is only necessary, then, to say with reference to these matters as well as to those of buildings, that our cooperative relations have been of a character to be looked back upon with pride and congratulation. Really, I think that it is a most satisfactory and encouraging circumstance that it could be found feasible for so many men of technical education and ability to be recruited and suitably organized so quickly and made to work together so well in so short a time. I think it a notable circumstance that there should have been so little friction, so little display of jealousy, envy and combativeness, as has appeared in the progress of this enterprise. Too high an estimate cannot be placed on the industry, skill and tact with which this result was secured by the master of us all, yet I venture to say that, considering the impromptu way in which Mr. Burnham had to go to work, and the extremely varied antecedents in the matter of education, custom and habit of those through whom he had to operate, equal success would have been possible only in a country which was, in a high degree socially, as well as politically, a republic.

I have only to add a few statements in respect to that part of the work of which the landscape architects were placed especially and more independently in general superintendence.

On this point I will observe, first, that we early recognized the importance of not entering upon undertakings which might lead to the requirement of outlays, the reasonableness of which could not be made plain to the directory, or which we could not be confident that in the progress of the work the financial department would fail to sustain. Also, we took well into account that various resources that would be available in any large capital of Europe would not in Chicago be at our command, and further, that we should have to push much of our work very rapidly with unknown and untrained men. After completing operations of grading, draining and the supplying of suitable soils we should have, for much of the ground, but one fall and spring for planting operations; for none of it more than two; and it is rare that a weak and sickly appearance can be avoided in freshly made plantations. We considered also, that we had to deal with many inexactly known conditions—conditions, I mean, of climate—as of the occurrence of rains and floods and sudden inroads of severe frosts in the planting season; conditions of uncertainties as to how the bottom and banks of our excavations would behave; as, for example, how they would be affected by subterranean springs. To illustrate this latter hazard, I will mention that at important points after our channels had been excavated there were movements, slips and uprisings of the sandy bottoms, forming shoals, and, as the result of the subsequent redredging of these places, adjoining banks and slopes slid away and caved off. Through this process, and from the effect of ice which formed to the depth [of] two feet along the shores and remained late in the spring, we lost, in spite of all precautions, many thousand water plants that had been collected, propagated and set with great painstaking.

From the start we took all these hazards and difficulties into account and devised our design at all points so that success in what we aimed at would not greatly depend on exact and defined local particulars, but on masses and broad general conditions.

One main difficulty to be considered was that of making sure of the clothing of several miles of newly made, raw sandy shores with a clean, graceful, intricate, picturesque, green drapery, varied in tints and pleasing in its shadows and reflections. We knew that we could depend but little on the ordinary commercial agencies for the materials required for this end, and within a week after the work was put under our direction we had begun the gathering, by special collecting agencies, of the plants required. We placed our dependence mainly on two classes of these: First, willows, chiefly of the shrubby sorts, but in large variety; second, herbaceous, bog and water side plants, principally such as are commonly known with us as flags, cattails, rushes, irises and pond lilies. Some of these were propagated on the Fair grounds; a few were bought from nurserymen and florists; much the larger part was obtained by parties organized and sent out for the purpose to various localities on the shores of lakes, rivers and swamps in Illinois and Wisconsin.

Altogether, we have planted on the shores of the lagoons one hundred thousand small willows; seventy-five large railway platform carloads of collected herbaceous aquatic plants, taken from the wild; one hundred and forty thousand other aquatic plants, largely native and Japanese irises, and two hundred and eighty-five thousand ferns and other perennial herbaceous plants. The whole number of plants transplanted to the ground has been a little over a million.

Our chief executive in the immediate direction of working operations has been Mr. Rudolph Ulrich.[11] He had never been employed under our direction before, but we had seen the results of rapid work carried on under difficulties by him and had formed a good opinion of his abilities to meet emergencies. On the very day of our appointment we telegraphed across the continent to ascertain if he would be available. Our message reached him at a moment when he happened to have just left a California work in which he had been engaged, and he was at once secured. It has been our policy to encumber him as little as possible with directions in detail, but to explain to him our aims and trust largely to his discretion as to particulars. He has entered admirably into the spirit of the design, and the zeal, activity, skill and industry with which he has labored to carry it out cannot be too highly esteemed.

NOTES

1. Sir Walter Scott (1771–1832), prolific Scottish prose and poetry writer on things historical, a landscape designer in his own right, and cofounder in 1808 of *Quarterly Review*, published therein an essay on landscape gardening in 1826 or 1828 but not, as Olmsted writes, in 1820, when there were no pages numbered in the 300s.

2. Beginning in 1782, the Reverend William Gilpin (1724–1804) published several books of "observations," "remarks," and "essays" on the "scenery" and "picturesque beauty" of "several parts of Great Britain"—based on his travels during the 1770s—that were influential in reshaping popular ideas about landscape. Philip Gilbert Hamerton (1834–94), landscape painter and art critic for the English *Saturday Review*, also wrote monographs, including *Imagination in Landscape Painting* (1877) from which Olmsted quotes.

3. An April 1890 act of Congress awarding the Columbian Exposition to Chicago established a national commission composed of eight at-large members plus two from each state and territory to oversee all aspects of the fair. The "directory" Olmsted mentions throughout is the local board of directors that oversaw the several departments as, for example, Publicity and Promotion, Traffic Management, and Landscape Architecture.

4. Olmsted and Vaux designed Jackson and Washington parks with its connecting Midway, collectively known as South Park, in 1871.

5. Chicago partners Daniel H. Burnham and John W. Root were the chief architects of the fair, Burnham supervising construction, Root artistic design. Root's untimely death on January 15, 1891, having turned forty-one only five days earlier, left Burnham solely in charge of architectural matters.

6. Harlow N. Higinbotham, a director of Marshall Field & Co., was the fair's president.

7. The Advisory Board of Architects consisted of Richard Morris Hunt, New York (chair); the firms of George B. Post and McKim, Meade & White, New York; Peabody & Stearns, Boston; Van Brunt & Howe, Kansas City; William Le Baron Jenney, Solon S. Bemen, Adler & Sullivan, Henry Ives Cobb, Burling & Whitehouse, and Holabird & Roche, Chicago.

8. Henry Sargent Codman (d. 1893), a brilliant young designer in Olmsted's firm, had spent three months in Paris in 1889 studying, among other things, that year's exposition. Codman died before completing his important work on the Chicago fair, much of which was taken over by Rudolph Ulrich (see n. 11)

9. The Administration building was designed by Richard Morris Hunt.

10. The Horticultural building was designed by William Le Baron Jenney.

11. Rudolph Ulrich (1841–1906), a New York City landscape architect and later superintendent of Olmsted and Vaux's Prospect Park in Brooklyn, had recently been and would continue designing in California. Despite what he writes here, Olmsted was not entirely satisfied with Ulrich's work at the fair, in particular, that he spent too much time on details. See Laura Wood Roper, *FLO: A Biography of Frederick Law Olmsted* (Baltimore: Johns Hopkins University Press, 1973), 446.

V

PARK DESIGN: HISTORY AND THEORY

TWELVE

Address to the Prospect Park Scientific Association

(1868)

Which "topographical conditions," Olmsted asks, are most suitable for a park? His answer is those that provide "an easy gratification of a great variety of the elementary human impulses" while simultaneously administering "to man's want of beauty." Thus it is the job of the landscape gardener, here referred to as both "scientist" and "engineer," to "stimulate the simplest, purest and most primeval action of the poetic element of human nature, . . . that which is most apt to be lost or to become diseased and debilitated among the dwellers in towns."

But this does not mean that a park should consist entirely of "easy flowing topography." The senses are stimulated and gracefulness enhanced by contrast, by natural and man-made "accessories": rocks, woods, shrubbery, and structures of useful sorts, all of which, however, should be "unmistakably auxiliary [and] subordinate . . . in every respect to the general design."

It is telling that Olmsted draws on his own experience traveling on horseback through the American Southwest to suggest what new parks might be like. Every day, he writes, he and his companions looked for campsites offering six conditions—he names them—which turned out to be some of the very same conditions found at "a pleasant family residence" and in old English parks. His point was not that those six conditions must be replicated in modern city parks, but that they addressed irreducible, elemental human needs, the satisfaction of which was the ultimate purpose, Olmsted firmly believed, of his own life's work.

Olmsted delivered this lecture on April 8, 1868, at the request of the Board of Control of the Prospect Park Association in Brooklyn, New York. A handwritten text found at the Frederick Law Olmsted National Historic Site—at "Fairsted," formerly Olmsted's own house and grounds in Brookline, Massachusetts—was first published in Charles E. Beveridge and Carolyn F. Hoffmann (eds.), Writings on Public Parks, Parkways, and Park Systems *(1997), which is supplementary series, v. I, of* The Papers of Frederick Law Olmsted.

The editor has taken the liberty of converting a lecturer's shortcuts into what better facilitates reading, for example, changing Olmsted's "&" into "and" and inserting necessary punctuation, along with other minor emendations that in no way alter his meaning.

You have asked me to talk to you upon the subject of the treatment of natural woods with reference to park-purposes. There is a difficulty which always stands in the way of useful debate of any of the elements by which our work here is distinguished from the great body of works in which the principles of engineering science and architectural art are more especially applied. A difficulty which arises from the insufficiency and chiefly from the looseness and vagueness of the nomenclature of the class of works in question [is that] we are prevented from comparing ideas, prevented from elaborating ideas by mutual efforts, prevented from giving and receiving instruction, by the want of words which are certain to call up in the minds of all of us or of any two of us, the same images or ideas. This arises from the fact that hitherto, there has been little occasion for exact discussion; that so far as works of this kind have been carried on at all they have been carried on without much careful thought, or at least without the benefit of exact thought in many minds. There has been but little criticism, little debate, consequently little explanation or occasion for explanation, of the principles of science and art upon which they are designed. In fact, public works of this class are new in the world. There have been public parks before now certainly, but [until] quite lately the construction of those parks has not been pursued fully and fairly as a public work, open to general, thorough and searching criticism, to anything like professional scientific criticism. Responsibility for these works has not been felt to be a responsibility to the public. Accountability has been felt only to some individual or to some few individuals and provided their intentions were realized, provided they were gratified, criticism of them has been regarded as nobody else's business. There has been no interest, therefore, demanding and leading to anything like precise, exact and searching debate and consequently precision of thought and clear means of expressing precise and thorough thought has not been developed.

Thus a necessity exists in the discussion of such a topic, for instance as this we have in hand, to use a great deal of circumlocution or to dwell a great deal upon elementary ideas and to define elementary terms. I must do so or I shall be liable to convey impressions to you very different from those I wish you to receive. To reach good results our process must be studious, elaborate, slow, perhaps tedious.

Take this term, park-purposes. What are we to understand by it? It is your business to plan and superintend constructions in which the materials of the earth's surface, clay, sand and stone, are to be largely and scientifically dealt with. You are called upon in your professional capacity to provide a certain town with a park as you might be to provide it with water-works, bridges, docks or canals. What is the idea your clients have when they demand of you a park? To begin let us say, they want a place of recreation? But that is a very insufficient definition. A theater is a place of recreation, so is a flower garden, so is a conservatory. The vacant lots between X and XI avenues and 3rd and 9th streets have been a place of recreation; of out of door recreation, for a long time, both the wooded parts and the open. But now we are asked to take this land and more and make a park of it. How shall we get at what it is they want? Where did they get the word? It is an English word and we must go to England if we would know to what it has been formerly applied. There are several thousand pieces of ground which for many centuries have been called parks—some of which were called parks at the period when, more especially, the English language was consolidated. The term park was not used to distinguish them as places set apart or fitted especially for recreation, certainly not for any kind of recreation that your modern townspeople want ground to be set apart and prepared for. What then is their common characteristic? In what did the park differ from other divisions of ground?

What was the *common quality* they possessed which made it necessary that they should have a *common designation*? They were not public properties but when the state of society was yet essentially barbarous were selected and taken possession of, prized, fought for and held solely by the rich and powerful—and when society became better organized and less rude, these same pieces of ground still remained a peculiar possession of the more fortunate and arrogant, who had residencies in the midst of them. It continued the same through all the changes of manners and customs, the increase of luxury and the progress of refinement to the present day, when at length we find people who cannot have a park for a private possession uniting with others to obtain one which can be used in common. Why should the particular pieces of land to which the term park was first applied have been regarded as choice and peculiarly desirable possessions for so long a time and by men of such very different wants and habits? Pretty certainly, it appears to me, because of some topographical conditions in which they originally differed from other pieces of land, which topographical conditions have all the time been found peculiarly convenient for the indulgence of certain propensities which are a part of human nature and which the progress of civilization does not affect, as it does mere manners and customs.

To illustrate and more fully fix in your minds this hypothesis, I shall narrate to you a personal experience. When I was a young man I made a long journey through England on foot, in company with my brother, in the course of which we became very familiar with the finest and most characteristic park scenery. A few years afterwards my brother and I started to go overland by the Southern or Gila route to the Pacific. On account of the outbreak of an Indian war and the refusal of parties which we had expected to join to take the risk without military escort, which could not be spared us, we were compelled to wait on the frontier during a period of several months. We undertook therefore, for our amusement and information, an exploration of so much of the country beyond settlements as it was at all safe for us to cruise in, as well as some of the border land a little beyond the line of safety, and of the other border a little within the line of outermost settlement.[1]

Traveling with a pack-mule and for the most part living on the country, being in no haste, we usually broke camp about 9 o'clock, and soon after noon began to look out for a new camping ground. That is to say, if at any time after noon we saw a promise anywhere to the right or left or right ahead of certain topographical conditions, we moved in that direction, and whenever we came upon a site which was particularly satisfactory to us as a place for camping, though it was but just after noon, there we would end our day's march. If we found nothing satisfactory we would keep on [until] dusk, and then do the best we could. If we were fortunate in this respect on Saturday we generally rested on Sunday, and sometimes at a camp that particularly pleased us, laid up for several days, it being our object to keep our stock in good condition. Thus I may say that it was our chief business for some months to study the topography of the country more especially with reference to the selection of satisfactory camping places. Now with fresh recollections of the old [English] country parks we found that the topographical conditions which we were accustomed to look for were such that we sometimes questioned whether if an Englishman had been brought blindfolded to our tent, and the scene disclosed to him, he would be readily persuaded that he was not in some one of those old parks. Yet I need not say the conditions were perfectly natural, that no engineer or gardener had had a hand in fashioning them—nay I suppose that sometimes no white man ever had before been on the ground.

What then were the governing circumstances of our selection?

First, we wanted good, clear water close at hand, both for bathing and for drinking.

2nd, good pasturage in which with little labor or care to us we could keep our cattle in good condition.

3rd, wood at convenient distance, both small wood to readily kindle up, and logs to keep the fire through the night.

4th, we preferred seclusion, partly because in seclusion there was greater safety, for though we did not fear the Indians or border ruffians by day light, the chance of an attempt to steal our horses at night was just enough to make us feel a little more comfortable if our situation was a somewhat cozy one. When at the greatest distance from settlements, the danger was sufficient to induce us to shift camp after cooking our supper lest the fire should have advertised us too closely. Partly for this reason we preferred seclusion, and partly because we were frequently visited after nightfall by the sudden blast of a northerner, in which case an elevated or exposed position was far from comfortable either for us or our horses, which whatever the range we gave them during daylight were always staked within close pistol shot of our bed at nightfall.

5th, we liked to have game near at hand, and

6th, we made it a point to secure if possible as much beauty as possible in the view from our tent door.

This last brings us to the question: What is the beautiful? but it is a question which we will not here discuss. I only wish you to observe that the beauty which we enjoyed in this case depended on elements of topography of a very simple character. I assume that such beauty of scenery gives pleasure even to savages.

Now, if you think of it, you will see that all these conditions of a pleasant camp would also be the conditions of a pleasant family residence of a more permanent character, provided that the wants of the family were very simple or rude; provided, [that is,] it was not greatly dependent for its comfort on the labor of others; provided it was prepared to live mainly within itself, as the phrase is.

In fact we found that wherever the pioneers were settling in this country, they were selecting just such places and plainly because the less artificial wants of men were in such situations more conveniently provided for, provided for with less exertion, effort and anxiety of mind, than in any other. For example, in such a situation it would be easy to get water when wanted, easy to get wood when wanted, easy to find shelter from wind, easy to find shelter from sun, easy to make shelter from rain, easy to spy game at a distance, easy to enclose stock, easy to keep watch of stock when turned out, easy to follow stock when strayed, easy for stock when turned out to find good grazing, water and shelter, easy, if desired, to enclose land, to cultivate it, and to house the crops from it.

In one word the topography of such a situation is of a character which suggests to an observer an easy gratification of a great variety of the elementary human impulses and thus, leaving out of consideration entirely the impulse to associate or marry with that quality of natural objects, whatever it is, which we describe as the beautiful.

And this topography as I have shown is also the characteristic topography of the old parks; this is what a park was, this and nothing more when certain pieces of land were first enclosed and called parks. This gives us, therefore, the original, radical and constant definition of the topography which is wanted to be selected or constructed when a park is called for. I do not mean that this is all of a park, but that an idea of a park centers and grows upon this. If it is an insufficient definition, it is because the condition of ease is merely a negative condition. The absence of obstruction is the condition of ease of movement, and a park as a work of design should be more than this; it should be a ground which invites, encourages and facilitates movement, its topographical conditions such as make movement a pleasure; such as offer inducements in variety, on one side and the other, for easy movement, first by one promise of pleasure then by another, yet all of a simple character and such as appeal to the common and elementary impulses of all classes of mankind. But this quality of ease must underlie the whole. You must first secure this, and if this is not all, it is at least the framework of all. But is a park, you may ask, a mere study of topography, the work merely of an engineer? I answer that that depends on what limit the engineer chooses to put upon the field of his professional study. My own opinion is that the science of the engineer is never more worthily employed than when it is made to administer to man's want of beauty. When it is carried into works not merely of art but of fine art.

Now Herbert Spencer in an essay on gracefulness says:

> grace as applied to motion, describes motion that is effected with an economy of muscular power, grace as applied to animal forms describes forms capable of this economy. Grace as applied to postures, describes postures which may be maintained with this economy, and grace as applied to inanimate objects, describes such as exhibit certain analogies to these attitudes and forms.
>
> That this generalization, if not the whole truth, contains at least a large part of it, will I think become obvious on considering how habitually we couple the words easy and graceful.[2]

Whether the philosophy here is perfect and the analysis final and complete or not, we must admit that the association of ideas pointed out is inevitable; and you will see that by simply substituting the word grace for the word ease in the statement of the conclusions to which we have arrived in our study of the engineering question which we have hitherto had before us, we raise our aim at once into the region of aesthetic art. Let us call grace the idealization of ease, and then let us take the final step, and add a positive quality to the negative one of ease or grace, and we shall find ourselves prepared to form what I consider to be the true conception or ideal of a park, in distinction from any other ground, or any other place of recreation.

That is to say, we must study to secure a combination of elements which shall invite and stimulate the simplest, purest and most primeval action of the poetic element of human nature, and thus tend to remove those who are affected by it to the greatest possible distance from the highly elaborate, sophistical and artificial conditions of their ordinary civilized life.

Thus it must be that parks are beyond anything else recreative, recreative of that which is most apt to be lost or to become diseased and debilitated among the dwellers in towns.

With reference to construction, or the artificial formation of topography then, we may say that park-purposes means a purpose to make gracefully beautiful in combination with a purpose to make interesting and inviting, or hospitable [places by offering] a succession of simple, natural pleasures as a result of easy movements.

These, I mean, are *park*-purposes, primarily, in distinction from all other pleasure-ground purposes. So far as we are to do anything at the ground for instance, it is with these purposes we are to do it. If we cannot make it more graceful, more interesting, more inviting, more convenient, then we are to do nothing.

It does not follow that all parts of our enclosure should be of this simple easy flowing topography which I have indicated. Grace like any other quality which acts upon us through our sense of vision is enhanced by contrast, and if we can employ accessories which will have this effect and at the same time serve a direct purpose of any value, they will be proper and desirable within our enclosure, but they will not be the characteristic features of the park. It is chiefly important that they do not become of so much relative importance as to lose their character as accessories.

Rocks for instance may be such accessories, so may thick wood, so may shrubbery. So may buildings, monuments, etc., but these are not what make a park; they are not characteristic of it.

The word park as a common noun, as a descriptive word, should indicate such graceful topography, such open pastoral, inviting hospitable scenery as I have indicated.

When I speak of the treatment of wood with reference to park purposes, I mean first of all with reference to the production or improvement of such scenery, and secondly with reference to the production of improvement of such accessories.

There may be another class of park-purposes, of a quite different character, and to discriminate between the two, you must recollect that the word park is used as a proper as well as a common noun.

Phoenix Park, for instance is *the* park of Dublin and includes, a vice-regal palace, with orchards and kitchen gardens; barracks, a magazine, an arsenal; parks of artillery, and other features which are far from being graceful and equally far from presenting inducements for an indulgence in simple natural enjoyments. Yet all of which are a part of what is called the Park when the word is used as a proper noun, as much as that which, using the word again as a common noun, is the park itself, which consists of few elements other than turf and trees.

When we know that such things as barracks, arsenals and buildings intended solely for domestic or public business purposes, which are wholly incongruous with the purposes of a park, are referred to under the same general head with turf and trees, we are in no danger of confusing the common and the proper noun. But there may be accessories of a park, which contribute to its main purpose by predisposing the mind or removing impediments of the mind to the kind of recreation which it is adapted to stimulate, as by means of relief from thirst or hunger or excessive fatigue or shelter from rain, and these may be included under the term park-purposes, even with reference to topographical construction and artistic design, though in themselves they are the reverse of graceful or suggestive of easy movement.

And it is possible to add these and many other auxiliaries to the means of accomplishing our primary purposes not only without lessening, but in such a manner as to positively increase the special value of the latter. For the influence of grace of topography, like any other quality which influences our minds through the senses, is enhanced by contrast.

Elements designed to *increase* park effects, by contrast, must, however, be used with caution, lest instead of heightening the impression sought to be primarily produced by certain elements of topography we obscure or confuse them. To this end it is chiefly important that the contrasting circumstances should be unmistakably auxiliary, subordinate, and accessory in every respect to the general design. This principle and this caution in the application of the principle, applies to the use of woods or trees as well as to more purely constructional objects.

What then is the part; what are the duties, of trees?

Christopher North asks:[3]

But the more important qualities of trees in landscape are those of termination and obscuration of the view of an observer, though the two may be considered as one, for the termination of landscape by trees is effected by a high degree of obscuration.

You will recollect that I used the term hospitable as descriptive of the essential characteristic of park topography, and that while I hinted at a more recondite significance, in the possible appeal of a hospitable landscape to the simplest instincts of our race, I also described this quality of hospitality to consist [of] conditions which make the ground appear pleasant to wander over. Among such conditions, one will be the absence of anything which should cause severe exertion to the wanderer and another the presence of opportunities for agreeable rest at convenient intervals. Together these conditions imply general openness and simplicity with occasional shelter and shade, which latter will result both from trees and from graceful undulations of the surface.

Bearing in mind this deduced significance of the term hospitable as descriptive of the general character of a park topography, you will see that the more unlimited the degree of hospitality of landscape, the more unmeasured the welcome which the broad face of your park can be made to express, the better will your purpose be fulfilled, and that it follows that all absolute limits should be so screened from view by trees that the imagination will be likely to assume no limit, but only acknowledge obscurity in whatever direction the eye may rove. As, however, to comply with the conditions previously established, [that] the range of clear vision must be constantly limited in most directions, it is desirable that there should be an occasional opportunity of looking upon a view over turf and between trees so extended that even obscurity, that is to say uncertainty of extent, to the hospitable elements of the topography, shall be impossible.

I trust you recognize the paramount importance of these purposes of trees, because ignorance of them or forgetfulness of them or the subordination of them to other purposes of trees is a besetting sin of most planters.

In subordination to them, strictly, strenuously, always and everywhere within a park, in subordination to them, trees are to be regarded as individuals, and as component parts of groups, which groups are again to be regarded both individually, and in relation one to another as components of landscapes as seen from special points of view.

I hope that you will see that I am not studying a mere word all this time. I want you to see that when people ask for a park, it may be perfectly possible to please them very much with something which is not a park or which is a very poor and much adulterated kind of park and that it would nevertheless be dishonest, quackish, to do so. A park is a work of art, designed to produce certain effects upon the mind of men. There should be nothing in it, absolutely nothing—not a foot of surface nor a spear of grass—which does not represent study, design, a sagacious consideration and application of known laws of cause and effect with reference to that end.

NOTES

1. Olmsted wrote about his tours in *Walks and Talks of an American Farmer in England* (1852) and *A Journey Through Texas* (1857).

2. Herbert Spencer (1820–1903), English philosopher, political and social theorist, published "Gracefulness" in *The Leader* magazine in 1852 and then in his *Essays: Scientific, Political and Speculative* (1854).

3. Scotsman John Wilson (1785–1854) wrote under the pseudonym Christopher North, on several occasions about trees. Olmsted evidently quoted him at this point in his lecture but excluded North's words from his handwritten text.

THIRTEEN

Public Parks and the Enlargement of Towns

(1870)

This is probably Olmsted's most impassioned plea for the creation of public recreation grounds and his most impassioned defense of Central Park. He opens by describing the international extent of and reasons for depopulation of small towns and rural areas, the consequent migration of people into cities, and the social problems that has caused. To ameliorate crime, disease, shorter life expectancy, the stressful pace of living, and other urban ills, what is needed, he says, is cleaner air, more sunlight, and more open space. To provide these he suggests increased tree planting, what might be considered an early call for municipal zoning, that is, dividing the city into commercial and residential districts, and more intelligent planning of new developing areas.

But his emphasis is on parks, places for recreation with or without strenuous physical activity, thus his suggestion that on small sites scattered around the city, but preferably in subdivisions of a single large park, there be provision for "exertive" and "receptive" recreation, the former more athletic in nature, the latter more contemplative.

Olmsted understands "receptive" recreation to be of two types: "neighborly," the gathering of friends, families, and lovers—that is, individuals known to each other—in appropriate pastoral settings, and "gregarious" or group activities of strangers centered primarily around promenading along shaded paths with well-planned vistas.

Olmsted's discussion of "gregarious" activities goes to the heart of his social philosophy: the mingling of all classes and religions on equal terms, "each individual adding by his mere presence to the pleasure of all others," the objective being not only increased mutual understanding among those whose contact is normally minimal, but also moral and physical improvement of the underprivileged.

He ends with a lengthy, candid discussion of Central Park: the financial and political difficulties involved with its establishment and administration, the benefits New York residents have and will receive from it, and how it might serve as a model for other cities contemplating parks of their own.

Originally given as a speech to the American Social Science Association in Boston in 1870, this document with Olmsted's subsequent emendations was then published in the association's annual Journal of Social Science *(1871).*

The last "Overland Monthly" tells us that in California "only an inferior class of people can be induced to live out of towns. There is something in the country which repels men. In the city alone can they nourish the juices of life."[1]

This of newly built and but half-equipped cities, where the people are never quite free from dread of earthquakes, and of a country in which the productions of agriculture and horticulture are more varied, and the rewards of rural enterprise larger, than in any other under civilized government! With a hundred million acres of arable and grazing land, with thousands of outcropping gold veins, with the finest forests in the world, fully half the white people live in towns, a quarter of all in one town, and this quarter pays more than half the taxes of all. "Over the mountains the miners," says Mr. Bowles, "talk of going to San Francisco as to Paradise, and the rural members of the Legislature declare that 'San Francisco sucks the life out of the country.' "[2]

Nearer home the newspapers again tell us that twenty-five thousand men, to say nothing of women, are asking for work in Chicago; each of the great cities of the Mississippi region is reported to be increasing in population at a wonderful rate; gold and wheat are fast falling in their markets, but rents keep up, and it is complained that builders do not supply the demand for dwellings suited to the requirements of new-comers, who are chiefly men of small capital and young families, anxious to make a lodgment in the city on almost any conditions which will leave them a chance of earning a right to remain.

To this I can add, from personal observation, that if we stand, any day before noon, at the railway stations of these cities, we may notice women and girls arriving by the score, who, it will be apparent, have just run in to do a little shopping, intending to return by supper time to farms perhaps a hundred miles away. We shall observe trains advertised with special reference to the attendance of country people upon the evening entertainments of the town. Leaving the cars at some remote and lonely station, we may find a poster in its waiting-room, announcing matinee performances at a city theater. If we push across the prairie, and call on a farmer who has been settled and doing well upon his land for twenty years, an intelligent and forehanded man, we shall hardly fail to see that very little remains to him or his family of what we formerly, and not very long ago, regarded as the most essential characteristics of rural life.

Formerly it was a matter of pride with the better sort of our country people that they could raise on their own land, and manufacture in their own household, almost everything needed for domestic consumption. Now their tables are furnished with all kinds of city delicacies. The housewife complains of her servants. There is no difficulty in getting them from the intelligence offices in town, such as they are; but only the poorest, who cannot find employment in the city, will come to the country, and these, as soon as they have got a few dollars ahead, are crazy to get back to town. It is much the same with the men, the farmer will add; he has to go up in the morning and find someone to take "Wolf's" place. You will find, too, that one of his sons is in a lawyer's office, another at a commercial college, and his oldest daughter at an "institute," all in town. I know several girls who travel eighty miles a day to attend school in Chicago. If under these circumstances the occupation of the country school-master, shoe-maker, and doctor, the country store-keeper, dress-maker and lawyer, is not actually gone, it must be that the business they have to do is much less relatively to the population about them than it used to be; not less in amount only, but less in importance. An inferior class of men will meet the requirements.

And how are things going here in Massachusetts? A correspondent of the "Springfield Republican" gave the other day an account of a visit lately made to two or three old agricultural neighborhoods, such as fifty years ago were the glory of New England. When he last knew them, their society was spoken of with pride, and the influence of not a few of their citizens was felt throughout the State, and indeed far beyond it. But as he found them now, they might almost be sung by Goldsmith.[3] The meeting-house closed, the church dilapidated; the famous old taverns, stores, shops, mills, and offices dropping to pieces and vacant, or perhaps with a mere corner occupied by day laborers; but a third as many children as formerly to be seen in the school-houses, and of these less than half of American-born parents.

Walking through such a district last summer, my eyes were gladdened by a single house with exceptional signs of thrift in fresh paint, roofs, and fences, and newly planted door-yard trees; but happening as I passed to speak to the owner, in the second sentence of our conversation he told me that he had been slicking his place up in hopes that some city gentleman would take a fancy to it for a country seat. He was getting old, had worked hard, and felt as if the time had fully come when he was entitled to take some enjoyment of what remained to him of life by retiring to the town. Nearly all his old neighbors were gone; his children had left years ago. His town-bred granddaughters were playing croquet in the front yard.

You know how it is here in Boston. Let us go on to the Old World. We read in our youth that among no other people were rural tastes so strong, and rural habits so fixed, as with those of Old England, and there is surely no other country where the rural life of the more fortunate classes compares so attractively with their town life. Yet in the "Transactions of the British Social Science Association," we find one debater asserting that there are now very few more persons living in the rural districts of England and Wales than there were fifty years ago; another referring to "the still increasing growth of our overgrown towns and the stationary or rather retrograding numbers of our rural population"; while a third remarks that the social and educational advantages of the towns are drawing to them a large proportion of "the wealthy and independent," as well as all of the working classes not required for field labor.[4]

When I was last in England, the change that had occurred even in ten years could be perceived by a rapid traveler. Not only had the country gentleman and especially the country gentlewoman of Irving[5] departed wholly with all their following, but the very embers had been swept away of that manner of life upon which, so little while ago, everything in England seemed to be dependent. In all the country I found a smack of the suburbs—hampers and packages from metropolitan tradesmen, and purveyors arriving by every train, and a constant communication kept up with town by penny-post and telegraph.

In the early part of the century, the continued growth of London was talked of as something marvelous and fearful; but where ten houses were then required to accommodate new residents, there are now a hundred. The average rate at which population increases in the six principal towns is twice as great as in the country at large, including the hundreds of other flourishing towns. So also Glasgow has been growing six times faster than all Scotland; and Dublin has held its own, while Ireland as a whole has been losing ground.

Crossing to the Continent, we find Paris absorbing half of all the increase of France in population; Berlin growing twice as fast as all Prussia; Hamburg, Stettin, Stuttgart, Brussels, and a score or two of other towns, all building out into the country at a rate never before known, while many agricultural districts are actually losing population. In Russia special provision is made in the laws to regulate the gradual compensation of the nobles for their losses by the emancipation of the serfs, to prevent the depopulation of certain parts of the country, which was in danger of occurring from the eagerness of the peasantry to move into the large towns.

Going still further to the eastward, we may find a people to whom the movement has not thus far been communicated; but it is only where obscurity affords the best hope of safety from oppression, where men number their women with their horses, and where labor-saving inventions are as inventions of the enemy.

Of the fact of the general townward movement of the civilized world, and its comprehensiveness, there can be no doubt. There is a difference of opinion apparently as to its causes and as to the probability of its continuance, for we hear anticipations of a reaction expressed. I see no grounds for them. It appears to me to look much more as if what we had thus far witnessed was but the beginning. I do not propose to go to the root of the matter; it is sufficient for our purpose to point out that the strength of the movement at any point seems to correspond closely with the degree in which the habits of the people have been recently changed by the abolition of feudalism, slavery, and government by divine right; by the multiplication and cheapening of schools, newspapers, and books; and by the introduction of labor-saving arrangements, especially of that class which are only available at all where they can be used to the direct benefit of many, such as railroads and telegraphs.

Consider that the standard of education is still advancing. There is yet no halt in the onward march of liberty of thought; telegraph stations are multiplying, new railroads are building, and the working capacity of old ones is increasing. Consider what we have been doing in our own country. Our public lands have been divided in square plats, so as to discourage the closer agricultural settlement which long and narrow divisions favor. We have given away the pick of them under a plan well adapted to induce a scattering settlement for a time, but also calculated to encourage waste of resources. We have no longer the best to offer.

Again, we have said to the world, "Here are countless deposits of the precious metals, scattered about over many millions of acres of wild land. We will give them away as fast as they can be found. First come, first served. Disperse then, and look for them." In spite of this policy, we find that the rate of increase of our principal towns is even now greater than that of the country.

But the same cause has also had the effect of giving us, for a time, great command of ready money and easy credit, and we have thus been induced to spend an immense sum—say two thousand millions—in providing ourselves with the fixtures and machinery of our railroad system. This system, while encouraging the greater dispersion of our food-producers, has tended most of all to render them, as we have seen, independent of all the old neighborhood agencies of demand and supply, manufacture and exchange, and to educate them and their children in familiarity with and dependence on the conveniences and habits of towns-people.

We all recognize that the tastes and dispositions of women are more and more potent in shaping the course of civilized progress, and again we must acknowledge that women are even more susceptible to this townward drift than men. Ofttimes the husband and father gives up his country occupations, taking others less attractive to him in town, out of consideration for his wife and daughters. Not long since I conveyed to a very sensible and provident man what I thought to be an offer of great preferment. I was surprised that he hesitated to accept it, until the question was referred to his wife, a bright, tidy American-born woman, who promptly said: "If I were offered a deed of the best farm that I ever saw, on condition of going back to the country to live, I would not take it. I would rather face starvation in town." She had been brought up and lived the greater part of her life in one of the most convenient and agreeable farming countries in the United States. Few have lived long in the city without having experiences of a similar feeling. Is it astonishing? Compare advantages in respect simply to schools, libraries, music and the fine arts. People of the greatest wealth can hardly command as much of these in the country as the poorest work-girl is offered here in Boston at the mere cost of a walk for a short distance over a good, firm, clean pathway, lighted at night and made interesting to her by shop fronts and the variety of people passing.

It is true the poorer work-girls make little use of these special advantages, but this simply because they are not yet educated up to them. When, however, they come from the country to town, are they not moving in the way of this education? In all probability, as is indicated by the report (in the "New York Tribune") of a recent skillful examination of the condition and habits of the poor sewing women of that city, a frantic desire to escape from the dull lives which they have seen before them in the country, a craving for recreation, especially for more companionship in yielding to playful girlish impulses, innocent in themselves, drives more young women to the town than anything else.[6] Dr. Holmes may exaggerate the clumsiness and dreariness of New England village social parties; but go further back into the country among the outlying farms, and if you have ever had part in the working up of some of the rare occasions in which what stands for festivity is attempted, you will hardly think that the ardent desire of a young woman to escape to the town is wholly unreasonable.[7]

The civilized woman is above all things a tidy woman. She enjoys being surrounded by bright and gay things perhaps not less than the savage, but she shrinks from draggling, smirching, fouling things and "things out of keeping" more. By the keenness with which she avoids subjecting herself to annoyances of this class, indeed, we may judge the degree in which a woman has advanced in civilization. Think what a country road and roadside, and what the back yard of a farm-house, commonly is, in winter and spring-time; and what far-away farmers' gardens are in haying time, or most of them at any time. Think, again, how hard it is when you city people go into the country for a few weeks in summer, to keep your things in order, to get a thousand little things done which you regard as trifles when at home, how far you have to go, and with how much uncertainty, how much unaccustomed management you have to exercise. For the perfection and delicacy—the cleanness—with which any human want is provided for depends on the concentration of human ingenuity and skill upon that particular want. The greater the division of labor at any point, the greater the perfection with which all wants may be satisfied. Everywhere in the country the number and variety of workmen, not agricultural laborers, proportionately to the population, is lessening as the facility for reaching workmen in town is increasing. In one year we find fifty-four new divisions of trade added to the "London Directory."[8]

Think of all these things, and you will possibly find yourself growing a little impatient of the common cant which assumes that the strong tendency of women to town life, even though it involves great privations and dangers, is a purely senseless, giddy, vain, frivolous, and degrading one.

The consideration which most influences this tendency of women in families, however, seems to be the amount of time and labor, and wear and tear of nerves and mind, which is saved to them by the organization of labor in those forms, more especially, by which the menial service of households is simplified and reduced. Consider, for instance, what is done (that in the country is not done at all or is done by each household for itself, and, if efficiently, with a wearing, constant effort of superintendence) by the butcher, baker, fishmonger, grocer, by the provision venders of all sorts, by the ice-man, dust-man, scavenger, by the postman, carrier, expressmen, and messengers, all serving you at your house when required; by the sewers, gutters, pavements, crossings, sidewalks, public conveyances, and gas and water works.

But here again there is every reason to suppose that what we see is but a foretaste of what is yet to come. Take the difference of demand upon invention in respect to cheap conveyance for example. We began experimentally with street railways twenty years ago. At present, in New York, one pair of horses serves to convey one hundred people, on an average, every day at a rate of fare about one fiftieth of the old hackney-coach rates, and the total number of fares collected annually is equal to that of the population of the United States. And yet thousands walk a number of miles every day because they cannot be seated in the cars. It is impossible to fix a limit to the amount of travel which really ample, convenient, and still cheap means of transportation for short distances would develop. Certain improvements have caused the whole number of people seeking conveyances in London to be doubled in the last five years, and yet the supply keeps nowhere near the demand.

See how rapidly we are really gaining and what we have to expect. Two recent inventions give us the means of reducing by a third, under favorable circumstances, the cost of good McAdam roads. There have been sixteen patents issued from one office for other new forms of perfectly smooth and nearly noiseless street pavement, some of which, after two or three years' trial, promise so well as to render it certain that some improvement will soon come by which more than one of the present special annoyances of town life will be abated. An improvement in our sewer system seems near at hand also, which will add considerably to the comparative advantages of a residence in towns, and especially the more open town suburbs.

Experiments indicate that it is feasible to send heated air through a town in pipes like water, and that it may be drawn upon, and the heat which is taken measured and paid for according to quantity required. Thus may come a great saving of fuel and trouble in a very difficult department of domestic economy. No one will think of applying such a system to farm-houses.

Again, it is plain that we have scarcely begun to turn to account the advantages offered to towns-people in the electric telegraph; we really have not made a beginning with those offered in the pneumatic tube, though their substantial character has been demonstrated. By the use of these two instruments, a tradesman ten miles away on the other side of a town may be communicated with, and goods obtained from him by a housekeeper, as quickly and with as little personal inconvenience as now if he were in the next block. A single tube station for five hundred families, acoustic pipes for the transmission of orders to it from each house, with a carriers' service for local distribution of packages, is all that is needed for this purpose.

As to the economy which comes by systematizing and concentrating, by the application of a large apparatus, of processes which are otherwise conducted in a desultory way, wasteful of human strength, as by public laundries, bakeries, and kitchens, we are yet, in America, even in our larger cities, far behind many of the smaller towns of the Old World.

While in all these directions enterprise and the progress of invention are quite sure to add rapidly to the economy and convenience of town life, and thus increase its comparative attractions, in other directions every step tends to reduce the man-power required on the farms for the production of a given amount of the raw material of food. Such is the effect, for instance, of every improvement of apparatus or process in plowing, mowing, reaping, curing, thrashing, and marketing.

Another tendency arising from the improvement of agricultural apparatus, and which will be much accelerated when steam shall have been as successfully applied to tillage as it is already to harvesting and marketing operations, is that [of] the enlargement of fields and of farms. From this will follow the reduction in number and the greater separation and greater isolation of rural homesteads; for with our long-fronted farms, it will be centuries before we can hope to have tolerable roads on which rapid steam traveling from farm to farm will be practicable, though we may be close upon it wherever hard, firm, and always smooth roads can be afforded.

It should be observed that possession of the various advantages of the town to which we have referred, and, indeed, of all the advantages which are peculiar to large towns, while it very certainly cannot be acquired by people living in houses a quarter or a half mile apart, does not, on the other hand, by any means involve an unhealthy density of population. Probably the advantages of civilization can be found illustrated and demonstrated under no other circumstances so completely as in some suburban neighborhoods where each family abode stands fifty or a hundred feet or more apart from all others, and at some distance from the public road. And it must be remembered, also, that man's enjoyment of rural beauty has clearly increased rather than diminished with his advance in civilization. There is no reason, except in the loss of time, the inconvenience, discomfort, and expense of our present arrangements for short travel, why suburban advantages should not be almost indefinitely extended. Let us have a cheap and enjoyable method of conveyance, and a building law like that of old Rome,[9] and they surely will be.

As railroads are improved, all the important stations will become centers or sub-centers of towns, and all the minor stations [of] suburbs. For most ordinary every-day purposes, especially house-keepers' purposes, these will need no very large population before they can obtain urban advantages. I have seen a settlement, the resident population of which was under three hundred, in which there was a public laundry, bath-house, barber's shop, billiard-room, beer-garden, and bakery. Fresh rolls and fresh milk were supplied to families before breakfast time every morning; fair fruit and succulent vegetables were delivered at house doors not half an hour after picking; and newspapers and magazines were distributed by a carrier. I have seen a town of not more than twelve hundred inhabitants, the streets and the yards, alleys, and places of which were swept every day as regularly as the house floors, and all dust removed by a public dust-man.

The construction of good roads and walks, the laying of sewer, water, and gas pipes, and the supplying of sufficiently cheap, rapid, and comfortable conveyances to town centers, is all that is necessary to give any farming land in a healthy and attractive situation the value of town lots. And whoever has observed in the French agricultural colonies how much more readily and cheaply railroads, telegraph, gas, water, sewer, and nearly all other advantages of towns may be made available to the whole population than under our present helter-skelter methods of settlement, will not believe that even the occupation of a farm laborer must necessarily and finally exclude his family from a very large share of urban conveniences.

But this opens a subject of speculation, which I am not now free to pursue. It is hardly a matter of speculation, I am disposed to think, but almost of demonstration, that the larger a town becomes because simply of its advantages for commercial purposes, the greater will be the convenience available to those who live in and near it for cooperation, as well with reference to the accumulation of wealth in the higher forms—as in seats of learning, of science, and of art—as with reference to merely domestic economy and the emancipation of both men and women from petty, confining, and narrowing cares.

It also appears to be nearly certain that the recent rapid enlargement of towns and withdrawal of people from rural conditions of living is the result mainly of circumstances of a permanent character.

We have reason to believe, then, that towns which of late have been increasing rapidly on account of their commercial advantages, are likely to be still more attractive to population in the future; that there will in consequence soon be larger towns than any the world has yet known, and that the further progress of civilization is to depend mainly upon the influences by which men's minds and characters will be affected while living in large towns.

Now, knowing that the average length of the life of mankind in towns has been much less than in the country, and that the average amount of disease and misery and of vice and crime has been much greater in towns, this would be a very dark prospect for civilization, if it were not that modern science has beyond all question determined many of the causes of the special evils by which men are afflicted in towns, and placed means in our hands for guarding against them. It has shown, for example, that under ordinary circumstances, in the interior parts of large and closely built towns, a given quantity of air contains considerably less of the elements which we require to receive through the lungs than the air of the country or even of the outer and more open parts of a town, and that instead of them it carries in to the lungs highly corrupt and irritating matters, the action of which tends strongly to vitiate all our sources of vigor—how strongly may perhaps be indicated in the shortest way by the statement that even metallic plates and statues corrode and wear away under the atmospheric influences which prevail in the midst of large towns, more rapidly than in the country.

The irritation and waste of the physical powers which result from the same cause, doubtless indirectly affect and very seriously affect the mind and the moral strength; but there is a general impression that a class of men are bred in towns whose peculiarities are not perhaps adequately accounted for in this way. We may understand these better if we consider that whenever we walk through the denser part of a town, to merely avoid collision with those we meet and pass upon the sidewalks, we have constantly to watch, to foresee, and to guard against their movements. This involves a consideration of their intentions, a calculation of their strength and weakness, which is not so much for their benefit as our own. Our minds are thus brought into close dealings with other minds without any friendly flowing toward them, but rather a drawing from them. Much of the intercourse between men when engaged in the pursuits of commerce has the same tendency—a tendency to regard others in a hard if not always hardening way. Each detail of observation and of the process of thought required in this kind of intercourse or contact of minds is so slight and so common in the experience of towns-people that they are seldom conscious of it. It certainly involves some expenditure nevertheless. People from the country are ever conscious of the effect on their nerves and minds of the street contact—often complaining that they feel confused by it; and if we had no relief from it at all during our waking hours, we should all be conscious of suffering from it. It is upon our opportunities of relief from it, therefore, that not only our comfort in town life, but our ability to maintain a temperate, good-natured, and healthy state of mind, depends. This is one of many ways in which it happens that men who have been brought up, as the saying is, in the streets, who have been the most directly and completely affected by town influences, so generally show, along with a remarkable quickness of apprehension, a peculiarly hard sort of selfishness. Every day of their lives they have seen thousands of their fellow-men, have met them face to face, have brushed against them, and yet have had no experience of anything in common with them.

It has happened several times within the last century, when old artificial obstructions to the spreading out of a city have been removed, and especially where there has been a demolition of and rebuilding on a new ground plan of some part which had previously been noted for the frequency of certain crimes, the prevalence of certain diseases, and the shortness of life among its inhabitants, that a marked improvement in all these respects has immediately followed, and has been maintained not alone in the dark parts, but in the city as a whole.

But although it has been demonstrated by such experiments that we have it in our power to greatly lessen and counteract the two classes of evils we have had under consideration, it must be remembered that these means are made use of only with great difficulty—how great, one or two illustrations from experience will enable us perhaps better to understand.

When the business quarter of New York was burnt over, thirty years ago, there was a rare opportunity for laying out a district expressly with a view to facilitate commerce.[10] The old plan had been arrived at in a desultory way; and so far as it had been the result of design, it had been with reference more especially to the residence of a semi-rural population. This had long since passed away; its inconvenience for commercial purposes had been experienced for many years; no one supposed from the relation of the ground to the adjacent navigable waters that it would ever be required for other than commercial purposes. Yet the difficulties of equalizing benefits and damages among the various owners of the land prevented any considerable change of the old street lines. Every working day thousands of dollars are subtracted from the profits of business, by the disadvantages thus reestablished. The annual loss amounts to millions.

Men of barbarous habits laid out a part of London in a way which a thousand years later was found to be a cause of immeasurable waste of life, strength, and property. There had been much talk, but no effective action, looking toward improvement, when the great fire came, and left every building a heap of ashes. Immediately upon this, while the fire was still burning, a great man, Sir Christopher Wren, prepared a plan for avoiding the old evils.[11] This plan, a simple, excellent, and economical one, he took to the king, who at once approved it, took a strong interest in it, and used all his royal power to have it carried out. It was hailed with satisfaction by all wise and good men, and yet so difficult was it to overcome the difficulties entailed by the original rural laying out of the ground, that the attempt was finally abandoned, and the new city was built with immaterial modifications under the old barbarous plan; and so it remains with only slight improvement, and that purchased at enormous cost, to this day.

Remedy for a bad plan, once built upon, being thus impracticable, now that we understand the matter we are surely bound, wherever it is by any means in our power, to prevent mistakes in the construction of towns. Strange to say, however, here in the New World, where great towns by the hundred are springing into existence, no care at all is taken to avoid bad plans. The most brutal Pagans to whom we have sent our missionaries have never shown greater indifference to the sufferings of others than is exhibited in the plans of some of our most promising cities, for which men now living in them are responsible.

Not long since I was asked by the mayor of one of these to go before its common council and explain the advantages of certain suggested changes, including especially the widening of two roads leading out of town and as yet but partially opened and not at all built upon. After I had done so, two of the aldermen in succession came to me, and each privately said in effect: "It is quite plain that the proposition is a good one, and it ought to be adopted; the city would undoubtedly gain by it; but the people of the ward I represent have less interest in it than some others: they do not look far ahead, and they are jealous of those who would be more directly benefited than themselves; consequently I don't think that they would like it if I voted for it, and I shall not, but I hope it will be carried."

They were unwilling that even a stranger should have so poor an opinion of their own intelligence as to suppose that they did not see the advantage of the change proposed; but it was not even suggested to their minds that there might be something shameful in repudiating their obligations to serve, according to the best of their judgment, the general and permanent interests committed to them as legislators of the city.

It is evident that if we go on in this way, the progress of civilized mankind in health, virtue, and happiness will be seriously endangered.

It is practically certain that the Boston of to-day is the mere nucleus of the Boston that is to be. It is practically certain that it is to extend over many miles of country now thoroughly rural in character, in parts of which farmers are now laying out roads with a view to shortening the teaming distance between their wood lots and a railway station, being governed in their courses by old property lines, which were first run simply with reference to the equitable division of heritages, and in other parts of which, perhaps, some wild speculators are having streets staked off from plans which they have formed with a rule and pencil in a broker's office, with a view chiefly to the impressions they would make when seen by other speculators on a lithographed map. And by this manner of planning, unless views of duty or of interest prevail that are not yet common, if Boston continues to grow at its present rate even for but a few generations longer, and then simply holds its own until it shall be as old as the Boston in Lincolnshire now is, more men, women, and children are to be seriously affected in health and morals than are now living on this Continent.

Is this a small matter—a mere matter of taste; a sentimental speculation?

It must be within the observation of most of us that where, in the city, wheel-ways originally twenty feet wide were with great difficulty and cost enlarged to thirty, the present width is already less nearly adequate to the present business than the former was to the former business; obstructions are more frequent, movements are slower and oftener arrested, and the liability to collision is greater. The same is true of sidewalks. Trees thus have been cut down, porches, bow-windows, and other encroachments removed but every year the walk is less sufficient for the comfortable passing of those who wish to use it.

It is certain that as the distance from the interior to the circumference of towns shall increase with the enlargement of their population, the less sufficient relatively to the service to be performed will be any given space between buildings.

In like manner every evil to which men are specially liable when living in towns, is likely to be aggravated in the future, unless means are devised and adapted in advance to prevent it.

Let us proceed, then, to the question of means, and with a seriousness in some degree befitting a question, upon our dealing with which we know the misery or happiness of many millions of our fellow-beings will depend.

We will for the present set before our minds the two sources of wear and corruption which we have seen to be remediable and therefore preventable. We may admit that commerce requires that in some parts of a town there shall be an arrangement of buildings, and a character of streets and of traffic in them which will establish conditions of corruption and of irritation, physical and mental. But commerce does not require the same conditions to be maintained in all parts of a town.

Air is disinfected by sunlight and foliage. Foliage also acts mechanically to purify the air by screening it. Opportunity and inducement to escape at frequent intervals from the confined and vitiated air of the commercial quarter, and to supply the lungs with air screened and purified by trees, and recently acted upon by sunlight, together with the opportunity and inducement to escape from conditions requiring vigilance, wariness, and activity toward other men—if these could be supplied economically, our problem would be solved.

In the old days of walled towns all tradesmen lived under the roof of their shops, and their children and apprentices and servants sat together with them in the evening about the kitchen fire. But now that the dwelling is built by itself and there is greater room, the inmates have a parlor to spend their evenings in; they spread carpets on the floor to gain in quiet, and hang drapery in their windows and papers on their walls to gain in seclusion and beauty. Now that our towns are built without walls, and we can have all the room that we like, is there any good reason why we should not make some similar difference between parts which are likely to be dwelt in, and those which will be required exclusively for commerce?

Would trees, for seclusion and shade and beauty, be out of place, for instance, by the side of certain of our streets? It will, perhaps, appear to you that it is hardly necessary to ask such a question, as throughout the United States trees are commonly planted at the sides of streets. Unfortunately, they are seldom so planted as to have fairly settled the question of the desirableness of systematically maintaining trees under these circumstances. In the first place, the streets are planned, wherever they are, essentially alike. Trees are planted in the space assigned for sidewalks, where at first, while they are saplings, and the vicinity is rural or suburban, they are not much in the way, but where, as they grow larger, and the vicinity becomes urban, they take up more and more space, while space is more and more required for passage. That is not all. Thousands and tens of thousands are planted every year in a manner and under conditions as nearly certain as possible either to kill them outright, or to so lessen their vitality as to prevent their natural and beautiful development, and to cause premature decrepitude. Often, too, as their lower limbs are found inconvenient, no space having been provided for trees in laying out the street, they are deformed by butcherly amputations. If by rare good fortune they are suffered to become beautiful, they still stand subject to be condemned to death at any time, as obstructions in the highway.*

What I would ask is, whether we might not with economy make special provision in some of our streets—in a twentieth or a fiftieth part, if you please, of all—for trees to remain as a permanent furniture of the city? I mean, to make a place for them in which they would have room to grow naturally and gracefully. Even if the distance between the houses should have to be made half as much again as it is required to be in our commercial streets, could not the space be afforded? Out of town space is not costly when measures to secure it are taken early. The assessments for benefit where such streets were provided for, would, in nearly all cases, defray the cost of the land required. The strips of ground reserved for the trees, six, twelve, twenty feet wide, would cost nothing for paving or flagging.

The change both of scene and of air which would be

*On the border of the first street laid out in the oldest town laid out in New England, there yet stands what has long been known as "the Town Tree," its trunk having served for generations as a publication post for official notices. "The selectmen," having last year removed the lower branches of all the younger roadside trees of the town, and thereby its chief beauty, have this year deliberately resolved that they would have this tree cut down, for no other reason, so far as appears in their official record, than that if two persons came carelessly together on the roadway side of it, one of them might chance to put his foot in the adjoining shallow street-gutter. It might cost ten dollars to deepen and bridge this gutter substantially. The call to arms for the Old French War, for the War of the Revolution, the war for the freedom of the seas, the Mexican War, and the War of the Rebellion, was first made in this town under the shade of this tree, which is an American elm, and, notwithstanding its great age, is perfectly healthy and almost as beautiful as it is venerable. [In this addendum added by Olmsted for publication, he was likely referring to the famous elm tree on Leyden Street in Plymouth, Massachusetts—R.T.]

obtained by people engaged for the most part in the necessarily confined interior commercial parts of the town, on passing into a street of this character after the trees had become stately and graceful, would be worth a good deal. If such streets were made still broader in some parts, with spacious malls, the advantage would be increased. If each of them were given the proper capacity, and laid out with laterals and connections in suitable directions to serve as a convenient trunk-line of communication between two large districts of the town or the business center and the suburbs, a very great number of people might thus be placed every day under influences counteracting those with which we desire to contend.

These, however, would be merely very simple improvements upon arrangements which are in common use in every considerable town. Their advantages would be incidental to the general uses of streets as they are. But people are willing very often to seek recreation as well as take it by the way. Provisions may indeed be made expressly for recreation, with certainty that if convenient, they will be used.

The various kinds of recreation may be divided primarily under two heads. Under one will be included all of which the predominating influence is to stimulate exertion of any part or parts needing it; under the other, all which cause us to receive pleasure or benefit without conscious exertion. Games chiefly of mental skill, as chess, or athletic sports, as base-ball, are examples of means of recreation of the first division, which may be termed that of *exertive* recreation; music and the fine arts generally, of the second or *receptive* division.

Considering the first by itself, it will be found not a very simple matter to determine for what forms of exertive recreations opportunities can be provided in a large town, consistently with good order, safety, and economy of management. Mr. Anthony Trollope[12] might recommend fox-hunting; hurdle-racing has been seriously urged by gentlemen who have given special attention to the advantages of that form of exercise. In New York, on the other hand, after several years' deliberation, and some experiments in a small way, it has been decided that the city cannot expediently undertake to provide grounds even for base-ball, cricket, and foot-ball clubs, to the great disappointment of a very large and influential element of the population.[13]

I do not propose now to discuss the various details of this question, but to leave out of consideration all that class of pastimes which, except in the open country, cannot easily be pursued without danger to persons not taking part in them, and to adopt the conclusion that only school-boys should be provided at public expense with every-day grounds for ball-playing, and this as a part of the educational rather than the recreative system of the town. I will only remark that you will find no purposes of athletic recreation which cannot be accommodated either by such trunk roads as I have suggested we should here and there introduce, or by a sufficient number of comparatively small spaces of open ground, and that, although there are certain advantages more particularly to be gained by pursuing the forms of exertive recreation named on grounds of large rather than small area, it would be better on the whole to have a number of small grounds than to establish any very large ground with special reference to them.

Let us now proceed to the consideration of receptive recreations. As we shall consider such forms of recreation as are pursued socially or by a number of persons together, it will be convenient to again divide our subjects into sub-heads, according to the degree in which the average enjoyment of them is greatest when a large congregation of persons is assembled, or when the number coming together is small, and the circumstances favorable to the exercise of personal friendliness. Our pleasure in recreations of the first of these classes appears to me to be dependent upon the existence of an instinct in us of which I think not enough account is commonly made, and I shall therefore term it the *gregarious* class of social receptive recreations. The other will be sufficiently distinguished from it by the term *neighborly*.

Purely gregarious recreation seems to be generally looked upon in New England society as childish and savage, because, I suppose, there is so little of what we call intellectual gratification in it. We are inclined to engage in it indirectly, furtively, and with complication. Yet there are certain forms of recreation, a large share of the attraction of which must, I think, lie in the gratification of the gregarious inclination, and which, with those who can afford to indulge in them, are so popular as to establish their importance of the requirement.

If I ask myself where I have experienced the most complete gratification of this instinct in public and out of doors, among trees, I find that it has been in the promenade of the Champs Elysées. As closely following it I should name other promenades of Europe, and our own upon the New York parks. I have studiously watched the latter for several years. I have several times seen fifty thousand people participating in them; and the more I have seen of them, the more highly have I been led to estimate their value as means of counteracting the evils of town life.

Consider that the New York Park and the Brooklyn Park[14] are the only places in those associated cities where, in this eighteen hundred and seventieth year after Christ, you will find a body of Christians coming together, and with an evident glee in the prospect of coming together, all classes largely represented, with a common purpose, not at all intellectual, competitive with none, disposing to jealousy and spiritual or intellectual pride toward none, each individual adding by his mere presence to the pleasure of all others, all helping to the greater happiness of each. You may thus often see vast numbers of persons brought closely together, poor and rich, young and old, Jew and Gentile. I have seen a hundred thousand thus congregated, and I assure you that though there have been not a few that seemed a little dazed, as if they did not quite understand it, and were, perhaps, a little ashamed of it, I have looked studiously but vainly among them for a single face completely unsympathetic with the prevailing expression of good nature and light-heartedness.

Is it doubtful that it does men good to come together in this way in pure air and under the light of heaven, or that it must have an influence directly counteractive to that of the ordinary hard, hustling working hours of town life?

You will agree with me, I am sure, that it is not, and that opportunity, convenient, attractive opportunity, for such congregation, is a very good thing to provide for, in planning the extension of a town.

I referred especially to the Champs Elysées, because the promenade there is a very old custom, not a fashion of the day, and because I must admit that this most striking example is one in which no large area of ground—nothing like a park—has been appropriated for the purpose. I must acknowledge, also, that the alamedas of Spain and Portugal supply another and very interesting instance of the same fact. You will observe, however, that small local grounds, such as we have said might be the best for most exertive recreations, are not at all adapted to receptive recreations of the type described.

One thing more under this head. I have but little personal familiarity with Boston customs; but I have lived or sojourned in several other towns of New England, as well as of other parts of the country. I have never been long in any one locality, south or north, east or west, without observing a *custom* of gregarious

out-of-door recreation in some miserably imperfect form, usually covered by a wretched pretext of a wholly different purpose, as perhaps, for instance, visiting a grave-yard. I am sure
that it would be much better, less expensive, less harmful in
all ways, more health-giving to body, mind, and soul, if it were
admitted to be a distinct requirement of all human beings, and
appropriately provided for.

I have next to see what opportunities are wanted to induce
people to engage in what I have termed neighborly receptive
recreations, under conditions which shall be highly counteractive to the prevailing bias to degeneration and demoralization
in large towns. To make clearer what I mean, I need an illustration which I find in a familiar domestic gathering, where the
prattle of the children mingles with the easy conversation of
the more sedate, the bodily requirements satisfied with good
cheer, fresh air, agreeable light, moderate temperature, snug
shelter, and furniture and decorations adapted to please the
eye, without calling for profound admiration on the one hand,
or tending to fatigue or disgust on the other. The circumstances
are all favorable to a pleasurable wakefulness of the mind without stimulating exertion; and the close relation of family life,
the association of children, of mothers, of lovers, or those who
may be lovers, stimulate and keep alive the more tender sympathies, and give play to faculties such as may be dormant in
business or on the promenade; while at the same time the cares
of providing in detail for all the wants of the family, guidance,
instruction, and reproof, and the dutiful reception of guidance,
instruction, and reproof, are, as matters of conscious exertion,
as far as possible laid aside.

There is an instinctive inclination to this social, neighborly,
unexertive form of recreation among all of us. In one way or
another it is sure to be constantly operating upon those millions on millions of men and women who are to pass their lives

within a few miles of where we now stand. To what extent it shall operate so as to develop health and virtue, will, on many occasions, be simply a question of opportunity and inducement. And this question is one for the determination of which for a thousand years we here to-day are largely responsible.

Think what the ordinary state of things to many is at this beginning of the town. The public is reading just now a little book in which some of your streets of which you are not proud are described. Go into one of those red cross streets[15] any fine evening next summer, and ask how it is with their residents? Oftentimes you will see half a dozen sitting together on the doorsteps, or, all in a row, on the curb-stones, with their feet in the gutter, driven out of doors by the closeness within; mothers among them anxiously regarding their children who are dodging about at their play, among the noisy wheels on the pavement.

Again, consider how often you see young men in knots of perhaps half a dozen in lounging attitudes rudely obstructing the sidewalks, chiefly led in their little conversation by the suggestions given to their minds by what or whom they may see passing in the street, men, women, or children, whom they do not know, and for whom they have no respect or sympathy. There is nothing among them or about them which is adapted to bring into play a spark of admiration, of delicacy, manliness, or tenderness. You see them presently descend in search of physical comfort to a brilliantly lighted basement, where they find others of their sort, see, hear, smell, drink, and eat all manner of vile things.

Whether on the curb-stones or in the dram-shops, these young men are all under the influence of the same impulse which some satisfy about the tea-table with neighbors and wives and mothers and children, and all things clean and wholesome, softening and refining.

If the great city to arise here is to be laid out little by little, and chiefly to suit the views of land-owners, acting only individually, and thinking only of how what they do is to affect the value in the next week or the next year of the few lots that each may hold at the time, the opportunities of so obeying this inclination as at the same time to give the lungs a bath of pure sunny air, to give the mind a suggestion of rest from the devouring eagerness and intellectual strife of town life, will always be few to any, to many will amount to nothing.

But is it possible to make public provision for recreation of this class, essentially domestic and secluded as it is?

It is a question which can, of course, be conclusively answered only from experience. And from experience in some slight degree I shall answer it. There is one large American town, in which it may happen that a man of any class shall say to his wife, when he is going out in the morning: "My dear, when the children come home from school, put some bread and butter and salad in a basket, and go to the spring under the chestnut-tree where we found the Johnsons last week. I will join you there as soon as I can get away from the office. We will walk to the dairy-man's cottage and get some tea, and some fresh milk for the children, and take our supper by the brook-side"; and this shall be no joke, but the most refreshing earnest.

There will be room enough in the Brooklyn Park, when it is finished, for several thousand little family and neighborly parties to bivouac at frequent intervals through the summer, without discommoding one another, or interfering with any other purpose, to say nothing of those who can be drawn out to make a day of it, as many thousand were last year. And although the arrangements for the purpose were yet very incomplete, and but little ground was at all prepared for such use, besides these small parties, consisting of one or two families, there came also, in companies of from thirty to a hundred and fifty, somewhere near twenty thousand children with their parents, Sunday-school teachers, or other guides and friends, who spent the best part of a day under the trees and on the turf, in recreations of which the predominating element was of this neighborly receptive class. Often they would bring a fiddle, flute, and harp, or other music. Tables, seats, shade, turf, swings, cool spring-water, and a pleasing rural prospect, stretching off half a mile or more each way, unbroken by a carriage road or the slightest evidence of the vicinity of the town, were supplied them without charge, and bread and milk and ice-cream at moderate fixed charges. In all my life I have never seen such joyous collections of people. I have, in fact, more than once observed tears of gratitude in the eyes of poor women, as they watched their children thus enjoying themselves.

The whole cost of such neighborly festivals, even when they include excursions by rail from the distant parts of the town, does not exceed for each person, on an average, a quarter of a dollar; and when the arrangements are complete, I see no reason why thousands should not come every day where hundreds come now to use them; and if so, who can measure the value, generation after generation, of such provisions for recreation to the overwrought, much-confined people of the great town that is to be?

For this purpose neither of the forms of ground we have heretofore considered are at all suitable. We want a ground to which people may easily go after their day's work is done, and where they may stroll for an hour, seeing, hearing, and feeling nothing of the bustle and jar of the streets, where they shall, in effect, find the city put far away from them. We want the greatest possible contrast with the streets and the shops and the rooms of the town which will be consistent with convenience and the preservation of good order and neatness. We want, especially, the greatest possible contrast with the restraining and confining conditions of the town, those conditions which compel us to walk circumspectly, watchfully, jealously, which compel us to look closely upon others without sympathy. Practically, what we most want is a simply, broad, open space of clean greensward, with sufficient play of surface and a sufficient number of trees about it to supply a variety of light and shade. This we want as a central feature. We want depth of wood enough about it not only for comfort in hot weather, but to completely shut out the city from our landscapes. These are the distinguishing elements of what is properly called a park.

There is no provision for recreation so valuable as this would be; there is none which will be so important to place judiciously in the plan of the city merely as a space, and as an interruption of direct communication between its different parts. There is nothing, therefore, for which we should be more anxious to find and early secure and hold in reserve a suitable site.

A Promenade may, with great advantage, be carried along the outer part of the surrounding groves of a park; and it will do no harm if here and there a broad opening among the trees discloses its open landscapes to those upon the promenade. But recollect that the object of the latter for the time being should be to see *congregated human life* under glorious and necessarily artificial conditions, and the natural landscape is not essential to them; though there is no more beautiful picture, and none can be more pleasing incidentally to the gregarious purpose, than that of beautiful meadows, over which clusters of level-armed sheltering trees cast broad shadows, and upon which are scattered dainty cows and flocks of black-faced sheep, while men, women, and children are seen sitting here and there forming groups in the shade, or moving in and out among the woody points and bays.

It may be inferred from what I have said, that very rugged ground, abrupt eminences, and what is technically called picturesque in distinction from merely beautiful or simply pleasing scenery, is not the most desirable for a town park. Decidedly not in my opinion. The park should, as far as possible, complement the town. Openness is the one thing you cannot get in buildings. Picturesqueness you can get. Let your buildings be as picturesque as your artists can make them. This is the beauty of a town. Consequently, the beauty of the park should be the other. It should be the beauty of the fields, the meadow, the prairie, of the green pastures, and the still waters. What we want to gain is tranquility and rest to the mind. Mountains suggest effort. But besides this objection there are others of what I may indicate as the house-keeping class. It is impossible to give the public range over a large extent of ground of a highly picturesque character, unless under very exceptional circumstances, and sufficiently guard against the occurrence of opportunities and temptations to shabbiness, disorder, indecorum, and indecency, that will be subversive of every good purpose the park should be designed to fulfill.

Nor can I think that in *the park proper*, what is called gardenesque[16] beauty is to be courted; still less that highly artificial and exotic form of it, which, under the name of subtropical planting, the French have lately introduced, and in suitable positions with interesting and charming results, but in following which indiscreetly, the English are sacrificing the peculiar beauty of their simple and useful parks of the old time. Both these may have places, and very important places, but they do not belong within a park, unless as side scenes and incidents. Twenty years ago Hyde Park had a most pleasing, open, free, and inviting expression, though certainly it was too rude, too much wanting in art; but now art is vexed with long harsh lines of repellent iron-work, and here and there behind it bouquets

of hot house plants, between which the public pass like hospital convalescents, who have been turned into the yard to walk
about while their beds are making. We should undertake nothing in a park which involves the treating of the public as prisoners or wild beasts. A great object of all that is done in a park,
of *all* the art of a park, is to influence the mind of men through
their imagination, and the influence of iron hurdles can never
be good.

We have, perhaps, sufficiently defined the ideal of a park
for a large town. It will seldom happen that this ideal can be
realized fully. The next thing is to select the situation in which
it can be most nearly approached without great cost; and by
cost I do not mean simply cost of land or of construction, but
cost of inconvenience and cost of keeping in order, which is a
very much more serious matter, and should have a great deal
more study.

A park fairly well managed near a large town, will surely
become a new center of that town. With the determination
of location, size, and boundaries should therefore be associated the duty of arranging new trunk routes of communication between it and the distant parts of the town existing and
forecasted.

These may be either narrow informal elongations of the
park, varying say from two to five hundred feet in width, and
radiating irregularly from it, or if, unfortunately, the town is
already laid out in the unhappy way that New York and Brooklyn, San Francisco and Chicago, are, and, I am glad to say, Boston is not, on a plan made long years ago by a man who never
saw a spring-carriage, and who had a conscientious dread of the
Graces,[17] then we must probably adopt formal Park-ways. They
should be so planned and constructed as never to be noisy and
seldom crowded, and so also that the straightforward movement of pleasure-carriages need never be obstructed, unless at

absolutely necessary crossings, by slow-going heavy vehicles used for commercial purposes. If possible, also, they should be branched or reticulated with other ways of a similar class, so that no part of the town should finally be many minutes' walk from some one of them; and they should be made interesting by a process of planting and decoration, so that in necessarily passing through them, whether in going to or from the park, or to and from business, some substantial recreative advantage may be incidentally gained. It is a common error to regard a park as something to be produced complete in itself, as a picture to be painted on canvas. It should rather be planned as one to be done in fresco, with constant consideration of exterior objects, some of them quite at a distance and even existing as yet only in the imagination of the painter.

I have thus barely indicated a few of the points from which we may perceive our duty to apply the means in our hands to ends far distant, with reference to this problem of public recreations. Large operations of construction may not soon be desirable, but I hope you will agree with me that there is little room for question, that reserves of ground for the purposes I have referred to should be fixed upon as soon as possible, before the difficulty of arranging them, which arises from private building, shall be greatly more formidable than now.

To these reserves—though not a dollar should be spent in construction during the present generation—the plans of private construction would necessarily, from the moment they were established, be conformed.

I by no means wish to suggest that nothing should be done for the present generation; but only, that whatever happens to the present generation, it should not be allowed to go on heaping up difficulties and expenses for its successors, for want of a little comprehensive and business-like foresight and study. In all probability it will be found that much can be done even for the present generation without greatly if at all increasing taxation, as has been found in New York.

But the question now perhaps comes up: How can a community best take this work in hand?

It is a work in which private and local and special interests will be found so antagonistic one to another, in which heated prejudices are so liable to be unconsciously established, and in which those who would be disappointed in their personal greed by whatever good scheme may be studied out, are so likely to combine and concentrate force to kill it (manufacture public opinion, as the phrase is), that the ordinary organizations for municipal business are unsuitable agencies for the purpose. It would, perhaps, be a bold thing to say that the public in its own interest, and in the interest of all of whom the present public are the trustees, should see to it that the problem is as soon as possible put clean out of its own hands, in order that it may be taken up efficiently by a small body of select men. But I will venture to say that until this in effect is done, the danger that public opinion may be led, by the application of industry, ingenuity, and business ability on the part of men whose real objects are perhaps unconsciously very close to their own pockets, to overrule the results of more comprehensive and impartial study, is much greater than in most questions of public interest.

You will not understand me as opposing or undervaluing the advantages of public discussion. What I would urge is, that park questions, and even the most elementary park questions, questions of site and outlines and approaches, are not questions to which the rule applies, that every man should look after his own interests, judge for himself what will favor his own interests, and exert his influence so as to favor them; but questions rather of that class, which in his private affairs every man of common sense is anxious, as soon as possible, to put into the hands of somebody who is able to take hold of them comprehensively as a matter of direct, grave, business responsibility.

It is upon this last point far more than upon any other that the experience of New York is instructive to other communities. I propose, therefore, to occupy your time a little while longer by a narration of those parts of this experience which bear most directly upon this point, and which will also supply certain other information which has been desired of me.

The New York legislature of 1851 passed a bill providing for a park on the east side of the island. Afterwards, the same legislature, precipitately and quite as an after-thought, passed the act under which the city took title to the site of the greater part of the present Central Park.

This final action is said to have been the result of a counter movement, started after the passage of the first bill merely to gratify a private grudge of one of the city aldermen.[18]

When in the formation of the counter project, the question was reached, what land shall be named in the second bill, the originator turned to a map and asked: *"Now where shall I go?"* His comrade, looking over his shoulder, without a moment's reflection, put his finger down and said, *"Go* there"; the point indicated appearing to be about the middle of the island, and therefore, as it occurred to him, one which would least excite local prejudices.

The primary selection of the site was thus made in an off-hand way, by a man who had no special responsibility in the premises, and whose previous studies had not at all led him to be well informed or interested in the purposes of a park.

It would have been difficult to find another body of land of six hundred acres upon the island (unless by taking a long narrow strip upon the precipitous side of a ridge), which possessed less of what we have seen to be the most desirable characteristics of a park, or upon which more time, labor, and expense would be required to establish them.

But besides the topographical objections, when the work of providing suitable facilities for the recreation of the people upon this ground came to be practically and definitely considered, defects of outline were discerned, the incomplete remedy for which has since cost the city more than a million of dollars. The amount which intelligent study would have saved in this way if applied at the outset, might have provided for an amplification of some one of the approaches to the Park, such as, if it were now possible to be gained at a cost of two or three million dollars, I am confident would, if fairly set forth, be ordered by an almost unanimous vote of the tax-payers of the city. Public discussion at the time utterly failed to set this blundering right. Nor was public opinion then clearly dissatisfied with what was done or with those who did it.

During the following six years there was much public and private discussion of park questions; but the progress of public opinion, judged simply by the standard which it has since formed for itself, seems to have been chiefly backward.

This may be, to a considerable degree, accounted for by the fact that many men of wealth and influence—who, through ignorance and lack of mature reflection on this subject, were unable to anticipate any personal advantage from the construction of a park—feared that it would only add to their taxes, and thus were led to form a habit of crying down any hopeful anticipations.

The argument that certain towns of the old country did obtain some advantage from their parks, could not be refuted, but it was easy to say, and it was said, that "our circumstances are very different: surrounded by broad waters on all sides, open to the sea breezes, we need no artificial breathing-places; even if we did, nothing like the parks of the old cities under aristocratic government would be at all practicable here."

This assertion made such an impression as to lead many to believe that little more had better be done than to give the name of park to the ground which it was now too late to avoid taking. A leading citizen suggested that nothing more was necessary than to plow up a strip just within the boundary of the ground and plant it with young trees, and chiefly with cuttings of the poplar, which afterwards, as they came to good size, could be transplanted to the interior, and thus the Park would be furnished economically and quite well enough for the purposes it would be required to serve.

Another of distinguished professional reputation seriously urged through the public press, that the ground should be rented as a sheep-walk. In going to and from their folds the flocks would be sure to form trails which would serve the public perfectly well for foot-paths; nature would in time supply whatever else was essential to form a quite picturesque and perfectly suitable strolling ground for such as would wish to resort to it.

It was frequently alleged, and with truth, that the use made of the existing public grounds was such as to develop riotous and licentious habits. A large park, it was argued, would inevitably present larger opportunities, and would be likely to exhibit an aggravated form of the same tendencies, consequently anything like refinement of treatment would be entirely wasted.

A few passages from a leading article of the "Herald" newspaper, in the seventh year of the enterprise, will indicate what estimate its astute editor had then formed of the prevailing convictions of the public on the subject:

It is all folly to expect in this country to have parks like those in old aristocratic countries. When we open a public park Sam will air himself in it. He will take his friends whether from church, street, or elsewhere. He will knock down any better dressed man who remonstrates with him. He will talk and sing, and fill his share of the bench, and flirt with the nursery-maids in his own coarse way. Now we ask what chance have William B. Astor and Edward Everett against this fellow-citizen of theirs? Can they and he enjoy the same place? Is it not obvious that he will turn them out, and that the great Central Park will be nothing but a great beer-garden for the lowest denizens of the city, of which we shall yet pray litanies to be delivered?[19]

In the same article it was argued that the effect of the construction of the Park would be unfavorable to the value of property in its neighborhood, except as, to a limited extent, it might be taken up by Irish and German liquor dealers as sites for dram-shops and lager-beer gardens.

There were many eminent citizens, who to my personal knowledge, in the sixth, seventh, and eighth year after the passage of the act, entertained similar views to those I have quoted.

I have been asked if I supposed that "gentlemen" would ever resort to the Park, or would allow their wives and daughters to visit it? I heard a renowned lawyer argue that it was preposterous to suppose that a police force would do anything toward preserving order and decency in any broad piece of ground open to the general public of New York. And after the work began, I often heard the conviction expressed that if what was called the reckless, extravagant, inconsiderate policy of those who had the making of the Park in charge, could not be arrested, the weight of taxation and the general disgust which would be aroused among the wealthy classes would drive them from the city, and thus prove a serious injury to its prosperity.

"Why," said one, a man whom you all know by reputation, and many personally, "I should not ask for anything finer in my private grounds for the use of my own family." To whom it was replied that possibly grounds might not unwisely be prepared even more carefully when designed for the use of two hundred thousand families and their guests, than when designed for the use of one.

The constantly growing conviction that it was a rash and ill-considered undertaking, and the apprehension that a great deal would be spent upon it for no good purpose, doubtless had something to do with the choice of men, who in the sixth year were appointed by the Governor of the State, commissioners to manage the work and the very extraordinary powers given them. At all events, it so happened that a majority of them were much better known from their places in the directory of banks, railroads, mining, and manufacturing enterprises, than from their previous services in politics; and their freedom to follow their own judgment and will, in respect to all the interior matters of the Park, was larger than had for a long time been given to any body of men charged with a public duty of similar importance.[20]

I suppose that few of them knew or cared more about the subject of their duties at the time of their appointment, than most other active business men. They probably embodied very fairly the average opinion of the public, as to the way in which it was desirable that the work should be managed. If, then, it is asked, how did they come to adopt and resolutely pursue a course so very different from that which the public opinion seemed to expect of them, I think that the answer must be found in the fact that they had not wanted or asked the appointment; that it was made absolutely free from any condition or obligation to serve a party, a faction, or a person; that owing to the extraordinary powers given them, their sense of responsibility in the matter was of an uncommonly simple and direct character, and led them with the trained skill of business men to go straight to the question:

"Here is a piece of property put into our hands. By what policy can we turn it to the best account for our stockholders?"

It has happened that instead of being turned out about the time they had got to know something about their special business, these commissioners have been allowed to remain in office to this time—a period of twelve years.

As to their method of work, it was as like as possible to that of a board of directors of a commercial corporation. They quite set at defiance the ordinary ideas of propriety applied to public servants, by holding their sessions with closed doors, their clerk being directed merely to supply the newspapers with reports of their acts. They spent the whole of the first year on questions simply of policy, organization, and plan, doing no practical work, as it was said, at all.

When the business of construction was taken hold of, they refused to occupy themselves personally with questions of the class which in New York usually take up nine tenths of the time and mind of all public servants, who have it in their power to arrange contracts and determine appointments, promotions, and discharges. All of these they turned over to the heads of the executive operations.

Now, when these deviations from usage were conjoined with the adoption of a policy of construction for which the public was entirely unprepared, and to which the largest taxpayers of the city were strongly opposed, when also those who had a variety of private axes to grind, found themselves and their influence, and their friends' influence, made nothing of by the commissioners, you may be sure that public opinion was manufactured against them at a great rate. The Mayor denounced them in his messages; the Common Council and other departments of the city government refused to cooperate with them, and were frequently induced to put obstructions in their way; they were threatened with impeachment and indictment; some of the city newspapers attacked them for a time in every issue; they were caricatured and lampooned; their session was once broken up by a mob, their business was five times examined (once or twice at great expense, lawyers, accountants, engineers, and other experts being employed for the purpose) by legislative investigating committees. Thus for a time public opinion, through nearly all the channels open to it, apparently set against them like a torrent.[21]

No men less strong, and no men less confident in their strength than these men—by virtue in part of personal character, in part of the extraordinary powers vested in them by the legislature, and in part by the accident of certain anomalous political circumstances—happened to be, could have carried through a policy and a method which commanded so little immediate public favor. As it was, nothing but personal character, the common impression that after all they were honest, saved them. By barely a saber's length they kept ahead of their pursuers, and of this you may still see evidence here and there in the park, chiefly where something left to stop a gap for the time being has been suffered to remain as if a permanence. At one time nearly four thousand laborers were employed; and for a year at one point, work went on night and day in order to put it as quickly as possible beyond the reach of those who were bent on stopping it. Necessarily, under such circumstances, the rule obtains: "Look out for the main chance; we may save the horses, we must save the guns"; and if now you do not find everything in perfect parade order, the guns, at all events, were saved.

To fully understand the significance of the result so far, it must be considered that the Park is to this day, at some points, incomplete; that from the center of population to the midst of the Park the distance is still four miles; that there is no steam transit; that other means of communication are indirect and excessively uncomfortable, or too expensive. For practical everyday purposes to the great mass of the people, the Park might as well be a hundred miles away. There are hundreds of thousands who have never seen it, more hundreds of thousands who have seen it only on a Sunday or holiday. The children of the city to whom it should be of the greatest use, can only get to it on holidays or in vacations, and then must pay car-fare both ways.

It must be remembered, also, that the Park is not planned for such use as is now made of it, but with regard to the future use, when it will be in the center of a population of two millions hemmed in by water at a short distance on all sides; and that much of the work done upon it is, for this reason, as yet quite barren of results.

The question of the relative value of what is called off-hand common sense, and of special, deliberate, business-like study, must be settled in the case of the Central Park, by a comparison of benefit with cost. During the last four years over thirty million visits have been made to the Park by actual count, and many have passed uncounted. From fifty to eighty thousand persons on foot, thirty thousand in carriages, and four to five thousand on horseback, have frequently entered it in a day.

Among the frequent visitors, I have found all those who, a few years ago, believed it impossible that there should ever be a park in this republican country—and especially in New York of all places in this country—which would be a suitable place of resort for "gentlemen." They, their wives and daughters, frequent the Park more than they do the opera or the church.

There are many men of wealth who resort to the Park habitually and regularly, as much so as business men to their places of business. Of course, there is a reason for it, and a reason based upon their experience.

As to the effect on public health, there is no question that it is already great. The testimony of the older physicians of the city will be found unanimous on this point. Says one: "Where I formerly ordered patients of a certain class to give up their business altogether and go out of town, I now often advise simply moderation, and prescribe a ride in the Park before going to their offices, and again a drive with their families before dinner. By simply adopting this course as a habit, men who have been breaking down frequently recover tone rapidly, and are able to retain an active and controlling influence in an important business, from which they would have otherwise been forced to retire. I direct school-girls, under certain circumstances, to be taken wholly, or in part, from their studies, and sent to spend several hours a day rambling on foot in the Park."

The lives of women and children too poor to be sent to the country, can now be saved in thousands of instances, by making them go to the Park. During a hot day in July last, I counted at one time in the Park eighteen separate groups, consisting of mothers with their children, most of whom were under school-age, taking picnic dinners which they had brought from home with them. The practice is increasing under medical advice, especially when summer complaint is rife.

The much greater rapidity with which patients convalesce, and may be returned with safety to their ordinary occupations after severe illness, when they can be sent to the Park for a few hours a day, is beginning to be understood. The addition thus made to the productive labor of the city is not unimportant.

The Park, moreover, has had a very marked effect in making the city attractive to visitors, and in thus increasing its trade, and causing many who have made fortunes elsewhere to take up their residence and become taxpayers in it—a much greater effect in this way, beyond all question, than all the colleges, schools, libraries, museums, and art-galleries which the city possesses. It has also induced many foreigners who have grown rich in the country, and who would otherwise have gone to Europe to enjoy their wealth, to settle permanently in the city.

And what has become of the great Bugaboo? This is what the "Herald" of later date answers:

> When one is inclined to despair of the country, let him go to the Central Park on a Saturday, and spend a few hours there in looking at the people, not at those who come in gorgeous carriages, but at those who arrive on foot, or in those exceedingly democratic conveyances, the street-cars; and if, when the sun begins to sink behind the trees, he does not arise and go homeward with a happy swelling heart [and so on, the effusion winding up thus—FLO]: We regret to say that the more brilliant becomes the display of vehicles and toilettes, the more shameful is the display of bad manners on the part of the—extremely fine-looking people who ride in carriages and wear the fine dresses. We must add that the pedestrians always behave well.[22]

Here we touch a fact of more value to social science than any other in the history of the Park; but to fully set it before you would take an evening by itself. The difficulty of preventing ruffianism and disorder in a park to be frequented indiscriminately by such a population as that of New York, was from the first regarded as the greatest of all those which the commission had to meet, and the means of overcoming it cost more study than all other things.

It is, perhaps, too soon to judge of the value of the expedients resorted to, but there are as yet a great many parents who are willing to trust their school-girl daughters to ramble without special protection in the Park, as they would almost nowhere else in New York. One is no more likely to see ruffianism or indecencies in the Park than in the churches, and the arrests for offenses of all classes, including the most venial, which arise simply from the ignorance of country people, have amounted to but twenty in the million of the number of visitors, and of these, an exceedingly small proportion have been of that class which was so confidently expected to take possession of the Park and make it a place unsafe and unfit for decent people.

There is a good deal of delicate work on the Park, some of it placed there by private liberality—much that a girl with a parasol, or a boy throwing a pebble, could render valueless in a minute. Except in one or two cases where the ruling policy of the management has been departed from—cases which prove the rule—not the slightest injury from wantonness, carelessness, or ruffianism has occurred.

Jeremy Bentham, in treating of "The Means of Preventing Crimes," remarks that any innocent amusement that the human heart can invent is useful under a double point of view: first, for the pleasure itself which results from it; second, from its tendency to weaken the dangerous inclinations which man derives from his nature.[23]

No one who has closely observed the conduct of the people who visit the Park, can doubt that it exercises a distinctly harmonizing and refining influence upon the most unfortunate and most lawless classes of the city—an influence favorable to courtesy, self-control, and temperance.

At three or four points in the midst of the Park, beer, wine, and cider are sold with other refreshments to visitors, not at bars, but served at tables where men sit in company with women. Whatever harm may have resulted, it has apparently had the good effect of preventing the establishment of drinking-places on the borders of the Park, these not having increased in number since it was opened, as it was originally supposed they would.

I have never seen or heard of a man or woman the worse for liquor taken at the Park, except in a few instances where visitors had brought it with them, and in which it had been drank secretly and unsocially. The present arrangements for refreshments I should say are temporary and imperfect.

Every Sunday in summer from thirty to forty thousand persons, on an average, enter the Park on foot, the number on a very fine day being sometimes nearly a hundred thousand. While most of the grog-shops of the city were effectually closed by the police under the Excise Law on Sunday, the number of visitors to the Park was considerably larger than before. There was no similar increase at the churches.

Shortly after the Park first became attractive, and before any serious attempt was made to interfere with the Sunday liquor trade, the head-keeper told me that he saw among the visitors the proprietor of one of the largest saloons in the city. He accosted him and expressed some surprise; the man replied, "I came to see what the devil you'd got here that took off so many of my Sunday customers."

I believe it may be justly inferred that the Park stands in competition with grog-shops and worse places, and not with the churches and Sunday-schools.

Land immediately about the Park, the frontage on it being seven miles in length, instead of taking the course anticipated by those opposed to the policy of the Commission, has advanced in value at the rate of two hundred per cent, per annum.

The cost of forming the Park, owing to the necessity of overcoming the special difficulties of the locality by extraordinary expedients, has been very great ($5,000,000); but the interest on it would even now be fully met by a toll of three cents on visitors coming on foot, and six cents on all others; and it should be remembered that nearly every visitor in coming from a distance voluntarily pays much more than this for the privilege.

It is universally admitted, however, that the cost, including that of the original off-hand common-sense blunders, has been long since much more than compensated by the additional capital drawn to the city through the influence of the Park.

Finally, to come back to the question of worldly wisdom. As soon as the Park came fairly into use, public opinion began to turn, and in a few months faced square about. The commissioners have long since, by simple persistence in minding their own proper business, come to be by far the most popular men who have had to do with any civic affairs in the time of the present generation. They have been, indeed, almost uncomfortably popular, having had need occasionally to "lobby" off some of the responsibilities which there was an effort to put upon them.

A few facts will show you what the change in public opinion has been. When the commissioners began their work, six hundred acres of ground was thought by many of the friends of the enterprise to be too much, by none too little for all park purposes. Since the Park has come into use, the amount of land laid out and reserved for parks in the two principal cities on the bay of New York has been increased to more than three times that amount, the total reserve for parks alone now being about two thousand acres, and the public demand is now for more, not less. Twelve years ago there was almost no pleasure-driving in New York. There are now, at least, ten thousand horses kept for pleasure-driving. Twelve years ago there were no roadways adapted to light carriages. There are now fourteen miles of rural drive within the parks complete and in use, and often crowded, and ground has been reserved in the two cities and their suburbs for fifty miles of park-ways, averaging, with their planted borders and inter-spaces, at least one hundred and fifty feet wide.

The land-owners had been trying for years to agree upon a new plan of roads for the upper part of Manhattan Island. A special commission of their own number had been appointed at their solicitation, but had utterly failed to harmonize conflicting interests. A year or two after the Park was opened, they went again to the Legislature and asked that the work might be put upon the Park Commissioners, which was done, giving them absolute control of the matter, and under them it has been arranged in a manner, which appears to be generally satisfactory, and has caused an enormous advance of the property of all those interested.

At the petition of the people of the adjoining counties, the field of the commissioners' operations has been extended over their territory, and their scheme of trunk-ways for pleasure-driving, riding, and walking has thus already been carried far out into what are still perfectly rural districts.

On the west side of the harbor there are other commissioners forming plans for extending a similar system thirty or forty miles back in to the country, and the Legislature of New Jersey has a bill before it for laying out another park of seven hundred acres.

In speaking of parks I have not had in mind the private enterprises, of which there are several. One of the very men who, twelve years ago, thought that anyone who pretended that the people of New York wanted a park must be more knave than fool, has himself lately devoted one hundred and fifty acres of his private property to a park designed for public use, and simply as a commercial operation, to improve the adjoining property.[24]

I could enforce the chief lesson of this history from other examples at home and abroad. I could show you that where parks have been laid out and managed in a temporary, off-hand, common-sense way, it has proved a penny-wise pound-foolish way, injurious to the property in their neighborhood. I could show you more particularly how the experience of New York, on the other hand, has been repeated over the river in Brooklyn.

But I have already held you too long. I hope that I have fully satisfied you that this problem of public recreation grounds is one which, from its necessary relation to the larger problem of the future growth of your honored city, should at once be made a subject of responsibility of a very definite, very exacting, and, consequently, very generous character. In no other way can it be adequately dealt with.

NOTES

1. Socrates Hyacinth, "A Flock of Wool," *Overland Monthly* (San Francisco), 4 (February 1870).

2. Olmsted's friend Samuel Bowles (1826–78) was editor of the *Springfield* (Massachusetts) *Republican*.

3. Olmsted refers to a February 5, 1870, article in the *Springfield Republican* about the nearby town of Blandford, Massachusetts, where farms and other enterprises had recently been abandoned. In "The Deserted Village" (1870), Irish-born poet Oliver Goldsmith (1730–74) mourns the destructive impact of early English industrialization on traditional farming villages.

4. From John Beddoe, "On the Physical Degeneration of Town Population," in George W. Hastings (ed.), *Transactions of the National Association for the Promotion of Social Science, 1861* (1862).

5. Olmsted refers to *Bracebridge Hall, or the Humourists* (1822), a short-story collection by American author Washington Irving (1783–1859).

6. Shirley Dare, "One End of the Thread," *New-York Daily Tribune*, February 26, 1870, on the city's seamstresses.

7. Olmsted may have been referring to the novel *Elsie Venner; a Romance of Destiny* (1861) by Oliver Wendell Holmes Sr. (1809–94), American physician,

lecturer, and author.

8. *Kelly's Post Office London Directory.*

9. Olmsted may be referring to the Roman building-code reforms of AD 64 prohibiting party wall construction, thereby making every new structure freestanding.

10. See Isaac Newton Phelps Stokes, *The Iconography of Manhattan Island, 1498–1909*, 6 vols. (1915–28), 5: 1735, for the December 16–17, 1835, fire that destroyed the packed-together buildings in New York's financial district.

11. English architect Christopher Wren (1632–1723) proposed a plan for reconfiguring London after the Great Fire of September 2–5, 1661, destroyed most of the city. The plan was not executed for fear of excessive cost.

12. Immensely popular novelist Anthony Trollope (1815–82) chronicled life in Victorian England.

13. The Central Park Commission would not allow adult sporting teams to play on The Green (now the Sheep Meadow) for fear of damage to plants and shrubs as well as concern about "objectionable features" accompanying such events.

14. Central Park in New York and Prospect Park in Brooklyn. The two cities were not consolidated until 1898.

15. Edward Everett Hale (1822–1909), a prominent Unitarian minister and author in Boston, published the novel *Sybaris and Other Homes* (1869), a utopian satire advocating healthful suburban communities for working-class families. A red cross was painted on doors of infected houses during the seventeenth-century London plagues. Two centuries later in the United States cities used crosses to mark streets and houses where infectious diseases were found.

16. The term "gardenesque" was coined in 1832 by John Claudius Loudon (1783–1843), Scottish landscape designer and magazine editor, to describe the deployment of formal or "artistic" plantings near the house and the focusing of attention on individual plant specimens scattered throughout an otherwise naturalistic setting. "Highly artificial and exotic" plants including "subtropical" varieties to which Olmsted objects were introduced at Parc Monceau in Paris in the 1860s by horticulturist Jean-Pierre Barillet-Des-

champs (dates unknown) and in London at almost the same moment by John Gibson (1815–75), supervisor of Battersea Park beginning in 1858.

17. In Greek mythology, Zeus had nine daughters, three of whom were the Graces or goddesses of beauty, mirth, and good cheer.

18. In 1851 the New York legislature passed a law providing for a city park at what was called Jones Wood on Manhattan's East Side. After opposition arose, a new law of 1853 authorized purchase of most of the land that is now Central Park.

19. "The Central Park and Other City Improvements," *New York Herald*, September 6, 1857, mentioned real estate speculator William Backhouse Astor (1792–1875) and Unitarian minister and orator Edward Everett (1794–1865).

20. Pursuant to an 1857 law, New York Governor John King (1788–1867) appointed eleven prominent men of wealth to the Central Park Board of Commissioners to dilute the influence of pork-barreling partisan politicians.

21. Shortly after taking office in 1858, Mayor Daniel Fawcett Tiemann (1805–90) announced that New York City building projects would henceforth be supervised by the mayor and city aldermen rather than independent commissions like that of Central Park.

22. Neither the editors of *The Papers of Frederick Law Olmsted* nor this editor were able to identify the source of this quote.

23. From *Principles of Penal Law*, part 3 (1843) by Jeremy Bentham (1748–1832), English jurist and philosopher.

24. Possibly Olmsted's friend, New York City banker Howard Potter (1826–77).

FOURTEEN

Park

(1875)

Olmsted begins his history of parks by describing how they came into being, what they are, and what they are not. Using England as his starting point, he differentiates among public gardens, places, place parks, parkways, parks, and woods, and there is much discussion here of how and why each had its own historical and contemporary purpose according to need and circumstance.

There follows a long review of European parks, some mentioned only in passing, others receiving lengthier scrutiny. "Every considerable town in Europe now possesses grounds . . . for public recreation," he begins this section, "and most have several different types specially prepared and kept at public expense." Because this essay was written for an American audience, Olmsted's intention is clear: to convince his fellow citizens that late in the nineteenth century it is almost barbaric not to follow Europe's example, and when they do, to ensure that parks are publicly owned and open to everyone.

When the scene shifts to the United States, Olmsted reviews recent developments in the same critically detached manner in which he discusses Europe. He closes by describing the principal features of his own and Calvert Vaux's parks, including Central and Prospect—as well as those designed by others—leaving it for readers to decide if the United States is at last beginning to match up to what exists overseas.

Originally published in George Ripley and Charles A. Dana (eds.),
The American Cyclopaedia: A Popular Dictionary of General
Knowledge, *v. 12 (1875), and in slightly different form in* The
Garden, *10 (March 25, 1876), this text is a longer and much revised
version of "Park" published in Ripley and Dana's earlier* American
Cyclopaedia, *v. 12 (1861). The editor has taken the liberty of break-
ing Olmsted's exceedingly long paragraphs—in one instance more
than three pages—into more manageable units.*

Park, a space of ground used for public or private recreation, differing from a garden in its spaciousness and the broad, simple,
and natural character of its scenery, and from a "wood" in the
more scattered arrangement of its trees and greater expanse
of its glades and consequently of its landscapes. For the sake
of completeness, recreation grounds not properly called parks
will be considered under the same title. The grounds of an old
English manorial seat are usually divided into two parts, one
enclosed within the other and separated from it by some form
of fence. The interior part, immediately around the dwelling, is
distinguished as the pleasure ground or kept ground, the outer
as the park. The park is commonly left open to the public, and
frequently the public have certain legal rights in it, especially
rights of way. A parish church is sometimes situated within the
park. The use of the park as part of a private property is to
put the possibilities of disagreeable neighborhood at a distance
from the house and the more domestic grounds, to supply a
pleasant place of escape from the confinement and orderliness
of the more artificial parts of the establishment, and for prolonged and vigorous out-of-door exercise. The kept grounds,
being used incidentally to in-door occupations, are designed in
close adaptation to the plan of the house, richly decorated, and

nicely, often exquisitely, ordered by the constant labor of gardeners. Anciently the kept grounds were designed as a part of the same general architectural plan with the house, and were enclosed and decorated with masses of foliage clipped in imitation of cut and sculptured stone. Their lofty hedges often completely intercepted the view from the house toward the park. A recognition of the fact that the parks were much more beautiful than the kept grounds when thus fashioned, led early in the 16th century to the art of landscape gardening, or, as it is more generally called out of England, landscape architecture.

The aim of the new art was, while still keeping the park fenced off, to manage the pleasure grounds in such a way that they would provide a harmonious and appropriate foreground to landscapes extending over the park, and to make such changes in the park itself as would improve the composition of these landscapes. The scenery of the old parks often has great beauty of a special character, which is the result of the circumstances under which the more ancient and famous of them have been formed. These were originally enclosed many centuries since for keeping deer. In choosing ground for this purpose, rich land having broad stretches of greensward pasturage, with trees more sparingly distributed than usually in the forest, was to be preferred, and this character would be increased intentionally by felling a portion of the trees, and unintentionally by the browsing of the deer; water, either flowing or still, was a necessity. In process of time the proprietors of parks established residences in them, and at length the size of their trees and the beauty of their grouping came to be matters of family pride. As the old decayed, new trees were planted, with the purpose of maintaining the original character, or perhaps of carrying it nearer its ideal. Properties of this class, being associated with that which was oldest and most respectable in the land, came to be eagerly sought for, and to be formed to order as nearly as possible after the older type; and they are to be seen now in England by thousands. As a general rule, each element in their scenery is simple, natural to the soil and climate, and unobtrusive; and yet the passing observer is very strongly impressed with the manner in which views are successively opened before him through the innumerable combinations into which the individually modest elements constantly rearrange themselves; views which often possess every quality of complete and impressive landscape compositions. It is chiefly in this character that the park has the advantage for public purposes over any other type of recreation ground, whether wilder or more artificial. Other forms of natural scenery stir the observer to warmer admiration, but it is doubtful if any, and certain that none which under ordinary circumstances man can of set purpose induce nature to supply him, are equally soothing and refreshing; equally adapted to stimulate simple, natural, and wholesome tastes and fancies, and thus to draw the mind from absorption in the interests of an intensely artificial habit of life.

Private and public parks differ only in the extent of their accommodations for certain purposes, and most of the public parks in Europe are old private parks adapted to public use. When this is not the case, and a park for public use has to be formed essentially from the bare ground, its value will chiefly depend on provisions that cannot be fully matured or have their best operation for many years after their groundwork is established. For this reason the selection of a site, the design for laying out, and the system of continuous management of a public park should be determined with great caution. The aim should be to produce the park rather than the more elaborate pleasure ground or garden style of scenery, not only for the reasons above indicated but because a ground of this character can be consistently and suitably maintained at much less cost;

because, also, it will allow the necessary conveniences for the enjoyment of it by large numbers of persons to be introduced in such a way as not to be unpleasantly conspicuous or disastrously incongruous; and because it favors such a distribution of those who visit it that few shall be seen at a time, and that the ground shall not seem overcrowded. It is a common impression that the loftier and more rugged and mountain-like the site of a public ground may be, and the more wild, picturesque, and grand scenery can be imitated in its improvement, the better it will answer its purpose. A principle of art however interposes, which M. Taine, in a discussion of the unimpressiveness of certain forms of mountain scenery, explains as follows: "A landscape in order to be beautiful must have all its parts stamped with a common idea and contributing to a single sensation. If it gives the lie here to what is said yonder, it destroys itself, and the spectator is in the presence of nothing but a mass of senseless objects."[1]

It is extremely difficult to provide suitably extensive and varied conveniences for the public use of a piece of ground, the elements of which are strongly picturesque with an approach to grandeur, without destroying much of its original character; and the result of such attempts, unless under unusually fortunate circumstances and the guidance of unusual taste and skill, with the use of large means, is sure to be confusing and ineffective. Sites of much natural grandeur or even of bold picturesqueness are, therefore, to be selected for a park only where all necessary improvements for the convenience of a great number of visitors can be so managed that they will in some way strengthen rather than weaken the prevailing character. No instance of a public park exists in which this has been accomplished, but the principle is illustrated in various landscapes of the great painters. Examples may be found, for instance, in almost any book of engravings after Turner,[2] in which the original effect of a crag of rock is shown to be augmented by buildings designed for the purpose, the bases of which are skillfully merged in its face, or where a single great building of very simple outline is given a firm and tranquil standing in a wild and broken landscape of steep declivities and rugged heights. Under good direction, sites with features of much natural grandeur, on a scale so large and of such a character that the necessary constructions for the intended visitors can be insignificant, are to be preferred to any other; but such sites have not yet been appropriated to the purpose with the advantage of a sufficiently long continued adequate direction of their improvement, and there can be but few cases where they will be.

After them, and more commonly attainable, are sites the natural character of which would usually and significantly be termed "park-like." If the ideal of the old English park scenery is kept in view, rather than either that of a more picturesque or more artificially refined, finical, and elaborately embellished kind, it will be readily seen that in the site for a public recreation ground it is desirable that views of considerable extent should be controllable within its borders, and that in order to command them it should not be necessary that views beyond its borders be opened, the elements of which cannot be controlled, and are liable, even in the distant future, to be made inharmonious with those of the park; especially so, where such elements will have urban rather than rural associations. It is generally better, therefore, that the outer parts should be the higher, the central parts the more depressed; that the surface should be tame rather than rugged, gently undulating rather than hilly. Water is desirable, and it will be best situated where it can be seen from the greatest number of widely distributed points of view. Relatively to the residences of those who are expected to benefit by it, the park will be best situated where there can be but little occasion to make thoroughfares through it. Otherwise, the less the distance and the more convenient and agreeable the intermediate roads, the better. As roads which radiate from a town are usually more important to be kept open than those which cross them, and as land near a town is relatively more needed for other uses than that more distant, it is commonly better that the breadth of the site should increase with its distance from the nearest point to the town, as in Prospect park, Brooklyn, N.Y. In the improvement of the site, attractive and suitable scenery has to be formed, and unsuitable elements of existing scenery changed or obscured; and at the same time and on the same ground accommodations of various kinds are to be prepared for great numbers of people, many in carriages and on horseback, many ignorant, selfish, and willful, of perverted tastes and lawless dispositions, each one of whom must be led as far as possible to enjoy and benefit by the scenery without preventing or seriously detracting from the enjoyment of it by all others.

The most essential element of park scenery is turf in broad, unbroken fields, because in this the antithesis of the confined spaces of the town is most marked. In the climate of Great Britain turf will endure on favorable soils twice as much foot wear as it will in that of Paris or northern France or the United States; yet in the more frequented London parks it is found necessary to surround with strong iron hurdles the glades on which their landscape attraction is dependent. For this and other obvious reasons, a great extent of ground must be prepared expressly for the wear of feet and wheels. In the two principal recreation grounds of Paris, the woods of Boulogne and Vincennes, though both are suburban parks and not readily used by the mass of the people, the extent of such flooring, prepared by macadamizing, paving, and otherwise, is 480 acres, or ten times the whole recreation ground of Boston, "the Common." In the Central park of New York it is 100 acres, and there is a constant public demand for its enlargement, which can only be met by reducing the verdant elements of landscape, and consequently the benefit to be obtained by the use of the park. In a public park for a city, therefore, the purpose of establishing such natural beauty as soil, climate, and topography would otherwise allow to be aimed at, must be greatly sacrificed under the necessity of providing accommodations for the travel and repose of many thousands of men and horses; and on the other hand, the extent of such accommodations must be made less than would otherwise be thought desirable, in order that the special objects of the park may be secured in a suitable degree.

A plan for a park is good, indifferent, or bad, mainly according to the ingenuity, tact, and taste with which these conflicting requirements are reconciled, and to the degree in which local circumstances are skillfully turned to account if they can be made favorable, or skillfully overcome if unfavorable for this purpose. The problem is sufficiently difficult under the simplest conditions, and it is undesirable that it should be unnecessarily complicated by a requirement to provide for various purposes which have nothing in common with that of tranquilizing rest and exercise, and to which the element of landscape beauty is not essential. Soldiers, for example, drill and maneuver, horses race, gymnasts and ball players exercise, on a piece of flat ground surrounded by buildings as well as in the glades of a wood. It is true that, when a suburban park is very spacious relatively to the number of people resorting to it for park recreation, a limited use of the larger turf areas for athletic exercises will injure it but little; but their frequent use for such purposes, especially if large assemblages of spectators are likely to be attracted, will be destructive of the value of the ground as a park, in the specific sense of the term. It is also to be considered that the proper rules and police arrangements for a park are different from those for a parade, ball, or gymnasium ground, or for a race course. Hence, when the most suitable ground near a town for these purposes adjoins that which is most suitable for a park, it is yet much better that there should be a marked division between them. Public buildings can be reconciled with the purposes of a park only in a limited degree. Ground about any building designed for an important public service should be laid out with a view, first, to convenience of communication with it; secondly, to its best exhibition as a work of architectural art. The neighboring grounds should be shaped and planted in strict subordination to these purposes, which will involve an entirely different arrangement from that which the purpose of forming a quiet rural retreat would prescribe. A similar consideration will prevent monuments and statues from being placed profusely in a park, or at all in situations where they will be obtrusive. The same cautions apply to the introduction of botanic, zoological, and other gardens. Their main object is as different from that of a park as that of a billiard room from a library. Both one and the other may serve for recreation, and there is an advantage in being able to pass from one to the other; but the kind of recreation to be gained by one is not that of the other, the appropriate furniture of the one is not that of the other; and their perfect combination being impracticable, the two can be much better used apart, one at a time.

In the larger part of the civilized world, circumstances are as unfavorable to park-like scenery as to grand scenery in the vicinity of large towns. The climate of France is nowhere as favorable to it as that of Great Britain, and even in the north it cannot be found in perfection unless on unusually suitable soil. In the south of France, in Italy, and on all the borders of the Mediterranean, in Mexico and California, and in short wherever a rich close perennial turf cannot be established, parks properly so called ought not to be attempted. In these cases, the two natural elements of scenery to be developed in a suburban public ground of great extent are forests (or "woods") and water. While trees in woods are by no means as beautiful as trees in parks, and a forest is apt to be gloomy and to produce an oppressive sense of confinement, the mystery of this confinement, so different from that of the walls of a town, makes it interesting and recreative. In the midst of well grown woods, public accommodations, no matter how obviously artificial, nor within reasonable limits how large they may be, detract but little from the main impression, and if fairly well designed supply a grateful relief to what might otherwise be too prolonged a mass and too nearly a monotone of color. The introduction of long strips of clear ground, even if covered with gravel or poor herbage (as at Versailles and most of the great old gardens), giving vistas through which the light may stream in visible beams, touching the walls of foliage at the side with an infinite number of lustrous flecks, produces a most agreeable impression. Bodies of water, whether formal or naturalistic in outline, in the midst of deep dark tall "woods," are still more effective. For the same reason statues, monuments, and gardens of highly colored flowers may be introduced in the midst of woods to much better advantage than in parks.

The use in America of the word park as a general designation for gardens, green courts, and all sorts of public places, is an exaggeration of a French application of the word to the more private or kept grounds of a château connected with a forest. To avoid confusion, open spaces for public use in a city may be termed "places"; grounds in turf and trees within places, "place parks"; and broad thoroughfares planted with trees and designed with special reference to recreation as well as for common street traffic, "parkways." The value of public gardens, places, place parks, and parkways, in distinction from parks and "woods," is dependent less on the extent of their sylvan elements than on the degree of convenience with which they may be used; those being the most valuable, other things being equal, through which the greatest number of people may be induced to pass while following their ordinary occupations and without serious hindrance or inconvenience.

Hence the most important improvement made of late in the general plan of cities has been the introduction or increase in number and breadth of parkways which, if judiciously laid out, become principal channels or trunk lines of common traffic, to which the ordinary streets serve as feeders, so that a man wishing to go to a considerable distance shall find it a saving of time and trouble to take one of them on his way.

In this respect Paris has taken the lead, having formed since 1855 over 80 m[iles] of such trunk lines of communication from 100 to 300 ft. in width, provided with borders of trees or shrubbery, walks and drives of a special character, seats, special lighting arrangements, and other conditions more interesting and agreeable than those of common streets. The total length of boulevards and avenues lined with trees under the direction of the municipality within the enceinte [wall] of Paris is 120 m[iles]. Most of the large towns of Europe are making similar improvements, and at Washington, Chicago, Cleveland, Buffalo, Syracuse, and Brooklyn excellent examples of them exist or are in process of formation. New York, with an area of about 42 sq[uare] m[iles], has 7 m[iles] of planted parkways, all of which are suburban and as yet but partly finished. Simple places, piazzas, or plazas (the two latter being equivalent terms derived from the Italian and Spanish) have the sanitary value of making a city more airy than it would be without them. If furnished with parks (place parks), they have the additional advantage of providing refreshment to the eye through the mind. If a piece of ground of one or two acres in the midst of a busy town is laid out and managed with a view to providing upon it the greatest practicable degree of plant beauty in trees, shrubs, flowers, and turf, and on the same general principles that a private garden for the same purpose would be, it will be of comparatively little use; for the walks will probably be indirect, the low planting of the outer parts will obscure the general view for passers by, and there will be frequent crowding and jostling and disturbance of quiet. Neatness and the maintenance of orderly conduct among visitors in such a ground becomes also exceedingly difficult. Hence, as a rule, at least in the United States, public grounds designed with this motive soon become more forlorn than open places would be. It is much better to decorate them in such a manner as will not destroy their openness or cause inconvenience to those who have occasion to cross them. For this purpose their plans should be simple and generally formal in style, their passages should be broad and direct, and they should be provided with seats in recesses or on the borders of the broader paved or graveled spaces, leaving ample room for free movement. Their trees should be high-stemmed and umbrageous; conifers, except in rare instances, as permanent dwarfs, should be excluded, and flowers and delicate plants little if at all used except in vases and baskets (*corbeilles*) or as fringes of architectural objects. Interest will desirably center in a fountain.

Every considerable town in Europe now possesses grounds which are resorted to for public recreation, and most have several different types specially prepared and kept at public expense. In France the state has long held and managed extensive "woods and forests," remnants of the original forests which covered the country in the time of Caesar. More than 20 such are found within a distance from Paris which makes them available for a day's pleasuring by means of railway excursion trains. They vary in extent from about 1,000 acres, as at St.

Cloud, to 41,000, as at Fountainebleau. Each of these contains a château which at some time has been a royal residence, in connection with which there is a "park" or garden of several acres, generally containing a lake, fountains, statuary, monuments, parterres, and sometimes conservatories, aviaries, or other interesting objects. More or less historical interest also attaches to each, and in some quaint old customs are maintained, by which visitors are attracted. The forest proper is wilder, and in its depths many animals are found in a state of nature. It is however divided, by a network of broad avenues crossed by first, second, and third class roads and walks, into spaces of five to ten acres, so that in passing through it vistas open at frequent intervals on both sides and in all directions. Some of these forests are distinguished for great rocks, trees, and picturesque scenery; some contain in their depths broad meadows and savannas, others lakes or streams with cascades; all are guarded from depredations and policed by an organized body of men thoroughly trained in their duties under a military discipline. Among the more noted of these suburban resorts around Paris are those of Boulogne, Vincennes, St. Cloud, Marly, St. Germain, Rambouillet, Chantilly, and Compiègne, which together contain more than 170,000 acres. The first five are within 10 m[iles] of the city, and may be reached by rail in less than half an hour. Versailles is another resort yet more famous, and in which the woods are of less importance than the palace and gardens. The woods of Boulogne and Vincennes, being nearest the city, one at its west and the other at its east side, have since 1854 been placed under the jurisdiction of the municipality, and fitted by extensive and important improvements, the better to serve as recreation grounds for the daily use of the citizens.

The wood of Boulogne contains about 2,500 acres, and the fortified line of the city forms its eastern boundary. The soil is naturally gravelly and poor, the trees are generally thickly sown, spindled, and weak, and the scenery flat and uninteresting. Several departmental roads (broad, straight, paved wagon ways) pass through it. Except in the refreshing wildness of a forest, it offered as late as 1855 but little to attract a visitor. Yet because of its close vicinity to the city it was already much frequented by the Parisians, and Napoleon III saw in the neglect to which it had been abandoned the opportunity of making one of those sensations, to the frequent succession of which he owed so much of his popularity. The coarse, siliceous soil was less costly to handle than better earth; good roads could be cheaply graded in it, and the materials of a sufficiently firm superstructure for so porous a base were to be had on the spot by simply screening its pebbles; for the same reason scarcely any artificial drainage was necessary. There were open meadows which could be extended to the banks of the Seine. The plan of improvement was adroitly adapted to turn all these advantages to account, so that in a short time, to those who kept to certain routes, the character of the wood seemed to have been completely changed. On the immediate borders of the new roads, and on the lines of certain vistas opening from them, the surface of the ground and the foliage appear varied and picturesque, and there are certain features of scenic interest, as a cascade and grotto, the rock of which was brought from the distant forest of Fontainebleau and skillfully wrought into masses with patches of concrete imitation of stone. The greater part of the old wood remained, as far as the operations of improvement are concerned, little changed and as uninteresting as a wood might be.

The approach to the improved ground from the central parts of the town is first through the Champs Elysées, afterward for a distance of 1 1/8 m[iles] by the new avenue Bois de Boulogne [now avenue Foch]. This consists of a driveway 60 ft. wide, a bridle road on one side of it 40 ft. wide, and a walk opposite of the same width, with borders of lawn-like ground on each side, the whole space being 300 ft. in width. In the original design this avenue was expected to become the fashionable promenade of Paris; but, probably because it was not in the outset sufficiently well shaded, fashion pushed further out to the road on the south bank of a new lake in the wood 1 2/3 m[iles] in length, where no tolerable provision had been made for it. To meet the demand, the original drive on the lake was widened to 45 ft., and a pad or bridle path introduced by its side, 40 ft. wide. Under ordinary circumstances the greater part of the visitors to the wood concentrate on these roads and the adjoining walk. There were in the whole wood of Boulogne before 1870, when a considerable space both of the old and new planting was cleared in preparation for the defense of Paris against the Germans, 1,009 acres of wooded land, 674 of unshaded turf, 75 of water surface, and 286 of drives, rides, and walks (not including the race track). The race ground of Longchamps, which is a part of the property, contains 195 acres, the ground leased to the [plant] acclimation society for a zoological garden, 50 acres, and the leased amusement garden, the Pré Catalan, in the midst of the wood, to which a charge for admission is made, 21 acres. There are 36 m[iles] of public drive (including the old straight forest and departmental highways), 7 m[iles] of ride, and 15 m[iles] of walk. The larger part of the pleasure drives are 25 to 36 ft. broad, the widest 48 ft.; the rides 12 to 17 ft.; the walks 8 to 12 ft.

The wood of Vincennes, similar in other respects to that of Boulogne, contained an ancient castle which was the center of a great military establishment, and a large plain in the midst of the wood, used as a training ground. This has been maintained, but in other respects the design for improvement has been similar to that for the wood of Boulogne, the principal difference being that the accommodations and attractions for foot visitors at Vincennes are relatively more important. The extent of the ground is 2,225 acres, of which about half is wooded. There is a race course on the plain, and a lake of 60 acres. The public ways, not including the race track, take up 183 acres. There are no large parks within the fortified lines of Paris, but several beautiful place parks and gardens. A detailed account of them and of their admirable method of administration may be found in Robinson's "Parks, Promenades, and Gardens of Paris" and one still more complete in *Les promenades de Paris*, by M. Alphonse, the chief designer of the recent improvements.[3] The extent of the public recreation grounds within the fortified lines of the city is about 250 acres. The area of suburban grounds commonly resorted to for recreation and maintained at public expense, not including those too far away for an afternoon excursion, may be estimated at 20,000 acres. The extent of pleasure drive maintained by the municipal government is 87 m[iles], being about 3 m[iles] of roadway to each square mile of the city, or, counting the parkways (boulevards) shaded and with asphalt driveways, over 7 m[iles] to the square mile. New York has less than a quarter of a mile to the square mile.

The parks and open spaces of London are very numerous, and their total extent is larger perhaps than that of those belonging to any other metropolis of the first magnitude. They are very various in area, ranging from one to several hundred acres. It has been long recognized that London owes a great deal of its physical and political health to its parks and open spaces. All the year round they act as great lungs to the mighty city, while in summer and even to a considerable extent in winter they are the Sunday resort of the weary workers. The open spaces of London are not confined to any quarter. The East End has Victoria park (300 acres); Finsbury park (115 acres), too new to be so pleasant to the eye, but still rapidly becoming what it is intended to be; and the half dozen "downs," "fields," and "commons" that go under the general name of Hackney Downs (50 acres). It has also, lying just outside its boundaries, the two forests of Epping and Hainault, and several green breadths that may be called everybody's and yet no man's land. South London has some of the finest of the parks and open spaces. To the southeast lie Woolwich common, Greenwich park (174 acres), and Greenwich common, and nearer at hand Lewisham common, Peckham Rye, and Southwark park (63 acres). Directly south lie Camberwell (55 acres) and various little remnants of ancient greens and commons, while the grounds of the Crystal palace may almost be said to answer as a park for the wide districts of Sydenham, Norwood, and Penge. Southwest lie Clapham common (10 acres), Wandsworth common (302), and Wimbledon common (628). Tooting Beck and Tooting Graveney commons and Battersea park (230 acres) also belong to this district. In the north lie Hampstead heath (240 acres), the Greenlanes, the grounds of Alexandra park (192), and Primrose hill. In the west are found Hyde park (about 400 acres), the Green park, St. James's park, Regent's park (450), Kensington gardens (290), and several small "greens," such as Shepherd's Bush. All these parks, commons, and open spaces are within the actual metropolitan district.

Taking in a little wider radius, the heaths, downs, parks, and greens within easy reach of London become almost innumerable. First, beginning at the southeast and sweeping round by the south, west, north, and east, we find Chiselhurst common; a little southwest of this Hayes common, a great resort of cockneys in summer, where any day a score of pleasure vans may be seen; a little further to the west Addington common, also much frequented; still further west Mitcham common and Banstead downs, not to speak of those of Epsom, famous for horse races, or of the score of small spaces kept "open" by the strong hand of the law and the general consent of the people. Approaching the Thames by a northwest course, we next meet with Richmond park (2,253 acres), the largest park near London except that at Windsor (3,800), Hampton Court park and Bushy parks (1,842), and Kew park and gardens (684), the finest botanic garden in England. Crossing the river, we come next upon Ealing and Acton greens (leaving Hownslow heath on the left as out of our radius), Wormwood Scrubs, and numerous little greens and commons. North of Hampstead and Alexandra park the open spaces are fewer and smaller, and owing to a more scattered population less required. Northeast lie Epping and Hainault forests, mentioned before, each of them very large and full of natural beauty.

Hyde park, the most noted of the public grounds of London, takes its name from the ancient manor of Hyde, which at one time belonged to the abbey of Westminster, became public property in 1535, was sold by order of parliament in 1652, and again recovered to the crown on the restoration in 1660. It was originally of the usual character of English private parks, a broad piece of quiet pasture ground, with numerous fine great trees scattered over it singly and in groups and masses. In 1730–33 a body of water was introduced (the Serpentine), but with no care to give it a natural or even a graceful outline. Roads have also been formed in the park from time to time, less with a view to public pleasure driving than for convenient passages. What is called the Rotten Row (a corruption of the French *route du roi*) was originally the passage for the king and his cavalcade between Westminster and his palace of Kensington; it is a mile long and 90 ft. wide, has a surface of loose fine gravel, and is used by the public only on horseback; it is separated from the Serpentine and "ladies' mile" (45 ft. wide), the fashionable drive of London, by a walk and strip of turf of variable width. It divides and overpowers what might otherwise be a pleasing landscape expanse, and no attempt has been made to mitigate the harshness of the invasion. Parts of Hyde park have lately been made into gardens, and in these during parts of the summer there is a very brilliant display of flowers, "specimens," and subtropical plants; but the old trees are disappearing more rapidly than the young ones are brought forward; the turf is not well kept, and to avoid its destruction in many parts iron hurdles are placed along the walks. It is thus gradually losing its beauty as a park, for which its streaks of fine gardening here and there offer no compensation. The Crystal Palace was erected in Hyde park in 1851, and on the site now stands the Albert memorial, completed in 1872.

Regent's park, formerly part of old Marylebone park, was laid out in 1812. There is a drive of nearly two miles around it, and within are the botanic and zoological gardens, and a lake. Victoria park in E. London was opened to the public in 1845. A fine drinking fountain, 60 ft. high and costing £5,000, given by Lady Burdette-Coutts, was erected in it in 1862. St. James's park was formed and walled in by Henry VIII, was much improved under Charles II, and was arranged as it now appears chiefly under George IV. The public property in many of the larger commons of London is so complicated by ancient manorial and local rights that its extent cannot be accurately stated. The aggregate area of the several public and crown parks that have been named, together with so much of the commons lying within the metropolitan district as is under the board of works, is about 13,000 acres. There is also in the squares and gardens (place parks), most of which have been established by landlords and are private property but of great public advantage, about 1,200 acres.

Liverpool and its suburb Birkenhead have six parks, five of which are recent acquisitions and yet incompletely prepared for public use. The largest, Sefton park, contains 387 acres.

Birkenhead park contains 120 acres, besides the leased villa grounds (60 acres) by which it is surrounded. It was undertaken as a land speculation, and though too small in scale and too garden-like for the general popular use of a large community, is very pleasing, and is one of the most instructive to study in Europe, having been laid out and the trees planted under the direction of the late Sir Joseph Paxton, over 30 years ago.[4] The corporation of Leeds has lately purchased a noble park of 800 acres, containing a fine stream of water and a lake, formed by the previous owner, of 33 acres. Its scenery is diversified, and it commands fine distant rural views. These advantages and its exemption from injury by factory smoke compensate for the necessity the citizens will be under of reaching it by rail, its distance from the town being 4 m[iles]. Birmingham, Manchester, Bradford, and other manufacturing towns of England have acquired parks by subscriptions of citizens or by joint-stock companies. At Halifax a park has been formed and given to the town by a benevolent citizen. Derby is provided in the same way with an arboretum. The city of Lincoln is forming an arboretum on land purchased for this purpose. Most of the small towns of England have some place of recreation, as for instance the old city walls and the river banks above the town at Chester, the common and the old castle grounds at Hereford, and the cathedral greens at Salisbury and Winchester. These consist in each case either of a long broad walk pleasantly bordered and leading to fine views, or a few acres of smooth turf with shaded borders. Most villages in England have a private park near them, which people are allowed to use. When this is not the case, even a hamlet almost invariably has at least a bit of cricket ground or common, where, on benches under a patriarchal oak or elm, the old people meet to gossip and watch the sports of the vigorous youth. Phoenix park at Dublin (1,752 acres) is a fine upland meadow fringed and dotted with trees, but badly laid out and badly kept, being much larger than the town requires or can afford to take suitable care of.

The old towns of the continent have generally provided themselves with recreation grounds by outgrowing their ancient borders of wall and moat and glacis [sloping hill], razing the wall, filling part of the moat, and so, with more or less skillful management of the materials, making the groundwork of a garden in the natural style. This is done admirably at Frankfort, Leipzig, and Vienna. Elsewhere simple broad walks bordered with trees have been laid out upon the leveled ramparts. The principal promenade of Vienna is the Prater, the chief feature of which is a straight carriage road over a mile long, with a walk on one side and a riding pad on the other. It contains near the town a great number of coffee houses and playhouses; but as it is 5 m[iles] long, considerable portions are thoroughly secluded and rural. Before the recent improvements of the Bois de Boulogne, it was the most frequented large recreation ground in the world. There are numerous other public grounds at Vienna, both urban and suburban. The English garden at Munich was laid out under the direction of Count Rumford by the baron von Skell.[5] It has serious defects, but its scenery in the English style has been considered more agreeable than that of any other public park on the continent; it is about 4 m[iles] long and half a mile wide. The Thiergarten at Berlin contains over 200 acres of perfectly flat land, chiefly a close wood, laid out in straight roads, walks, and riding pads; its scenery is uninteresting. The Prussian royal gardens of Sans Souci, Charlottenburg, and Heiligensee are all extensive grounds, the two former in mixed, the latter in natural style. Public gardens worthy of a traveler's attention exist at Cologne, Dresden, Düsseldorf, Stuttgart, Hanover, Brunswick, Baden, Cassel, Darmstadt, Gotha, Weimar, Wörlitz, Schwetzingen, Teplitz, Prague, and Hamburg. Coffee or beer houses are important adjuncts of

German public gardens. The refreshments furnished are plain and wholesome, and the prices moderate. Many families habitually resort to these for their evening meal, especially when, as is usually the case, there is the additional attraction of excellent music furnished by the government.

The gardens of Antwerp, the Hague, and Warsaw, and the "city grove" of Pesth, are also remarkable. The famous summer gardens of St. Petersburg are not extensive, being but half a mile long by a quarter of a mile wide, and formal in style. They contain fine trees, are rich in statuary (boxed up in winter), and are the most carefully kept public gardens in the world, as shown in the exceeding freshness and vigor of the plants and flowers and in the deep vivid green of the turf. The more fashionable promenade of St. Petersburg is in the gardens of Katharinenhof, where on the first of May an annual procession of private carriages of almost endless length is headed by that of the emperor. A remarkable ground is that of Tzarskoye Selo, in which is the residence of the imperial family, about two hours from St. Petersburg. Besides the palace, it contains temples, banqueting houses, and theaters, a complete village in the Chinese style, a Turkish mosque, a hermitage, and numerous monuments of military and other achievements. But beyond this museum of incongruous objects there is a part in which there is natural and very beautiful scenery both open and wooded, and much of it is simple. The keeping of the ground employs 600 men. Stockholm has a great variety of delightful waterside rural walks; but the chief object of pride with its people is the Djurgard or deer park, which is a large tract of undulating ground about 3 m[iles] in circumference, containing grand masses of rock and some fine old trees. The Haga park, also at Stockholm, is picturesque, and has the peculiarity of natural water communications between its different parts and the city, so that it is much visited in boats. The environs of Copenhagen contain many grounds of public resort, but the notable promenade of the city is the royal deer park (*Dyrhave*). In all the Italian cities, the chief public rural resorts are gardens attached to the villas of ancient noble families.

The Cascine of Florence is an old pasture of the dairy of the former grand dukes on the banks of the Arno, passing through which are broad straight carriage drives. It contains little that is attractive, but commands delicious views. At a space whence several roads radiate, a band of music usually performs at intervals during the promenade hours. The municipality is now preparing promenades and recreation grounds which promise to be of remarkable interest. The fashionable promenade of Rome has been on the Pincian hill, which has few attractions except in its magnificent distant views. Since Rome was made the capital of the new kingdom of Italy, large public grounds in other quarters have been projected and in great part formed by the municipality. At Naples the fashionable promenade is the Riviera di Chiaja, a public street. It is divided into a ride, a drive, and a walk, and is nearly a mile in length, with a breadth of 200 ft. A part of it is separated from the shore of the bay of Naples by the villa Reale, planted in the garden style. Most towns of Spanish or Portuguese origin are provided with a promenade of formal avenues, to which, generally at dusk, custom brings the ladies in open carriages and the gentlemen on foot or on horseback.

Until some years after the middle of the present century no city in North America had begun to make provision for a park. To a certain extent cemeteries were made to serve the purpose. In 1849 Mr. A. J. Downing began in the "Horticulturist" a series of papers which were widely copied and did much to create a demand on this subject. At length a large tract of land was provided in New York, upon which in 1858 the preparation of the present Central park was begun. The topography of the ground was in all important respects the reverse of that which would have been chosen with an intelligent understanding of the desiderata of a park. The difficulties presented could only have been tolerably overcome by an enormous outlay. The popularity of the parts of the park first prepared, however, was so great that the necessary means for improvements on a large scale were readily granted. The magnitude of the operations (nearly 4,000 men being at one time employed on the works), the rapidity of the changes wrought, and the novelty of the scenes presented, soon gave the enterprise great celebrity; and the rapid rise in the taxable value of the land near it more than met the interest on its cost. An efficient management of its public use was maintained, and though frequented by great crowds of people it was found, contrary to general expectation, that a degree of good order and of social amenity prevailed, nowhere surpassed and rarely equaled in the public places of Europe. Philadelphia, Brooklyn, Albany, Providence, Baltimore, Buffalo, Chicago, St. Louis, Cincinnati, Montreal, and San Francisco have since each acquired land for one or more parks of considerable extent, the average being over 500 acres. As in the case of New York, the selection of ground has often been made more with reference to other considerations than to that of fitness for the intended use. Some are as yet only held for future use, while in others provisions essentially temporary, and which will be in the way of substantial improvement, are made; none are so far complete and well fitted as fairly to illustrate the ends which a park should be designed to serve.

The Central park of New York is 2 1/2 miles long and half a mile wide, but this space is practically divided by the reservoirs of the city water works, which are elevated above its general level and occupy 142 acres. Deducting besides this certain other spaces occupied for special public purposes, the area of the park proper is 683 acres. Of this, 55 acres is meadow-like ground, 54 in smaller glades of turf, 400 of rocky and wooded surface, 43 in six pieces of water, the largest being of 20 acres, 15 in riding ways, 52 in carriage ways, and 39 in walks. There are 5 1/2 m[iles] of rides, 9 1/2 m[iles] of drives, and 28 m[iles] of walks. Omitting a few by-roads, the average breadth of the drives is 50 ft., and of the walks 13 ft. There are 8 bridges (over water) and 38 tunnels and subway arches, 15 of which are concealed from view by plantations carried over them, and all of which are expedients for reconciling within narrow limits the large amount of foot, horse, and wheel room required with sylvan and pastoral landscapes. On the east side, near the middle of the parallelogram containing the park and reservoirs, ground is reserved for a great museum of art; and beyond its boundary on the west side another plot is held for a museum of natural history. The first block of each is now building. There are carriage and foot entrances at the two southern corners, and between them on the south end, at the termini of street railroads, there are two foot entrances; and 14 other entrances are in use or provided for. From the [southeast] or Fifth avenue approach, which is most used, the visitor is led by a nearly direct course to a slightly elevated point in the interior of the park, northwardly from which, at great cost in reducing the original rocky knolls, broad green surfaces have been prepared, and views of a tranquil landscape character obtained of considerable extent. At the most distant visible point a small tower of gray stone has been built to draw the eye, and the perspective effect is aided by the character and disposition of the foliage, and especially by an avenue of elms leading toward it. At the end of this avenue, termed the mall, the ground falls rapidly to the arm of a lake, and here a structure called the terrace has been introduced, which, though mainly below the general plane of the landscape and unobtrusive, supplies a considerable shelter and place of reunion. It is designed to be richly decorated with sculptured works. On one side of it is the concert ground of the park, on the other a fountain surmounted by a bronze typifying the angel of Bethesda.[6] The concert ground is overlooked by a shaded gallery called the Pergola, back of which is a small house of refreshment in cottage style. On the opposite side of the water is a rocky and wooded slope, threaded by numerous paths, called the Ramble. These with the green, play ground reserved for the scholars of the public schools, two irregular bodies of water, and several rocky knolls (on one of which is the Kinderberg, a place for little children), form the chief features of the south park. Those of the north are a central meadow divided by a rocky spur, the high wooded ground beyond it, with a steep rocky face on the north, and an intermediate glen with a chain of waters. The number of visits to the park sometimes exceeds 100,000 in a day, and is about 10,000,000 a year.

Prospect park of Brooklyn, N.Y., contains, with the adjoining parade ground, 550 acres. There is included in it a considerable amount of old wood, and for this reason, and because of the better soil, climate, and early horticultural management, it has a finer rural and more mature character than the New York park, though its construction was begun eight years later. It has about 6 m[iles] of drives, 4 m[iles] of ride, and 20 m[iles] of walks. Its artificial water covers a space of 50 acres, and is supplied from a well by a steam pump. It commands a fine view over the ocean. There are 33 smaller public grounds in New York and Brooklyn, all but three of which are improved and in use, the total pleasure ground space of the two cities being 1,600 acres.

Fairmount park of Philadelphia is a body of land 2,740 acres in extent, having a great variety of surface, all of it of considerable natural beauty. The heights command fine distant prospects; it bears many noble trees, and at the part most remote from the city there is a glen through which dashes a charmingly picturesque stream. It is divided by the Schuylkill river and crossed by a common highway and in two directions by railroads, the cuttings and embankments of which unfortunately completely break the naturally most quiet scenes. These with other structures, some of which have been recently erected and are designed to be permanent, greatly disturb its natural beauty. The object of the city in acquiring the ground was to control it against such occupations as would peril its water supply, and its permanent disposition is not fully determined. Appropriations have been already made for two large reservoirs, for pumping works, and for a zoological garden. No measure has yet been taken looking to the permanent preservation or special preparation of any considerable part distinctly as a park; but drives, rides, and walks have been formed, mainly temporary, by which all parts are traversed or laid open to view. Several houses which were originally private villas are used as refectories; the river is well adapted to pleasure boating; the spaces are so large that few restrictions on the movements of visitors are necessary; and in spite of the defects to which allusion has been made, the ground offers better and larger opportunities for popular rural recreation than are possessed in a single property by any other city in the world.

Druid Hill park in Baltimore, of 600 acres, is a very beautiful old wood, acquired by the city in 1860, the original private improvements of which have been enlarged and extended for public use. Buffalo is forming the most complete system of recreation grounds of any city in the United States. It will consist of an inland suburban park of 300 acres, of very quiet rural character, with an ample approach from the center of the city, and parkways 200 ft. wide extending from it in opposite directions, one to a promenade overlooking Lake Erie, the other to a parade ground and a garden on the opposite side of the town. There is a fine natural growth of trees in the main park, a lake of 46 acres has been formed, and several miles of fair macadamized roads and walks constructed, together with various suitable buildings. The work was begun in 1871, and has been advanced very steadily and economically. The aggregate area of ground occupied, including the parkways, is 530 acres.

Chicago is situated in a region most unfavorable to parks, and should she ever have any that are deserving the name, it will be because of a persistent wisdom of administration and a scientific skill as well as art in the constant management of those which she is setting about, such as has been nowhere else applied to a similar purpose. The grounds appropriated are flat, poor in soil, and devoid of desirable natural growth, or, except two which look upon Lake Michigan, of any natural features of interest. In one it is proposed to transform a series of marshes partly overflowed by high water of the lake into lagoons, the quiet water surface of which is designed to take the place ordinarily given to lawns in sylvan landscapes; this, if the idea is consistently carried out, will be unique and interesting. The Chicago park system contains nearly 1,900 acres of land in six parks of an average extent of 250 acres each, three in one chain, and all with one exception connected by parkways. About 20 m[iles] of parkway, from 200 to 250 ft. wide, has been laid out (in the city and suburbs), nearly half of which is already provided with good macadamized or concrete roads and well planted.

St. Louis now controls 2,100 acres of lands held for recreation grounds, of which about 100 are in place parks, the greater part improved and in use, and the remainder suitable for parks proper, the smallest field being of 180 acres and the largest of 1,350. Of the latter, one only, Tower Grove park, containing 277 acres, is yet at all adapted to use. A parkway 120 ft. wide and 12 m[iles] long is under construction.

Cincinnati has a little over 400 acres of public recreation

ground, 207 being in Eden park, which lies on undulating ground commanding fine distant views, and 168 in Burnett wood, which has a similar surface with a fine growth of indigenous trees. There will be about 3 m[iles] of pleasure road in each. Cincinnati possesses in Spring Grove cemetery the best example in the world, probably, of landscape gardening applied to a burial place; and her parks are likely to be improved with the same taste and skill.

San Francisco holds 1,100 acres of land for recreation grounds, of which over 1,000 acres is in one body, called the Golden Gate park. This borders on the ocean, and is very bleak and partly covered with drift sand; no trees grow upon it except in an extremely dwarfed and distorted form, and turf can only be maintained by profuse artificial watering; but wherever shelter, fertility, and sufficient root moisture can be secured, a low, southern, almost subtropical vegetation may be maintained throughout the year, of striking luxuriance and beauty. Experiments in arresting the sand and forming a screen of foliage on the shore have been made with promising success. If steadily, boldly, and generously pursued, with a cautious humoring of the design to the unique natural conditions, and skillful adaptation of available means, a pleasure ground not at all park-like, but strikingly original and highly attractive, may be expected. Nearly 7 m[iles] of carriage road has already been formed on the ground, and it is much used. A parkway stretching 3 m[iles] along the shore is provided for, the reservation for it ranging from 200 to 400 ft. in breadth.

NOTES

1. Hippolyte Adolphe Taine (1828–93), French historian and literary critic, *A Tour through the Pyrenees* (1855), translated into English in 1874.

2. Joseph Mallord William Turner (1775–1851), the most famous of English landscape painters.

3. William Robinson (1838–1935), Irish journalist and gardener, published

The Parks, Promenades, and Gardens of Paris in 1869; Jean-Charles-Adolphe Alphand (1871–91), a French civil engineer in charge of improving Paris parks during the 1850s, published *Les promenades de Paris* between 1867 and 1873.

4. On Joseph Paxton, see Document 1, n. 5.

5. Count Rumford was born William Thompson (1753–1814) in Woburn, Massachusetts, but because of Loyalist sympathies he fled to England and in 1785 moved to Bavaria, where as Minister of War he established the Englischer Garten in 1789 for soldier rest and recreation. Soon, however, under the design direction of landscape gardener Friedrich Ludwig von Sckell (1754–1823), the garden was reconceived as a public park.

6. In 1873 New York sculptor Emma Stebbins (1815–82) unveiled her "Angel of the Waters" symbolizing the healing powers of Jerusalem's Pool of Bethesda. It is now popularly known as Bethesda Fountain.

FIFTEEN

A Consideration of the Justifying Value of a Public Park

(1881)

The worth of a park does not lie in the market value of its land, Olm-sted says, not for the first or last time, but in how well it serves the public over the long term, which cannot be measured monetarily, even though cost is inevitably at issue. Political administrations and park superintendents come and go, sometimes undoing their predecessors' work, so the public is never sure if park appropriations are wisely spent. This is problem number one.

Problem number two is that despite growing popular demand across Europe and the United States—a "park movement," Olm-sted calls it—the public is uncertain about what a park should be other than a generically vague "ground appropriated to public recre-ation." But there is no agreement about what that term means, and he points out that facilities other than, or opposed to, "public recreation" are found in most parks anyway. How they are actually used varies widely. No wonder people are confused.

To end confusion, then, it must be made perfectly clear to everyone exactly what a park is. If twenty-five years ago "I was right in say-ing that . . . the leading idea popularly attached to the word [park] . . . was one of certain influences of scenery—soothing and reposeful influences," then it is proper for him to contend, he thinks, that the growing attraction to natural scenery he sees everywhere around him is au fond "a self-preserving instinct of civilization" in the face of the "great enlargements of towns and development of urban habits" in an age, quoting John Ruskin now, "in which we grow more and more artificial day by day."

The purpose of a park is therefore to offer all urban dwellers "the contemplation of beauty in natural scenery"—as opposed to nature itself—artfully arranged by a landscape designer, Olmsted insists (for after all, only the privileged could afford to visit the country) scenery he believes will alleviate "vital exhaustion," "nervous irritation," "constitutional depression," "excessive materialism," "loss of faith and lowness of spirit."

This recurring theme in Olmsted's mature writings, appearing in other documents in this volume, is the primary motivation behind his design philosophy: city life offers great advantages, opportunities, and pleasures, to be sure, but it also has serious "drawbacks"—his word—of which those listed above are only representative. The extent to which his parks ameliorated those drawbacks, as he believed they did, was also the extent to which people lived happier, healthier, saner, and more productive lives. Parks are morally, spiritually, and physically therapeutic, he might have said, and badly needed right now, hence the urgency with which he makes his case.

Originally a lecture to the American Social Science Association meeting at Saratoga, New York, in September 1880, and published as "The Justifying Value of a Public Park," Journal of Social Science, *12 (December 1880), this text with Olmsted's introduction and footnotes added is taken from his pamphlet,* A Consideration of the Justifying Value of a Public Park *(1881).*

Our large town parks are public trusts, so loosely defined as to fix no clear limits to the use which may be legitimately or honorably made of the lands, materials, funds, or official "influence," which belong to them. The most essential duty under them may be neglected without wreck of character or sense of shame. To say as to any point in question of their management "it is a matter of taste," generally means that every trustee is as to that point a law unto himself. This paper, which touches the question of a possible basis of stricter accountability, has been printed in the Journal of the American Social Science Association, but with such errors, owing to a miscarriage of proofs, that I wish to offer corrected copies to those having a special interest in the topic discussed. The feeling which has lately been evinced against plans urged by able and worthy men for subverting the most important features of the Central Park of New York by buildings, roads, walks, and decorative garden-work suitable to a world's fair ground, and a growing dislike shown elsewhere to the introduction of objects and methods of decoration in public grounds thought to be incongruous with their character, may be hoped to indicate a ripening of public opinion favorable to the ends of the paper.

A bill has just been introduced in the Legislature of New York by Senator Astor, entitled "An Act to Define and Limit the Uses of Public Parks,"[1] which declares that all properties so classed under the laws of the State, when exceeding 100 acres in extent, "are intended and shall be appropriated for the recreation of the people by means of their rural, sylvan, and natural scenery and character," that they must be used and managed in accordance with this definition and that "no ground in them shall be appropriated or used in such a manner as to lessen their value and advantages for such recreation."

A striking illustration of the equivocal use which prevails of the word park and of the harm liable to result from it, has recently occurred. Lord Dufferin, deploring the destruction of the appropriate scenery of Niagara Falls, and seeking means to arrest it and restore a natural aspect to the shores, suggested a scheme for what he, unfortunately, though with strict propriety, termed an international park.[2] It is a serious obstacle to the purpose which he had in view, that under this term few seem to suppose that anything can be intended which does not involve costly gardening "decoration" which would be simply savage.

F.L.O.

The Justifying Value of a Public Park

After the Paper now to be read had been mainly prepared I was advised of a wish that it might lead on to a discussion of the subject of parks at low cost for small towns. The topic which I had adopted being a more comprehensive one, I will introduce it by a few observations, showing how the question of cost for parks of any class, for towns large or small, cannot well be discussed independently of it.

The cost of a park depends on two considerations back of economy of management; back, also, of a plan as commonly understood: the first is the use intended to be made of it, or the general aims of the undertaking; the second, the degree in which the site to be improved is adapted to these aims. As to the first, it is liable to be overlooked that the aims of a park may be so low that the result will be of less value than no park at all. This has been proved over and over again. As to adaptation of site, it is also liable to be forgotten that a hundred acres of land in one situation may be turned, at a given cost, into a more useful park than two hundred in another; and that two hundred acres of land, of one sort, may be prepared for a given use, of a given population, at less cost than one hundred of another sort.

These considerations being recognized, the special perplexity of park business will be understood to lie in the fact that, whatever determinations as to use you set out with, whatever aims control your choice of site and your plan of improvements; whatever rules for economy you fix upon, you have no assurance in law, custom or public common sense, that they will not soon be thrown overboard. This, again, being understood, it will not be difficult to realize that the great danger to be guarded against in setting about a park, is one which is commonly disguised under the phrase, "practical business tact," or "practical common-sense," meaning a habit of mind, cultivated in commercial life, of judging values by the market estimate. What answers to the market estimate, in park values, is commonly a guess as to what the public will think of the results of a proposed operation at a time when these results, although the operation shall be apparently complete, are yet immature, provisional and tentative; and, as in this condition, they will be regarded from the point of view, not of mental relaxation, but of commercial competition. Under these circumstances, most important elements of value are liable to be wholly disregarded.

For example, in any well-designed park-work, the character of each of several parts is largely determined with a motive (over and above any that appears in the work as seen by itself) of enhancing the value of all other parts, and of gaining enhancement of value by the character to be given all other parts. Again, much the larger share of the value to be ultimately earned by the park, depends on the gradual merging together of elements of value originally detached, and which, as seen in this detached condition (as they must be for years after work has apparently ceased with reference to them), show nothing, and to most minds, suggest nothing of the value which they potentially possess.

These, I think, are two plain reasons, but as it happens to apply more directly to my main purpose, I should like to refer also to another embarrassment of the ordinary pleasure-seeker's judgment, which is not so plain. I may, indeed, be excused for doubting if, in this scientific audience, there are many who suspect the degree in which considerations of stability and endurance enter into any sound estimate of the value of park-work, or who realize in what manner these elements of value may be represented in objects which, to the mind seeking relaxation, exhibit qualities of an entirely different character; objects of little more apparent stability than the maize in the farmer's field, which next month is to be cleared of it, and plowed over for a spring sowing of oats. So few are prepared to accept what is sound in this respect and it has so much to do with the question, what it is worthwhile for a small but promising town to undertake in a park, and of what is low cost with reference to it, that I beg to offer a little evidence bearing on the point.

It is more than two hundred years since Mr. Pepys wrote of going in his new coach to the King's Park, and of the "innumerable appearance of gallants," which he there found, sauntering among the trees.[3] Of those trees it is possible that some have not yet succumbed to the acrid atmosphere of London. It is certain that many held their own long enough, and were enough valued, to preserve the general outlines and surface of the park against all suggestions of change, and thus indirectly to influence the leading lines of miles of streets, and establish the position of later park plantings, of which we now have the result. What had then been done, determines where today shade shall be found, where prospects screened or opened, where millions of men and women are yet to direct their steps. Mr. Pepys's road is still in use, and not many years ago it was plainly to be seen where its grade was affected, its breadth contracted, and its course deflected, out of respect to a single tree which he probably saw as a sapling, the trunk and roots of which had grown into it. Of most of the bridges, conduits, markets, and landing-places of London of that period, only curious fragments remain. The King's Park was never as much, or as well used as it is at present, and for the purposes of its most important use, has few substantial advantages or disadvantages not to be traced to determinations formed long, long ago; when London, in comparison with its present state, was a very small town.

In Paris, the series of groves and greens which lie between the ruins of the Tuileries and the long-since leveled gate toward the Woods of Boulogne had its beginning as far back, at least, as the sixteenth century, when, as we now reckon, Paris, also, was a small town; and no motive has had more weight in determining the plan of the great town growing from it, than that of sparing and providing for the extension and uninterrupted use of these grounds.

The present town park of Dijon was laid out by Le Nôtre before these waters of Saratoga had been tasted by a white man, and its plan is as different from any modern park as the personal costume of that day differs from that we are wearing. But, visiting it not long since, I found the town forester following orders which Le Nôtre had given, and the ground better realizing the pictures which must have been in his mind, than it could possibly have done while he lived.[4] The roads, walks, seats; the verdant carpets, the leafy vistas—in none of these had the original work lost value. Never before were they as well adapted to their designed use, or worth as much for it. Where is the public building of the same date, of which, as a town property, the same can be said?

Most old, large towns would supply some like evidence; there are woody resorts in Rome which have been woody resorts from the time of the Cæsars. The Mount of Olives still serves as a place of retreat from the confinement and bustle of

the streets of Jerusalem, and its present groves are believed to
have sprung from the roots of trees planted centuries before
the summer days when the humble friends of a certain unpractical Jew were apt to look for him among the afternoon strollers
under their shade.[5]

There is no people in the world who would take more honest and respectable pride and satisfaction in having their work
done with a view to considerations of intrinsic and lasting value
than our own; but it is at present impossible that the impression
we casually form of our inceptive park-work shall take fairly
into account its substantial merits or short-comings. Parks, of
all things, should not be taken hold of as frontier expedients.
Makeshift, temporizing, catch-penny work upon them is always
extravagant work. The men hitherto more directly in trust of
our parks have not been specially prone to the trading view of
them. Though raw in respect to park service, they have usually
been high-minded servants of the public. But they have been
constrained by public opinion to waste much of what their free
judgment would secure, and there is but one way in which the
difficulty can be got over. It is by bringing public opinion itself
to take a larger interest in the lasting conditions of accruing
value in a park; and experience suggests that this is of even
more importance, and of greater difficulty, in small towns, and
in regard to parks for moderate use, than with respect to undertakings the magnitude and costliness of which is better fitted
to affect the imagination in this respect.

One of the chemists engaged in the discussion of this
Association on the subject of the Adulterations of Food, the
other night, said that all were agreed that everything should
be known in the market by its own name: that if we wanted
glucose we should not have to take it with the name of sugar;
if oleomargarine, not as butter. There is a difficulty in discussing questions of cost and value in parks, lying in the fact that

the public is so far from a common understanding of what the unadulterated substance of a park may be. If I now proceed upon my own notion in this respect, I may be met, as a dealer once told me that he had been by a young housekeeper who complained that if she left the stuff which he sold her for milk to stand a little while "a nasty yellow scum rose on it." "So it always does, madam, on good milk." "Never, sir," she rejoined, "never, on what I call milk."

I have lately known the word "park" applied to the protecting belt of a reservoir, to a fish-pond, a sea beach, and a jail yard; to scores of things which have the least possible public interest in common. I have seen a low rocky shore having what I regard as park-value beyond estimate, in tints, lights and shadows and reflections of translucent and opaque foliage over rippling water, and full of poetic mystery—of beauty such as no painter can render. I have seen such a shore so changed that the water lay dead upon a wall of raw stone, capped by an inclined plane of turf; all possible architectural beauty lost through meaningless meanderings; all value which might have been in a simple breadth of turf, destroyed by pinning it down with prim pegs of living spruce and arbor vitae. And this result I have heard praised as park-like.

Therefore, I had begun my paper (which I now reach) with some observations on this point, recalling the fact that while the few public properties which had the name of park with us, twenty-five years ago, did not differ from others known as greens, commons, or yards; yet the word had a meaning by no other so well given. Scores of times I have heard plain country people, Northern and Southern, Eastern and Western, describe something they had seen as "park-like," or "pretty as a park," or as "a perfect natural park." It might be Blue Ridge table-lands, oak openings further west, mesquite-grass prairies beyond the Trinity, or passages of the Genesee Flats or Connecticut Bottoms. What did the word mean? Nothing in the least practical. It reported nothing of the soil, of the water-power, of quarries or quartz lodes. It told of a certain influence of *conditions solely of scenery*—soothing and reposeful influences. If we trace back this use of the word, it will carry us to the immigrations of the early part of the seventeenth century, before the replanting of English parks under the urgings of Evelyn, the Royal Society and the Admiralty, when there were generally broader spaces of greensward within them, and yet more of spacious seclusion from all without than even at present.[6]

I beg that this significance of the word may be kept in mind a little while.

Twenty-five years ago we had no parks, park-like or otherwise, which might not better have been called something else. Since then a class of works so called has been undertaken which, to begin with, are at least spacious, and which hold possibilities of all park-like qualities. Upon twenty of these works in progress, there has been thus far expended upwards of forty millions of dollars—well nigh if not fully fifty millions—and this figure does not tell the whole story of cost, as I will later show. Considering that in none of the towns making this outlay the necessity of a park was a little while ago at all felt, a remarkable progress of public demand is thus manifested. It will be found the more remarkable when it is considered that, in all Europe, but one notable public park had been laid out in the first half of this century; that this was formed on ground previously a royal hunting park, not by the government of the town, not by taxing the town, and not with an eye single to the town's advantage.[7] But to see the full significance of the fact it is further necessary to consider that within the same period, since 1850, as many parks have been laid out for the people of large towns in Europe as with us, and that the area which has been for the first time legally and definitely appropriated to that end is larger there than here. What has been secured for London alone is of greater extent than all the town parks of America together.* At the same time there has been a radical change in the management of many of the old parks.

Allow me to use the term *park movement*, with reference to what has thus recently occurred on both continents. With us, it dates from Mr. Downing's writings on the subject in 1849.[8] But these could not have obtained the public attention they did, nor have proved the seed of so large a harvest, but for their timeliness, and a condition of expectancy in the soil upon which they fell.

Our first act of park legislation was in 1851. In 1853, the first Commissioners for the Central Park entered upon their duties. It was only in the latter year that some ill-considered steps were taken toward supplying Paris with its first public park. It was not till 1855 that Mr. Alphand came from Bordeaux, and gave the work its final form and impetus. A little earlier, three small park undertakings had been entered upon in England, the leading one under the direction of Paxton, afterwards Sir Joseph. I know of none in Germany, Italy or Belgium; but a few years afterward, I saw in each of these countries evidence that, about the same time, planting and gardening for the public benefit had taken new life.[9]

Parks have plainly not come as the direct result of any of the great inventions or discoveries of the century. They are not, with us, simply an improvement on what we had before, growing out of a general advance of the arts applicable to them. It is not evident that the movement was taken up in any country from any other, however it may have been influenced or accelerated. It did not run like a fashion. It would seem rather

---

*Chiefly in recent action in respect to Epping Forest. [The forest was purchased in 1878 by the city of London—R.T.]

to have been a common, spontaneous movement of that sort which we conveniently refer to the "Genius of Civilization."

I do not take this way of disposing of the question of its origin, impulse and aim, which I will discuss later. I wish here only that the reflection may be made that a wide-spread popular movement is not, naturally, all at once perfectly clear-headed, coherent and perspicuous in its demands. In other words, it is hardly to be supposed that the popular demand represented in parks has yet taken the fully mature, self-conscious form of thoroughly-reasoned purposes and principles, and has insisted on an accurate embodiment of them in the works ordered. It is more reasonable to assume that it has not.

I wish to present this assumption in a practical form. Let me suppose that a man has become possessed, near a town, of adjoining properties comprising one or two farms, with marsh land, wood-land, pastures, mill-pond, quarry and brickyard. It is crossed by roads, upon which there is some pleasure-driving; the pond is used for skating, the hill-sides for coasting, the pastures for kite-flying, base ball and target-firing; snipe are shot in the marshes, rabbits trapped in the woods. There are neglected private properties so used for recreation by the public near most of our towns. Now, suppose that the man dies, leaving an infant heir; twenty years afterwards the heir dies, and the entire property is to come by will to the town on condition that the town spends half a million dollars to make it a park. Suppose the old roads are improved and furnished with sidewalks and shade trees; the brickyard fitted for a parade ground, the marsh for a rifle range; and that the quarry, with masonry and gates added, becomes a town reservoir. Part of the ground is taken for a cemetery; a statue of the former owner is set on the highest hill; a museum and public library take the place of the homestead; an armory is provided, a hospital, poor-house, high school, conservatory, camera-obscura, prospect tower, botanic and zoological garden, archery, lawn-tennis and croquet-grounds, billiard-house, skating-rink, racket court, ten-pin alley, riding-school, Turkish bath, mineral springs, restaurants, pagodas, pavilions, and a mall, terrace and concert garden. Suppose that the town has spent its half million, several times over, in these things, and that the courts can have found reason (I know not how) to decide that the condition of the bequest has been complied with. Suppose that a due part of all the town outlay in the premises has been set down in the town books to old accounts, so far as applicable, as to account of waterworks, street improvements, schools, hospitals, and so on; and that, after all, there is found something which must be charged under the new head of "parks."

Now, suppose that a question is raised whether this expenditure has been made in good faith, with reference to the proper objects and distinctive value of a park, and has been judiciously and economically directed, and that a popular judgment (not a technical court judgment) is asked upon this issue, what would be the result? Few men would have a sufficiently clear idea of the objects and the conditions of value of a park to form a judgment; those who had would differ widely in their ideas, and most of the more judicial and properly leading minds would hold such ideas as they had with enough of doubt to make them slow either to fully support or decisively condemn those responsible. This, unquestionably, would be the case much more than it would be in regard to any other large matter of town expenditure.

Let this unreadiness of popular judgment be considered for a moment in connection with certain faults in our methods of public business. This Association needs no explanation of them. It is sufficient to say that changes in the fundamental laws of our parks, in the boards governing them, or in the bodies governing these boards, occur annually. A certain weakness of human nature, usually exhibited in some degree after such changes, is expressed in the proverb, "New brooms sweep clean." There is generally a disposition with each new man in office to find an *ex post facto* reason for his being there. In the absence of any restraint, such as lies with reference to other public works, in a definite and well established public understanding of what is to be accomplished, there is nothing to prevent a novice in a park board, or in the office of mayor, comptroller or member of city council, from aiming to make changes of organization, and to force a course of operations adapted to discountenance some of the aims of work previously done, and with this motive to lay waste what funds under the same trust had before been used to obtain. There have already been such cases. In one a large outlay has been made, and the money is claimed to have been honestly used, with the unquestionable intent of nullifying what at least half a million dollars had been previously spent to gain. It has happened more than once that plans have been adopted, work advanced under them, then thrown aside by new men, new plans adopted, and, after some years, these in their turn abandoned, and the original plans resumed. The change of purpose in such cases will have been deliberate and intentional. But changes as great and as wasteful are more likely to occur through the passing of park works under the control, direct or indirect, of men who, through simple ignorance, forgetfulness, or indifference to such aims as have before-time been had in view, let a large share of the value that has been once secured slip through their fingers.[*]

---

[*] In the short history of one of our parks, a change in the immediate direction of the plantations has occurred not less than six times, and in each case the new appointee has shown a disposition to upset the methods of his predecessor, and twice, at least, such changes have been thus accomplished, amounting to serious changes of general design. Upon another park, for which I am supposed to have some responsibility, the resident professional superintendent was changed five times in three years. [It is unclear to which parks Olmsted is referring—R.T.]

But now, if I have suggested the special hazard under our special political customs, of the lack of a well-understood central and distinctive purpose in the management of these large town properties, I wish to add that, back of this, but closely united with it, there is a more positive and a deeper seated difficulty. Briefly, it is the difficulty of dispossessing the mind of ideas which are associated with an object when, through lapse of time and change of circumstances, the nature of that object and its conditions of value have been radically changed. This difficulty, in individual experience, is not an uncommon one, but, with regard to this matter of parks, it is largely a transmitted experience, and I can think of no quite parallel case by which to explain it.

Its full elucidation would carry me into a history of a class of property unknown with us, but which, throughout the Old World, has for many centuries been of importance. Its value has been in two kinds; forest materials and game. It has been managed with reference to each, systematically, by classes of men specially trained to their duties, and since no other equally extensive property has had so much of what is called sentimental value, as to none has service been so much handed down from father to son, and as to none have traditional ideas been more persistent. There are many thousands of such properties, of which the character and methods of management and use have changed little since the period of the Crusades. In England they are mostly called parks, and there the changes have been greater, as a rule, than on the continent. Still, in some essential particulars, the sentiment of conservatism with regard to them, not only with their owners for the time being, but with the people at large, is very strong.

Some few of these old forest and hunting properties, once belonging to kings, and situated near growing towns, came after a time to be used by the townspeople for their own amusement, much as neglected private lands near our towns often are now. Gradually such use of them established something like a vested right, and so, by very slow degrees, from kings' parks, they came to be regarded as at least pseudo-public parks.

I say by slow degrees. A single fact will indicate how slowly, and suggest, with reference to their management, how imperfectly. That great park which we know so well for its Merry Wives' recreations; with its antlered stags in waiting for royal hunting parties; its phantom huntsman; its foresters' saw-pits with children hiding in them; is now surrounded with towns and villages, and is an important feature of suburban London. It is nearer to the West End than Long Branch to the Battery, and is accessible by boats and three lines of railway, running cheap excursion trains. It is an object not simply of town but of national pride. In its use and value as a public park, a thousand times more than anything else, lies the proper concern of government with it. Yet, as late as four years ago, the only allusion to it as a public park, in the stated report to Parliament of the commissioner in charge, was contained in two lines, in which the extent to which it is used for public recreation is mentioned as a reason why the commissioner cannot make a better return from the sale of timber and other forest products, the letting of pasturage, and so on. It will be remembered, also, that yet every year a somewhat ridiculous public ceremony is performed in this park, called a hunt with the royal hounds, in which a venerable stag is turned out of a wagon and set after with great outcry, but with special precautions against his being seriously hurt when overtaken. These two facts suggest the degree in which the ancient theory of the use, value and economic management of this property has had influence with those in charge of it down to this very day.[10]

Hyde Park, which may be considered as more particularly the progenitor of modern public parks, is now in the midst of London (the town having grown around it since the time of Mr. Pepys). But Hyde Park was classed with Windsor and under the same management when I first visited it, only thirty years ago. I believe that it was transferred to a special commission, appointed, not by the local authorities, but by Parliament, at the time of the first International Exhibition, but, though the deer and kennels have been removed, some of the rangers or gamekeepers are still living upon it and there is an attractive private residence in the middle of it, with stables and gardens, occupied by a gentleman who represents the office corresponding for this park to that held for Woodstock Chase by The Loyal Lee in the seventeenth century, as described by Scott.[11]

One of the two great parks of Paris was an imperial forest and hunting ground as late as 1850, the other still later. The public park of Florence was the grand duke's private property until the last revolution. The greater part of it is a dense wood, managed on the principles of economic forestry. The park of Munich, which people say was laid out by Rumford as a sanitary measure, is of the same character; it is still stocked with deer for the king's hunting, and its resident superintendent is a gamekeeper, as his father was before him. I saw him inspecting the repair of roads after a storm; he carried a gun in his hand, and was followed by aged hounds.

The names of the parks of Berlin and Stockholm indicate what they have been; each, in a different language, meaning a place for keeping deer.[12]

I could show from facts of personal observation how, much more than it is easy to realize, the present condition of even the most changed of these old parks has thus been determined by motives as foreign to the forms of recreation in which their public value now lies, as the motives of a cotton mill are from those of a cathedral, and how the customs of management and of use now prevailing, have been *perforce*, largely fitted to these traditional motives. Also, how some of these customs, foreign in every sense to us, have lately emigrated and are crowding out that which is natural to us and belongs to our common sense.

I hope I have said enough to make it plain that during the long process through which the present ideas of the value of a park were gaining upon those which they have at last mainly superseded, the public demands, expectations and standards of value in respect to these grounds have been mixed, inconsistent and contradictory. This being realized, it will next be evident that the inherited and transmitted idea of a public park has been one of a body of land held for no clearly defined purposes, which is equivalent to saying, held for purposes always remaining to be determined. It also follows that the inherited and transmitted idea of the responsibilities of those in immediate direction of these parks has been a corresponding one, and that they have been little subject to popular criticism based on fixed, just and sound principles applicable to public recreation.

Lastly, it follows that the idea fitted to the word park in our minds, when, twenty-two years ago, we began, here in America, dealing with the subject—having come to us much less from anything that we had seen, or from any dictionary, than through that marvelous process of race nutrition which gives every man his native tongue—was an idea largely made up of irreconcilable impressions.

The fact remains to be more distinctly emphasized, that it is only through the use of this word of vague and inconstant significance that any limit has been placed upon the purposes to which public money, appropriated to parks, shall be applied. The simplest statement of purpose that courts would unhesitatingly accept or public opinion stand agreed upon, and, even then, not as a complete statement, but only as true so far as it goes, would be this: "A public park is a ground appropriated to public recreation."

Observe, then, that most of the public properties known as parks contain provisions for other purposes than recreation, and even opposed to recreation. Again, waiving the question how far these are legitimate parts of them, observe that recreation is so broad a term, and means so much more to some than to others, that to devote public funds to recreation is little less than to give a free rein to the personal tastes, whims and speculations of those entrusted with the administration of them.

We must fall back on usage. What, then, does usage prescribe?

In one European public park we find a race-course, with its grandstand, stables, pool-room and betting ring; in another, popular diversions of the class which we elsewhere look to Barnum to provide.[13] In one there is a theater with ballet-dancing; in another, soldiers firing field-pieces at a target, with a detail of cavalry to keep the public at a distance.

Attempts to introduce like provisions in several of our American parks have been resisted under the personal conviction that they would tend to subvert their more important purpose. In some of our parks, nevertheless, arrangements have been made for various games; concerts and shows have been admitted; there have been military parades; and it is impossible to find any line of principle between many favored and neglected propositions.

Usage, therefore, in this respect, decides nothing.

Asking what usage prescribes as to the simpler forms of recreation, we shall find that one ground, classed among public parks, consists of dense woods, with a few nearly straight roads through it, while others have open, pastoral landscapes, with circuitous drives, rides and walks; that the interest of one centers in an extremely artificial display of exotics and bedding plants, while another bids fair to be equally distinguished for its fountains, monuments, statues and other means of recreation in stone, concrete and bronze. Yet another is so natural and unsophisticated you can hardly use it in dry weather without choking with dust, or in wet weather without wading in mud.

Again, usage determines nothing.

What this laxity leaves us liable to, and how much may be safely presumed upon the public's confusion of mind, is shown by the fact that in one case, when local opposition was found to be inconveniently strong against the location of a small-pox hospital anywhere else, the difficulty was overcome by placing it in the midst of a park.[14]

I have known orders given in a park, and carried out at considerable expense, the motive and origin of which could be explained only by reference to an idiosyncracy of that class which, to some men, causes eggs or strawberries to be loathsome, and makes cats or curs objects of an irresistible, undefined terror.

The choice of site of most of our parks, and the definition of their boundaries, have been made without the slightest regard for any object of a park, except, possibly, that of securing an air space. Even as with a view to air spaces the locality, in some cases, is nearly the last that should have been selected, and the area taken much broader and greatly more costly than necessary to the purpose.

No one can for a moment suppose that the state of public opinion exemplified in the facts which have been stated, is one favorable to securing what the public wants most in a park, or, if at all, to its obtaining it at reasonable cost.

But the true state of the case will not be fully realized without taking into account certain elements of possible cost of a park which have hitherto had little general consideration.

A town is built to meet the demands of commerce—of commerce in a large sense. As these demands successively arise and their pressure is felt, street is added to street, building to building; railroads, canals and docks are introduced; sewers, water-pipes and gas-lights are pushed out here and there, and thus, not only the extent but the direction of the town's growth is in a large degree controlled by natural laws, the acts of government following much more than leading, directing, or resisting, the movements of supply and demand.

It will be evident that this element of security against injudicious municipal enterprise applies not at all to our great park trusts. A town does not grow into parks, as it does, by the law of its existence, into buildings and streets; on the contrary, when a great body of land is used as a park in the borders of a town, it will be a serious disturbance of what would otherwise be the natural development of the town.

See, for illustration, how Hyde Park has elbowed out the streets of London. See how the street system of Paris has been kept from its natural development because Catherine de Medici turned a tile-yard into a pleasaunce;[15] or, to take the nearest example, see how the park of New York brings suddenly to a full stop more than ninety streets, which would otherwise constitute forty thoroughfares of commerce, at the very center of an island which may yet be the most important point of commercial transfer in the world.

That when land is to be bought, or even accepted as a free gift, by a town for a park, its adaptation to the purpose of a park should first of all be considered, and that then none and no more should be taken than is necessary, or at least desirable, for that purpose, will be conceded.

A little consideration, then, will satisfy the Association that a large proportion of the objects which are more or less provided for in our parks might, at less cost and greater value, be provided for in a series of smaller grounds placed as nearly as practicable at regular distances through or around the town.

The argument is briefly this: That such scattered, smaller grounds would be more accessible; would less embarrass other interests of the town; would less interfere with its natural development; would involve less contention with local jealousies and consequent wasteful compromises; and would, on the whole, be less costly.

There is, however, an important element of value in most parks which could not be well provided for in such small local grounds. What is desirable in this respect is a long, unbroken, spacious drive, ride and walk, offering suitable conditions to a large number of people to obtain together moderate exercise in the open air, with such other conditions favorable to gaiety as can be conveniently associated with them.

To a great many persons, perhaps the most of those who have much active influence upon the management of parks, the value of a park lies mainly, and to some it would seem exclusively, in the advantages it offers in this respect. Yet, as affecting these advantages, it will be obvious that the larger part of every park is waste land. Besides which, regarding this object from a point of view commonly taken by many intelligent people, and taking it up as a professional problem, it is little less than absurd to say that it might not be much better met, and at less cost, than it ever has been on any park, new or old. Indeed, from the accounts we have, it would seem that in some southern towns it has been so taken up, not in as clear-headed and bold a way as it might have been, but sufficiently to demonstrate that a result is easily attainable [and] better adapted to the end in view than any we have hoped to attain in our parks.

An arrangement of the general type of the Spanish alamedas, developed with anything like the enterprise and outlay which we have been willing to put on our parks, would, for the purpose in question, be more commodious; its use simpler and more easily and efficiently regulated; there would be less liability to accidents upon it; it might be more effectively decorated, and thus in every way be made to present a gayer, more brilliant and festive scene.

Such an affair, without making half as great a break in our towns as, sooner or later, their parks will, would open a splendid field for the great and admirable enterprise, erudition and skill, which are now given to decorative gardening—a perfectly suitable field for it, which a park seldom offers. It would give fine show room for all the novelties on the market, and would allow a fine scenic arrangement to be made of the superb tropical and subtropical beauties which are just now in fashion, and the best use possible of floral ribbons, embroidery and gew-gaudry which, after doing their worst to degrade and destroy art in landscape gardening, are now, if not wholly going out of fashion, I am glad to say, tending to lapse more nearly to their proper places.

With these advantages, it would cost not nearly as much for land, for construction, for maintenance, or in readjustment of the natural plan of a town.

But, plainly, it is not for this that the "Genius of Civilization" has called for these broad spaces termed parks. In what, then, shall we find the originating impulse, aim and justification of the park-movement?

May we not, perhaps, wisely seek an answer to this question by considering whether there are any other movements of our times with which the park-movement, as we know it, may seem to be related?

If I was right in saying that twenty-five years ago, when we began discussing parks as something to be made for us, the leading idea popularly attached to the word, throughout this country, was one of certain influences of scenery—soothing and reposeful influences—then it is reasonable to suppose that there was something in our motive very closely allied to a social force which, in this same quarter of a century, has had a very remarkable development—a force which has directed the investment of hundreds of millions of private capital in traveling machinery, built up many towns, replenished many treasuries, enriched kingdoms, been a practical matter for statesmanship, and swayed every commercial exchange in the world.

It is open to question whether we care much more than our ancestors did for all manner of beauty of nature; whether we appreciate leaf and flower form and flower color, for instance, more than they. We have a greater variety of flowers; our curiosity about them is more stimulated, our science advanced, we take more interest in them from the point of view of the collector and classifier; they are matters of fashion; we use them more profusely. But there is room for doubt if they act more powerfully upon our sensibilities, and if we make on the whole a more fitting use of them. There can be no like question as to our more general susceptibility to the beauty of clouds, snowy peaks, mountain gorges, forests, meadows and brooks, as we know them in *the broad combining way of scenery*. Even if this doubt should not have weight, it would be much easier to see something akin to regard for scenery in the demand which has led our cities to obtain possession of the broad bodies of land in our parks, than that of interest in the beauty of nature such as may be gratified in a conservatory, a garden, a flower-pot or a posy, saying nothing of natural beauty such as exists even in jewels, furs, fruits, or plumage, or in trees individually regarded and as they grow on the lawn of a cottage.

But now, if we call this force interest in the beauty of natural scenery (to distinguish it from interest in the beauty of nature) we shall find another form of its operation from that evinced by tourists and sojourning seekers of scenery in the more general development of talent in landscape-painting and in the demand for education in landscape-judgment, such as is met by works like those of Ruskin, Taine and Hamerton, of which more are now read by Americans in every year than were all works of similar aims by all the world in a hundred years before we began our first park.[16]

Why this great development of interest in natural landscape and all that pertains to it; to the art of it and the literature of it?

Considering that it has occurred simultaneously with a great enlargement of towns and development of urban habits, is it not reasonable to regard it as a self-preserving instinct of civilization?

Mr. Ruskin may be thought not only unpractical but fanatical, and many of his sayings may be regarded as wild, but that he is inspired by a great and good motive, few will doubt. What is the ruling conviction of his zeal? In his own bitter words, it is that "This is an age in which we grow more and more artificial day by day, and see less and less worthiness in those pleasures which bring with them no marked excitement; in knowledge which affords no opportunity of display."

This is true, though a man ten times more unpractical and fanatical than Mr. Ruskin can be thought to be, had said it; and it is also true, that to all the economical advantages we have gained through modern discoveries and inventions, the great enlargement of the field of commerce, the growth of towns and the spread of town ways of living, there are some grave drawbacks. We may yet understand them so imperfectly that we but little more than veil our ignorance when we talk of what is lost and suffered under the name of "vital exhaustion," "nervous irritation" and "constitutional depression"; when we speak of tendencies, through excessive materialism, to loss of faith and lowness of spirit, by which life is made, to some, questionably worth the living. But that there are actual drawbacks which we thus vaguely indicate to the prosperity of large towns, and that they deduct much from the wealth-producing and tax-bearing capacity of their people, as well as from the wealth-enjoying capacity, there can be no doubt.

The question remains whether the contemplation of beauty in natural scenery is practically of much value in counteracting and alleviating these evils, and whether it is possible, at reasonable cost, to make such beauty available to the daily use of great numbers of townspeople? I do not propose to argue this question. I submit it to the Association as one needing discussion; for if the object of parks is not that thus suggested, I know of none which justifies their cost. On the other hand, if the object of parks is thus indicated, I know of no justification for a great deal that is done with them, and a great deal more that many men are bent on doing. That other objects than the cultivation of beauty of natural scenery may be associated with it economically, in a park, I am not disposed to deny; but that all such other objects should be held strictly subordinate to that, in order to justify the purchase and holding of these large properties, I am inclined to think, cannot be successfully disputed.

I will but add that the problem of a park, as it would appear, under the view which I have aimed to suggest, clear of unfortunate, temporary political necessities, is mainly the reconciliation of adequate beauty of nature in scenery with adequate means in artificial constructions of protecting the conditions of such beauty, and holding it available to the use, in a convenient and orderly way, of those needing it; and in the employment of such means for both purposes, as will make the park steadily gainful of that quality of beauty which comes only with age.

NOTES

1. Olmsted opposed the movement, begun in 1879, to hold a world's fair in Central Park in 1883, fearing construction of buildings and access routes would disfigure it beyond recognition. William Waldorf Astor (1848–1919), estate manager for his father, John Jacob Astor II (1822–90), and state senator at the time, introduced "An Act Restricting the Right to Grant, Use or Occupy the Central Park, in the City of New York, for the Purposes of a Public Fair or Exhibition" that became law in 1881, ending the threat that so worried Olmsted, who here shortens name of the act.

2. Frederick Temple Hamilton-Temple-Blackwood (1826–1902), known as Lord Dufferin, English politician and diplomat, was governor-general of Canada from 1872 to 1878.

3. Samuel Pepys (1633–1703), English naval administrator and Member of Parliament, is best remembered for his diaries chronicling the 1660s first published in 1825. The editors of *The Papers of Frederick Law Olmsted* point out (in v. 3, p. 347, f. 5) that Olmsted's quote is not from Pepys but from John Evelyn (1620–1706), English writer and garden designer, who is also best remembered for his *Diary and Correspondence* (1872). The passage reads: "I went to Hyde Park to take the air, where was his Majesty and an innumerable appearance of gallants and rich coaches."

4. It is not certain that André Le Nôtre (1613–1700), French landscape architect and gardener for Louis XIV, was in fact responsible for designing Parc de la Colombiere.

5. Jesus Christ was the "unpractical Jew."

6. John Evelyn (n. 3 above) was a tireless advocate of reforestation.

7. St. James Park in London's West End was reconfigured in 1826–27 by John Nash (1752–1835), English architect and town planner.

8. Andrew Jackson Downing (1815–52) championed the creation of urban parks in *The Horticulturist*, subtitled *A Journal of Rural Art and Rural Taste*, of which he was founding editor from 1846 until his death.

9. Emperor Napoleon III granted Bois de Boulogne on the western edge of Paris to the city for a public grounds in 1852, charging Baron Georges-

Eugène Haussmann (1809–91), prefect of the Seine, with its development. In 1854, Haussmann appointed Jean-Charles-Adolphe Alphand (1817–91), French military engineer and landscape designer, to plan the park's layout and oversee its construction. For Paxton see Document 1, n. 5.

10. The reference is to Shakespeare's *The Merry Wives of Windsor* (ca. 1597), part of which takes place in Great Park in the city of Windsor, which is five miles farther away from London than the seaside resort, Long Branch, New Jersey, is from Manhattan.

11. In Hyde Park, London, 1851. The reference is to the novel *Woodstock* (1826) by Sir Walter Scott (1771–1832) wherein the "Loyal Lee" is Sir Henry Lee, keeper of the King's Lodge in Woodstock, an actual small town near Oxford.

12. Olmsted refers above to the Bois de Boulogne and Bois de Vincennes in Paris, the Cascine in Florence, the English Garden in Munich, the Thiergarten in Berlin, and the Djurgarden in Stockholm. For Rumford, see Document 14, n. 5.

13. That is, P. T., or Phineas Taylor Barnum (1850–1891), American circus impresario.

14. Mount Royal Park in Montreal, one of the first two parks he designed after the breakup of Olmsted, Vaux, & Company in 1872.

15. Catherine de Médici (1519–1589), wife of Henry II, was responsible for the creation in 1564 of the Tuilleries Garden to which Olmsted refers.

16. Olmsted read and admired John Ruskin (1818–1900), Hippolyte-Adolphe Taine (1828–93), and Philip Gilbert Hamerton (1834–94)—from England, France, and England, respectively—who, among their many accomplishments, were all widely read art critics. The Ruskin quote that follows is from the first volume of *Modern Painters*, published anonymously in 1843.

SIXTEEN

Parks, Parkways, and Pleasure-Grounds
(1895)

In unusually straightforward prose, Olmsted offers what is virtually a primer on landscape architecture, as if he were writing for design students or beginning professionals. He discusses the importance of various kinds of municipal "pleasure-grounds" including outlying nature preserves, but concentrates on what he variously terms "scenic," "rural," or "landscape" parks, which is to say, the urban parks for which he is best known, offering common-sense advice about governance, siting, design, and construction. His essay is packed with useful "tips": why meadow concavity is sometimes preferable to convexity, where to place roadways, when to use perimeter plantings, how to frame vistas within parks and to their exteriors, under what circumstances to permit internal structures, and more.

Perhaps Olmsted's plain style derived from a late discovery that his earlier writing had been somewhat verbose, or perhaps at age seventy-seven, beginning to fail physically and mentally—he knew he was losing his memory by 1895—he wished to make a kind of final, easily comprehensible statement (this was one of his last written works) to a larger-than-usual and different kind of readership, which might explain why he published this essay where he did.

In any event, it could be argued that this document might better introduce than close this volume, given its accessibility. But then again, perhaps it was worth the wait.

Originally published in Engineering Magazine, *9 (May 1895).*

The aggregation of men in great cities practically necessitates the common or public ownership, or control, of streets, sewers, water pipes, and pleasure-grounds. Municipal pleasure-grounds comprise all such public open spaces as are acquired and arranged for the purpose of providing favorable opportunities for healthful recreation in the open air. As there are many modes and means of open-air recreation, so there are many kinds of public pleasure-grounds. The formal promenade or plaza is perhaps the simplest type. Broad gravel-ways well shaded by trees afford pleasant out-of-door halls where crowds may mingle in an easy social life, the value of which is better understood in Southern Europe and in Spanish America than in the United States. Agreeable and numerous open-air nurseries and playgrounds for small children present a more complex, but perhaps more necessary, type of public ground. Very few public open spaces suitably arranged for this special purpose are to be found in American cities, and yet it goes without saying that every crowded neighborhood ought to be provided with a place removed from the paved streets, in which mothers, babies, and small children may find opportunity to rest and sleep and play in the open air. Playgrounds for youths are needed, but these may be further removed from the crowded parts of towns. Public open-air gymnasia have proved valuable in Europe and in Boston. Public flower-gardens are sometimes provided, but these are luxuries, and ought to be opened at the public expense only after the more essential kinds of public grounds have been secured. Promenades, gardens, concert-grounds, out-door halls, nurseries, playgrounds, gymnasia, and gardens may, of course, be combined one with another, as opportunity offers. To properly fulfill their several functions none of them need take out more than a small space from the income-producing area of a town.

There remains another less obvious, but very valuable, source of refreshment for townspeople, which only considerable areas of open space can supply. The well-to-do people of all large towns seek in travel the recreation which comes from change of scene and contemplation of scenery. For those who cannot travel, free admission to the best scenery of their neighborhood is desirable. It is, indeed, necessary, if life is to be more than the meat. Cities are now grown so great that hours are consumed in gaining the "country," and, when the fields are reached, entrance is forbidden. Accordingly it becomes necessary to acquire, for the free use and enjoyment of all, such neighboring fields, woods, pond-sides, river-banks, valleys, or hills as may present, or may be made to present, fine scenery of one type or another. This providing of scenery calls for the separation of large bodies of land from the financially productive area of a town, county, or district; and, conversely, such setting apart of large areas is justifiable only when "scenery" is secured or made obtainable thereby.

Having thus made note of the main purposes of public pleasure-grounds, we pass now to consider (1) Government; (2) Sites and Boundaries; (3) General Plans or Designs; and (4) Construction.

Park Government

The providing and managing of reservations of scenery is the highest function and most difficult task of the commissioners or directors of park works. Public squares, gardens, playgrounds, and promenades may be well or badly constructed, but no questions are likely to arise in connection therewith which are beyond the comprehension of the ordinary man of affairs. If scenic parks, on the other hand, are to be well placed, well bounded, well arranged, and, above all, well preserved, the directors of the work need to be more than ordinary men. Real-estate dealers must necessarily be excluded from the management. Politicians, also, if the work is to run smoothly. The work is not purely executive, like the work of directing sewer-construction or street cleaning, which may best be done by single responsible chiefs. The direction of park works may probably best rest with a small body of cultivated men, public-spirited enough to serve without pay, who should regard themselves and be regarded as a board of trustees, and who, as such, should make it their first duty to hand down unharmed from one generation to the next the treasure of scenery which the city has placed in their care. Public libraries and public art museums are created and managed by boards of trustees. For similar reasons public parks should be similarly governed.

A landscape park requires, more than most works of men, continuity of management. Its perfecting is a slow process. Its directors must thoroughly apprehend the fact that the beauty of its landscape is all that justifies the existence of a large public open space in the midst, or even on the immediate borders, of a town; and they must see to it that each newly-appointed member of the governing body shall be grounded in this truth. Holding to the supreme value of fine scenery, they will take pains to subordinate every necessary construction, and to perfect the essence of the park, which is its landscape, before elaborating details or accessories, such as sculptured gates or gilded fountains, however appropriately or beautifully they may be designed. As trustees of park scenery, they will be especially watchful to prevent injury thereto from the intrusion of incongruous or obtrusive structures, statues, gardens (whether floral, botanic, or zoologic), speedways, or any other instruments of special modes of recreation, however desirable such may be in their proper place. If men can be found to thus serve cities as trustees of scenic or rural parks, they will assuredly be entirely competent to serve at the same time as providers and guardians of those smaller and more numerous urban spaces in which every means of recreation, excepting scenery, may best be provided.

Park Sites and Boundaries

It is much to be desired that newly-created park commissions should be provided at the beginning, by loan or otherwise, with a supply of money sufficient to meet the cost of all probably desirable lands. Purchases or seizures of land should be made as nearly contemporaneously as possible. Before making any purchases, ample time should, however, be taken for investigation, which should be directed both to the study of the scenery of the district in question and to a comparison of land values. The first problem usually is to choose from the lands sufficiently vacant or cheap to be considered: (1) those reasonably accessible and moderately large tracts which are capable of presenting agreeable secluded scenery, and (2) those easily accessible or intervening small tracts which may most cheaply be adapted to serve as local playgrounds or the like. A visit and report from a professional park-designer will prove valuable, even at this earliest stage of operations. Grounds of the local playground class may safely be selected in accordance with considerations of cheapness and a reasonably equitable distribution, but the wise selection of even small landscape parks requires much careful study. It is desirable that a city's parks of this class should present scenery of differing types. It is desirable that the boundaries of each should be so placed as to include all essential elements of the local scenery and to produce the utmost possible seclusion and sense of indefinite extent, as well as to make it possible to build boundary roads or streets upon good lines and fair grades. Public grounds of every class are best bounded by streets; otherwise, there is no means of insuring the desirable fronting of buildings towards the public domain. In spite of a common popular prejudice to the contrary, it will generally be found that concave, rather than convex, portions of the earth's surface are to be preferred for park-sites. If the courses of brooks, streams, or rivers can be included in parks, or in strips of public land connecting park with park or park with town, several advantages will be secured at one stroke. The natural surface-drainage channels will be retained under public control where they belong; they will be surely defended from pollution; their banks will offer agreeable public promenades; while the adjacent boundary roads, one on either hand, will furnish the contiguous building land with an attractive frontage. Where such stream-including strips are broad enough to permit the opening of a distinctively pleasure drive entirely separate from the boundary roads, the ground should be classed as a park. Where the boundary roads are the only roads, the whole strip is properly called a parkway; and this name is retained even when the space between the boundary roads is reduced to lowest terms and becomes nothing more than a shaded green ribbon, devoted perhaps to the separate use of the otherwise dangerous electric cars. In other words, parkways, like parks, may be absolutely formal or strikingly picturesque, according to circumstances. Both will generally be formal when they occupy confined urban spaces bounded by dominating buildings. Both will generally become picturesque as soon as, or wherever, opportunity offers.

After adequate squares and playgrounds, two or three local landscape parks, and the most necessary connecting parkways shall have been provided, it may next be advisable to secure one or more large parks, or even one or more reservations of remoter and wilder lands. In a city of five hundred thousand inhabitants a park of five hundred acres, however judiciously located, is soon so much frequented as necessarily to lose much of its rurality; in other words, much of its special power to refresh and charm. The necessarily broad roads, the numerous footways, the swarms of carriages and people, all call to mind the town, and in a measure offset the good effect of the park scenery. It is then that it becomes advisable to go still further afield, in order to acquire and hold in reserve additional domains of scenery, such as Boston has lately acquired in the Blue Hills and the Middlesex Fells. In selecting such domains, however, no new principles come into play. As in selecting sites for parks, so here it is always to be borne in mind that provision and preservation of scenery is the purpose held in view, and that demarcation of acquired lands is to be determined accordingly.

Park Plans or Designs

To "plan" something means to devise ways of effecting some particular purpose. It has not always been thought necessary to "plan" the various kinds of pleasure-grounds. With no consistent end or purpose in mind, the members of some park commissions attempt to direct from day to day and from year to year such "improvements" as they may from time to time decide upon. That the results of this method of procedure are confused, inadequate, and unimpressive is not to be wondered at.

In order to be able to devise a consistent plan, such as may be followed during a long period of years with surety that the result will be both useful and beautiful, it is necessary, in the first place, to define as accurately as possible the ends or purposes to be achieved. As already remarked, these ends or purposes are as numerous as are the various modes of recreation in the open air. Thus a small tract of harbor-side land at the North End of Boston has been acquired by the park commission, in order to supply the inhabitants of a poor and crowded quarter with a pleasant resting-place overlooking the water, and with opportunities for boating and bathing. Accordingly, the plan provides a formal elevated stone terrace, connecting by a bridge spanning an intervening traffic-street with a double decked pleasure-pier, which in turn forms a breakwater enclosing a little port, the shore of which will be a bathing beach. In the adjacent city of Cambridge a rectangular, level, and street-bounded open space has been ordered to be arranged to serve as a general meeting-place or promenade, a concert-ground, a boys' playground, and an out-door nursery. Accordingly, the adopted plan suggests a centrally-placed building which will serve as a shelter from showers and as a house of public convenience, in which the boys will find lockers and the babies a room of their own, from which also the head keeper of the ground shall be able to command the whole scene. South of the house a broad, but shaded, gravel space will provide room for such crowds as may gather when the band plays on a platform attached to the veranda of the building. Beyond this concert-ground is placed the ball-field, which, because of the impossibility of maintaining good turf, will be of fine gravel firmly compacted. Surrounding the ball-ground and the whole public domain is a broad, formal, and shaded mall. At one end of the central building is found room for a shrub-surrounded playground and sand-court for babies and small children. At the other end of the house is a similarly secluded out-door gymnasium for girls. Lastly, between the administration house and the northern mall and street, there will be found an open lawn, shut off from the malls by banks of shrubbery and surrounded by a path with seats where mothers, nurses, and the public generally may find a pleasant resting-place.

Plans for those larger public domains in which scenery is the main object of pursuit need to be devised with similarly strict attention to the loftier purpose in view. The type of scenery to be preserved or created ought to be that which is developed naturally from the local circumstances of each case. Rocky or steep slopes suggest tangled thickets or forests. Smooth hollows of good soil hint at open or "park-like" scenery. Swamps and an abundant water-supply suggest ponds, pools, or lagoons. If distant views of regions outside the park are likely to be permanently attractive, the beauty thereof may be enhanced by supplying stronger foregrounds; and, conversely, all ugly or town-like surroundings ought, if possible, to be "planted out." The paths and roads of landscape parks are to be regarded simply as instruments by which the scenery is made accessible and enjoyable. They may not be needed at first, but, when the people visiting a park become so numerous that the trampling of their feet destroys the beauty of the ground cover, it becomes necessary to confine them to the use of chosen lines and spots. These lines ought obviously to be determined with careful reference to the most advantageous exhibition of the available scenery. The scenery also should be developed with reference to the views thereof to be obtained from these lines. This point may be illustrated by assuming the simplest possible case—namely, that of a landscape park to be created upon a parallelogram of level prairie. To conceal the formality of the boundaries, as well as to shut out the view of surrounding buildings, an informal "border plantation" will be required. Within this irregular frame or screen the broader the unbroken meadow or field may be, the more restful and impressive will be the landscape. To obtain the broadest and finest views of this central meadow, as well as to avoid shattering its unity, roads and paths should obviously be placed near the edges of the framing woods. In the typical case a "circuit road" results. It is wholly impossible to frame rules for the planning of rural parks; local circumstances ought to guide and govern the designer in every case; but it may be remarked that there are few situations in which the principle of unity will not call for something, at least, of the "border plantation" and something of the "circuit road."

Within large rural parks economy sometimes demands that provision should be made for some of those modes of recreation which small spaces are capable of supplying. Special playgrounds for children, ball or tennis grounds, even formal arrangements such as are most suitable for concert-grounds and decorative gardens, may each and all find place within the rural park, provided they are so devised as not to conflict with or detract from the breadth and quietness of the general landscape. If boating can be provided, a suitable boating-house will be desirable; the same house will serve for the use of skaters in winter. In small parks economy of administration demands that one building should serve all purposes and supply accommodations for boating parties, skaters, tennis-players, ball-players, and all other visitors, as well as administrative offices. In large parks separate buildings serving as restaurants, boat-houses, bathing-houses, and the like may be allowable. It is most important, however, to remember that these buildings, like the roads and paths, are only subsidiary, though necessary, adjuncts to the park scenery; and, consequently, that they should not be placed or designed so as to be obtrusive or conspicuous. Large public buildings, such as museums, concert halls, schools, and the like, may best find place in town streets or squares. They may wisely perhaps be placed near, or facing upon, the park, but to place them within it is simply to defeat the highest service which the park can render the community. Large and conspicuous buildings, as well as statues and other monuments, are completely subversive of that rural quality of landscape the presentation and preservation of which is the one justifying purpose of the undertaking by a town of a large public park.

Park Construction

That the man who thinks out the general plan of a park ought to have daily supervision of the working-out of that plan is undoubtedly theoretically true. It is impossible to represent in drawings all the nice details of good work in grading and planting, and yet no work is more dependent for its effect upon finishing touches.

On the other hand, however desirable the constant over-sight of the landscape architect may be, it is impracticable under modern conditions. The education of a designer of parks consumes so much time, strength, and money that no existing American park commission, unless it be that of New York, can as yet afford to engage the whole time of a competent man. Consequently, it is the usual practice for the landscape architect to present his design in the form of a drawing or drawings, and to supplement the drawings by occasional visits for conference with those in immediate charge, by descriptive reports, and by correspondence.

The prime requisite in the resident superintendent of park work is efficiency. Naturally enough, most of the superintendents of parks in the United States have been trained either as horticulturists or as engineers, but it is not necessary or even desirable that such should be the case. Probably the best results will be achieved by men who, possessing the organizing faculty and a realizing sense of the importance of their work, shall, with the assistance of an engineer and a plantsman, labor to execute faithfully designs which they thoroughly understand and approve.

Most men of specialized training, such is architects, engineers, and all grades of horticulturists, stand in need of an awakening before they are really competent to have to do with park work. Each has to learn that his building, his bridge or road, his tree or flower, which he has been accustomed to think of as an end in itself, is, in the park, only a means auxiliary and contributive to a larger end—namely, the general landscape. It is hard for most gardeners to forego the use of plants which, however lovely or marvelous they may be as individuals, are only blots in landscape. It is hard for most engineers to conform their ideas of straightforward construction to a due regard for appearance and the preservation of the charm of scenery. Neatness of finish in slopes adjacent to roads is not sufficient; such slopes must be contrived so as to avoid formality and all likeness to railroad cuts or fills. Road lines and grades which may be practicable in the ordinary world are to be avoided in the park, because the pleasure of the visitor is the one object held in view. Roads, walls, bridges, water-supply, drainage, and grading—such of these works as may be necessary are to be executed with all technical skill, as in the outer world; but the engineer in charge should be a man who will see to it that the work is done with constant regard to the object of a park as distinguished from the object of a city street or square or railroad.

Similarly, the park planter should be a man capable of holding fast to the idea that the value of a rural park consists in landscape, and not in gardening or the exhibition of specimen plants. Guided by this idea, he will avoid such absurd traces of formality as the too common practice of planting trees in rows beside curving driveways. In devising necessary plantations he will give preference to native plants, without avoiding exotics of kinds which blend easily. Thus, where a banana would be out of place, the equally foreign barberry, privet, or buckthorn may be admissible and useful. Influenced by the same principle, he will confine flower-gardening to the secluded garden, for which space may perhaps be found in some corner of the park.

If men can be found who will thus cooperate with park commissioners to the end that the lands and landscapes which the latter hold in trust shall be cared for and made available in strict accordance with that trust, excellent results can be hoped for in American parks. As before remarked, men who are capable of such work may certainly be trusted to construct and manage town spaces—squares, playgrounds, and the like—with due regard to their special purposes and to the satisfaction of all concerned.

For Further Reading

Since 1977, the Johns Hopkins University Press has been releasing *The Papers of Frederick Law Olmsted*, which at this writing consists of seven volumes covering 1822 to 1882, plus volume I of a supplementary series, *Writings on Public Parks, Parkways, and Park Systems* (1997). These "papers" are not intended to constitute a "complete works," but they nevertheless provide an extensive selection of correspondence, published and unpublished lectures and essays, and proposals for and reports on executed and unexecuted commissions, many jointly authored with Calvert Vaux.

Laura Wood Roper, *FLO: A Biography of Frederick Law Olmsted* (Baltimore: Johns Hopkins University Press, 1973), remains the most comprehensive treatment of his life and work. Elizabeth Stevenson, *Park Maker: A Life of Frederick Law Olmsted* (New York: Macmillan, 1977), is especially insightful about his ideas and motivations, more so than Melvin Kalfus, *Frederick Law Olmsted: The Passion of a Public Artist* (New York: New York University Press, 1990), whose "psycho-history," while illuminating, is questionably speculative.

More recent overviews of Olmsted's life, while not strictly biographies, assess the sources of his ideas and the significance of his work for his day and ours: Lee Hall, *Olmsted's America: An*

"Unpractical" Man and His Vision of Civilization (Boston: Bulfinch Press, 1995); Charles E. Beveridge and Paul Rocheleau, *Frederick Law Olmsted: Designing the American Landscape* (New York: Rizzoli, 1995), which also features Rocheleau's stunning photographs; and Witold Rybczynski, *A Clearing in the Distance: Frederick Law Olmsted and North America in the Nineteenth Century* (New York: Scribner's, 1999).

Two additional books deserve mention: Frederick Law Olmsted Jr. and Theodora Kimball, *Forty Years of Landscape Architecture* (New York: G. P. Putnam's Sons, 1928), and Albert Fein, *Frederick Law Olmsted and the American Environmental Tradition* (New York: George Braziller, 1972).

It is virtually impossible to photograph large landscapes, designed or not, if the purpose is to get a sense of the whole that mattered so much to Olmsted. Aside from spending time in his creations, the best alternatives for understanding his work are plans and their accompanying documents, and most of the books listed above are sprinkled with the former. As yet, however, no published compilation contains all, or even a significant sample of plans, in part because there are so many. The most comprehensive listing of his works is Lucy Lawliss, Caroline Loughlin, and Lauren Meier (eds.), *The Master List of Design Projects of the Olmsted Firm, 1857–1979* (rev. ed. 2008). With photographs unable to do his work justice, except for bits and pieces, and relatively few plans easily accessible, the serious student will need to visit the archives at "Fairsted," formerly his estate in Brookline, Massachusetts, now the Frederick Law Olmsted National Historic Site. For those unengaged in scholarly research, the beautifully restored and maintained house and grounds are more than worth the trip.

Index

Italics indicate the editor's commentary; boldface indicates illustrations.